ZODIAC™
STARFORCE

CRIES OF THE FIRE PRINCE

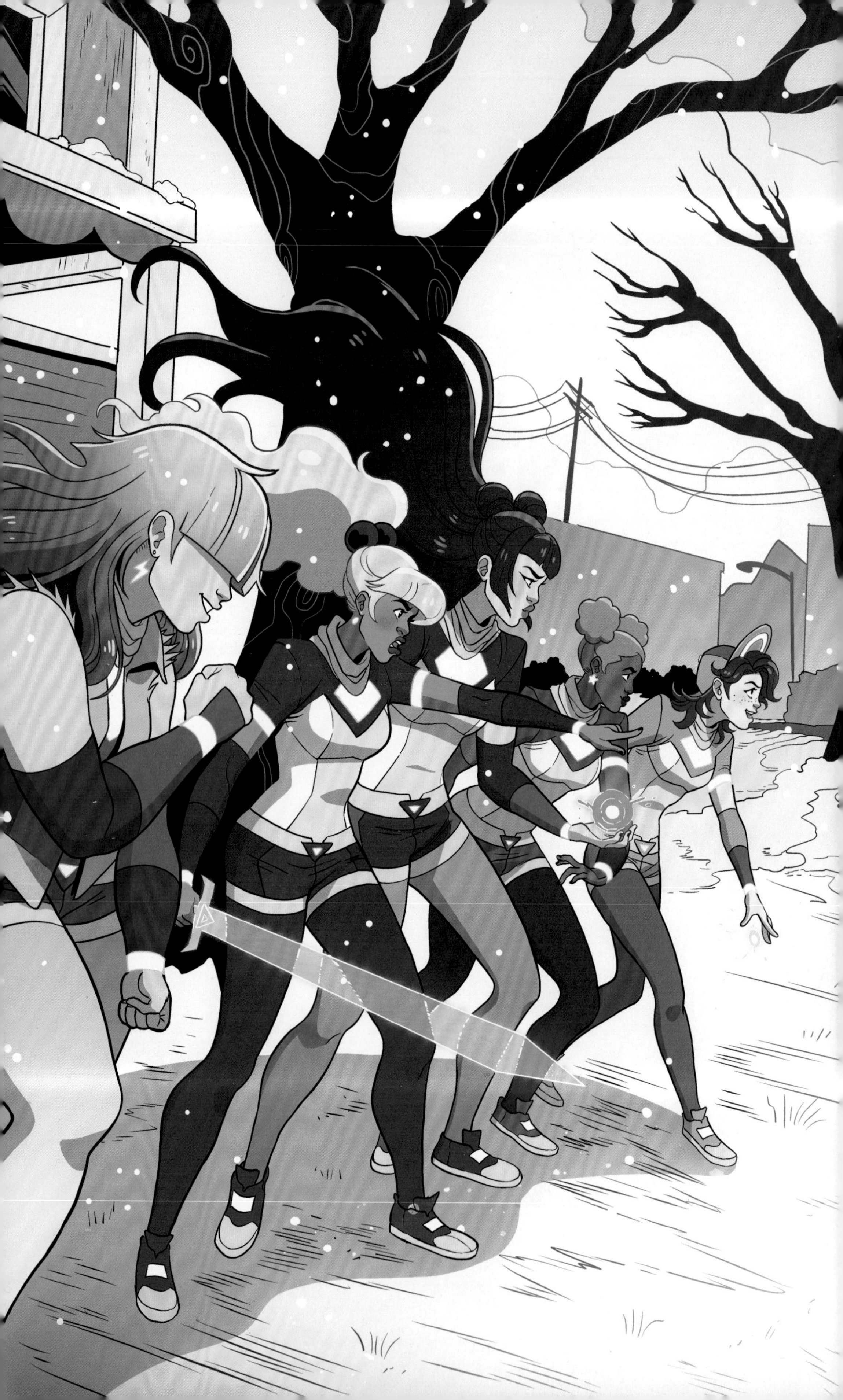

ZODIAC™
STARFORCE

CRIES OF THE FIRE PRINCE

SCRIPT BY
KEVIN PANETTA

ART AND COVER BY
PAULINA GANUCHEAU

COLORS BY
SARAH STERN

LETTERS BY
CHRISTY SAWYER
AND **NIKKI FOXROBOT**

DARK HORSE BOOKS

PRESIDENT AND PUBLISHER
MIKE RICHARDSON

EDITOR
SHANTEL LaROCQUE

ASSISTANT EDITORS
KATII O'BRIEN AND **BRETT ISRAEL**

DIGITAL ART TECHNICIAN
CHRISTIANNE GOUDREAU

COLLECTION DESIGNER
ETHAN KIMBERLING

Neil Hankerson Executive Vice President **Tom Weddle** Chief Financial Officer **Randy Stradley** Vice President of Publishing **Nick McWhorter** Chief Business Development Officer **Matt Parkinson** Vice President of Marketing **Dale LaFountain** Vice President of Information Technology **Cara Niece** Vice President of Production and Scheduling **Mark Bernardi** Vice President of Book Trade and Digital Sales **Ken Lizzi** General Counsel **Dave Marshall** Editor in Chief **Davey Estrada** Editorial Director **Chris Warner** Senior Books Editor **Cary Grazzini** Director of Specialty Projects **Lia Ribacchi** Art Director **Vanessa Todd-Holmes** Director of Print Purchasing **Matt Dryer** Director of Digital Art and Prepress **Michael Gombos** Director of International Publishing and Licensing **Kari Yadro** Director of Custom Programs

Published by Dark Horse Books
A division of Dark Horse Comics, Inc.
10956 SE Main Street
Milwaukie, OR 97222

First edition: August 2018
ISBN 978-1-50670-310-7
Digital ISBN 978-1-63008-794-4

10 9 8 7 6 5 4 3 2 1
Printed in China

Comic Shop Locator Service: comicshoplocator.com

This volume collects and reprints the comic book series Zodiac Starforce: Cries of the Fire Prince #1–#4.

Library of Congress Cataloging-in-Publication Data

Names: Panetta, Kevin, author. | Ganucheau, Paulina, artist. | Stern, Sarah (Colorist), colourist. | Sawyer, Christy, letterer. | Foxrobot, Nikki, letterer.
Title: Cries of the Fire Prince / script by Kevin Panetta ; art and cover by Paulina Ganucheau ; colors by Sarah Stern ; letters by Christy Sawyer and Nikki Foxrobot.
Description: First edition. | Milwaukie, OR : Dark Horse Books, August 2018. | Series: Zodiac Starforce ; Volume 2 | "This volume collects and reprints the comic book series Zodiac Starforce: Cries of the Fire Prince #1-#4." | Summary: "After defeating a former Zodiac Starforce member and her mean-girl minions the girls thought they would get a break, but a new big-bad has come out to play and demons are overrunning the town!"-- Provided by publisher.
Identifiers: LCCN 2018019960 | ISBN 9781506703107 (paperback)
Subjects: LCSH: Graphic novels. | CYAC: Graphic novels. | Women superheroes--Fiction. | Magic--Fiction. | Demonology--Fiction. | BISAC: COMICS & GRAPHIC NOVELS / Superheroes. | COMICS & GRAPHIC NOVELS / Contemporary Women. | COMICS & GRAPHIC NOVELS / Gay & Lesbian.
Classification: LCC PZ7.7.P22 Cr 2018 | DDC 741.5/973--dc23
LC record available at https://lccn.loc.gov/2018019960

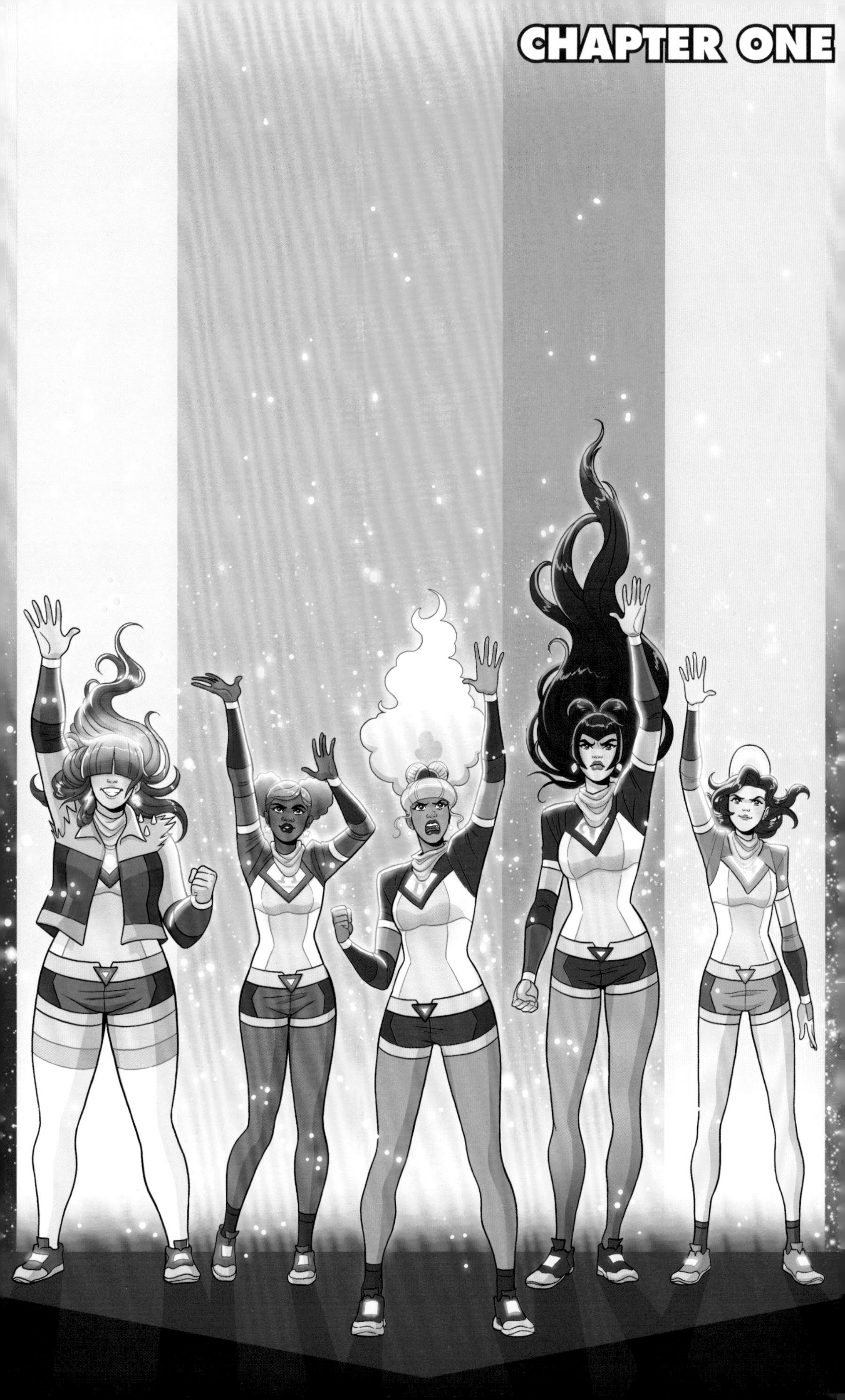
CHAPTER ONE

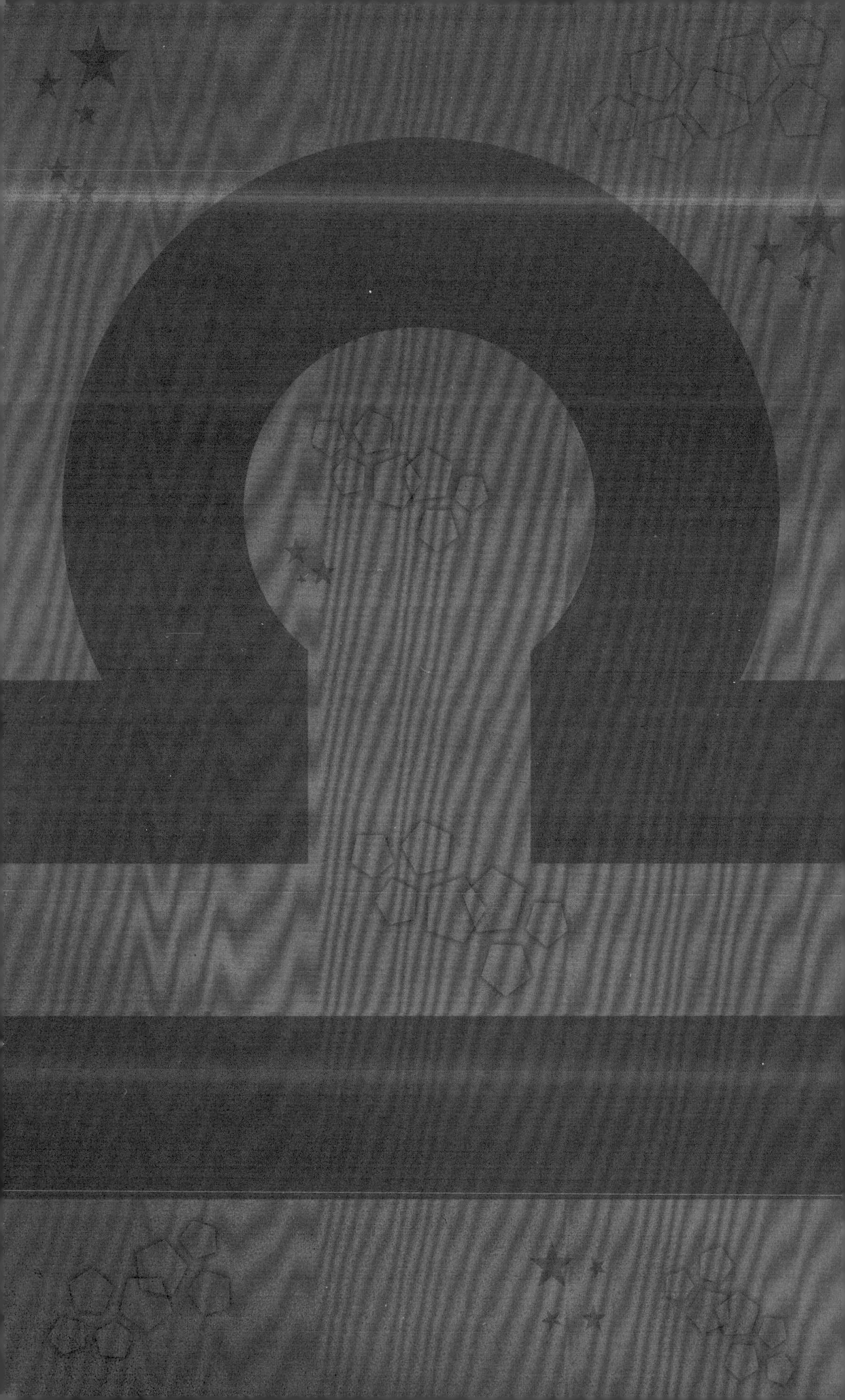

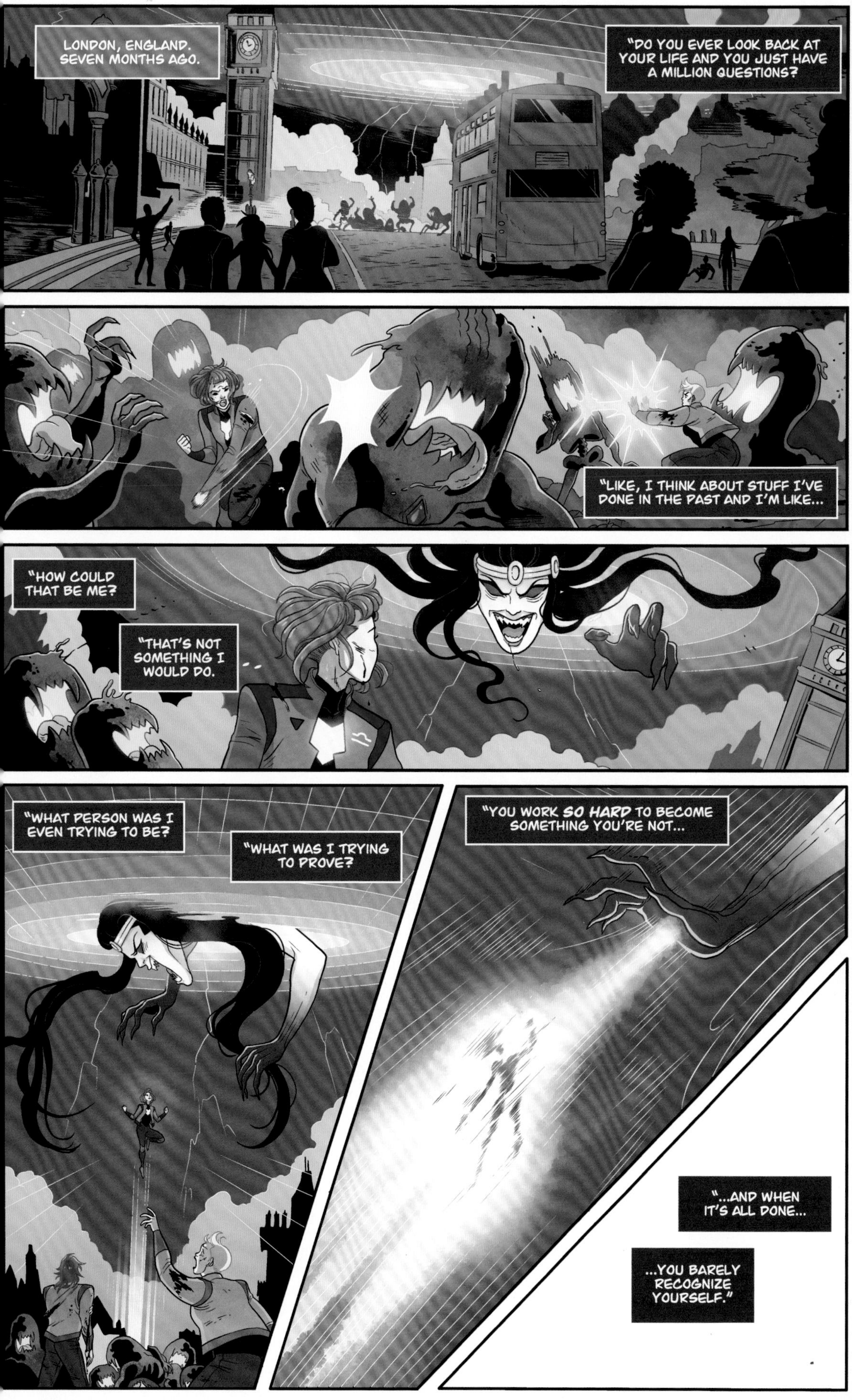
LONDON, ENGLAND. SEVEN MONTHS AGO.
"DO YOU EVER LOOK BACK AT YOUR LIFE AND YOU JUST HAVE A MILLION QUESTIONS?
"LIKE, I THINK ABOUT STUFF I'VE DONE IN THE PAST AND I'M LIKE...
"HOW COULD THAT BE ME?
"THAT'S NOT SOMETHING I WOULD DO.
"WHAT PERSON WAS I EVEN TRYING TO BE?
"WHAT WAS I TRYING TO PROVE?
"YOU WORK SO HARD TO BECOME SOMETHING YOU'RE NOT...
"...AND WHEN IT'S ALL DONE...
...YOU BARELY RECOGNIZE YOURSELF."

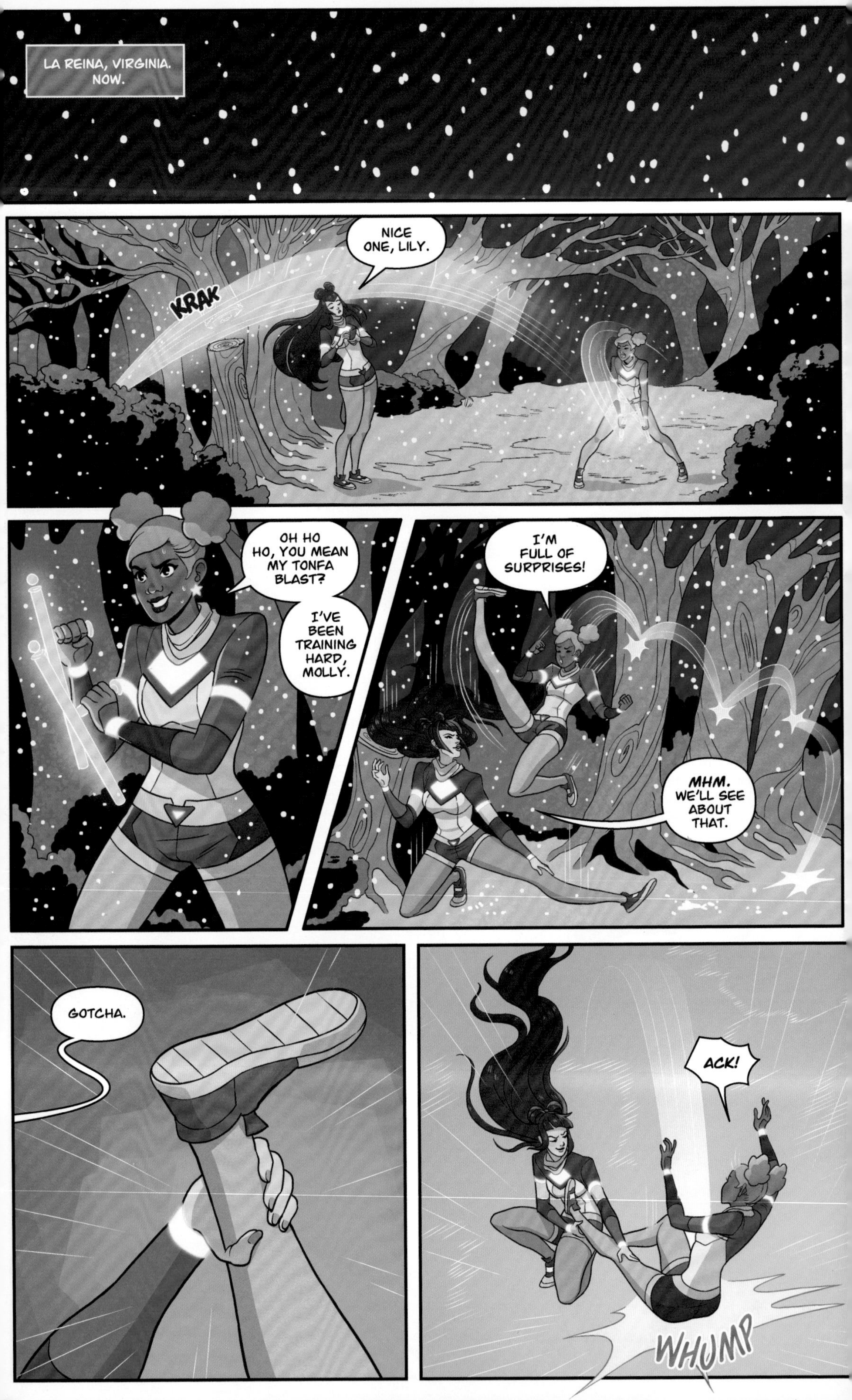
LA REINA, VIRGINIA.
NOW.
NICE ONE, LILY.
KRAK
OH HO HO, YOU MEAN MY TONFA BLAST?
I'VE BEEN TRAINING HARD, MOLLY.
I'M FULL OF SURPRISES!
MHM. WE'LL SEE ABOUT THAT.
GOTCHA.
ACK!
WHUMP

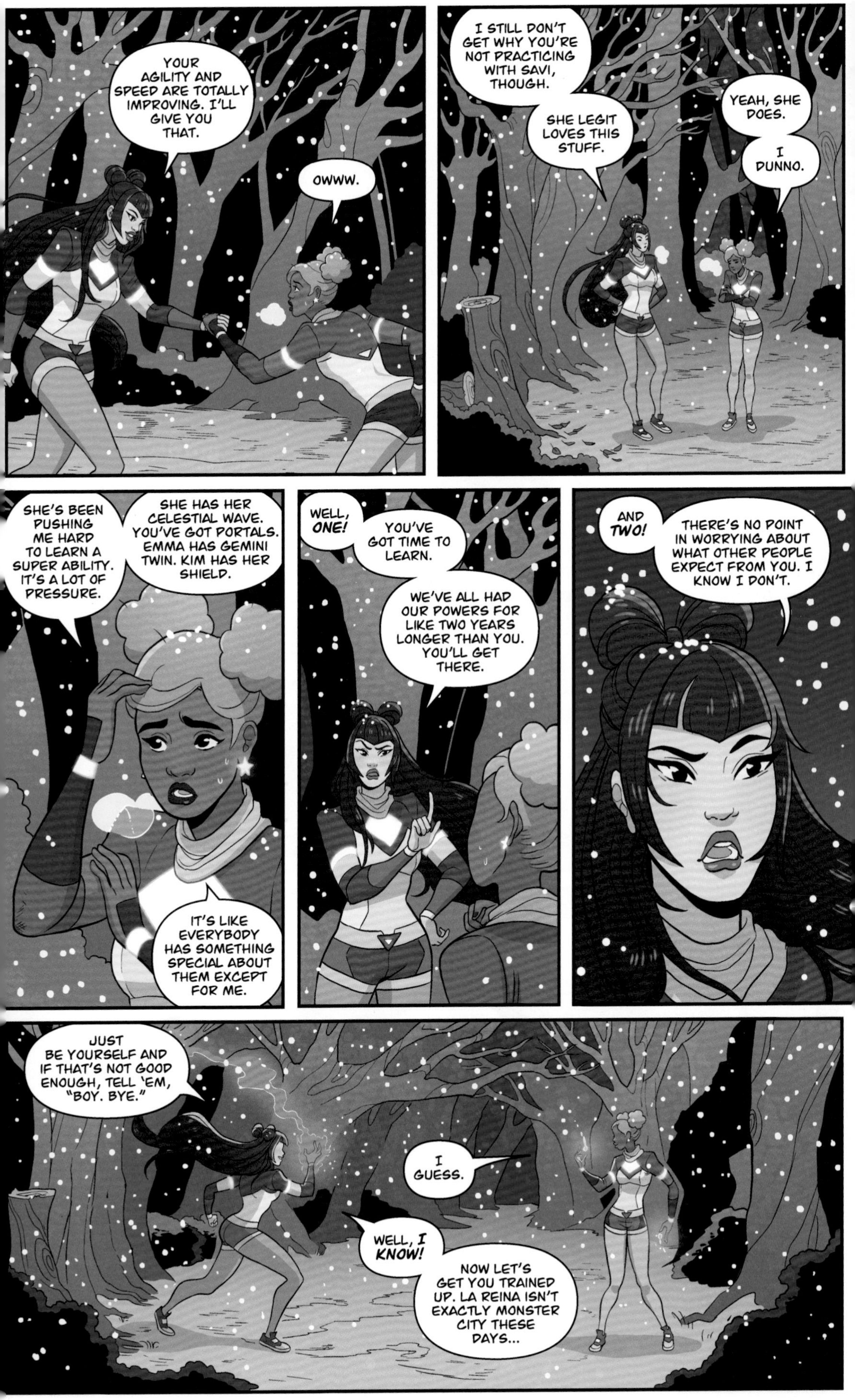
YOUR AGILITY AND SPEED ARE TOTALLY IMPROVING. I'LL GIVE YOU THAT.
OWWW.
I STILL DON'T GET WHY YOU'RE NOT PRACTICING WITH SAVI, THOUGH.
SHE LEGIT LOVES THIS STUFF.
YEAH, SHE DOES.
I DUNNO.
SHE'S BEEN PUSHING ME HARD TO LEARN A SUPER ABILITY. IT'S A LOT OF PRESSURE.
SHE HAS HER CELESTIAL WAVE. YOU'VE GOT PORTALS. EMMA HAS GEMINI TWIN. KIM HAS HER SHIELD.
IT'S LIKE EVERYBODY HAS SOMETHING SPECIAL ABOUT THEM EXCEPT FOR ME.
WELL, ONE!
YOU'VE GOT TIME TO LEARN.
WE'VE ALL HAD OUR POWERS FOR LIKE TWO YEARS LONGER THAN YOU. YOU'LL GET THERE.
AND TWO!
THERE'S NO POINT IN WORRYING ABOUT WHAT OTHER PEOPLE EXPECT FROM YOU. I KNOW I DON'T.
JUST BE YOURSELF AND IF THAT'S NOT GOOD ENOUGH, TELL 'EM, "BOY. BYE."
I GUESS.
WELL, I KNOW!
NOW LET'S GET YOU TRAINED UP. LA REINA ISN'T EXACTLY MONSTER CITY THESE DAYS...

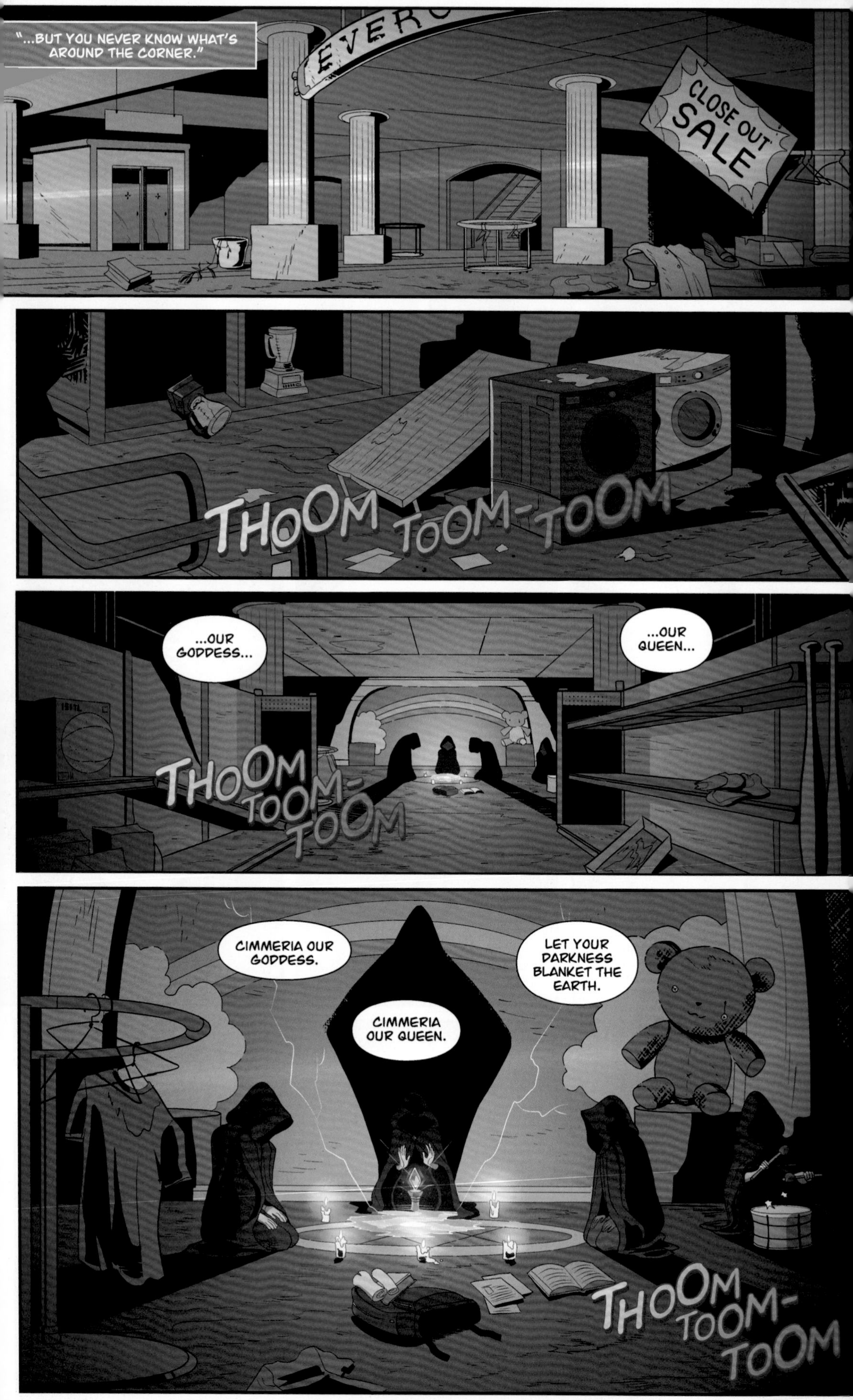
"...BUT YOU NEVER KNOW WHAT'S AROUND THE CORNER."
EVER
CLOSE OUT SALE
THOOM TOOM-TOOM
...OUR GODDESS...
...OUR QUEEN...
THOOM-TOOM-TOOM
CIMMERIA OUR GODDESS.
CIMMERIA OUR QUEEN.
LET YOUR DARKNESS BLANKET THE EARTH.
THOOM-TOOM-TOOM

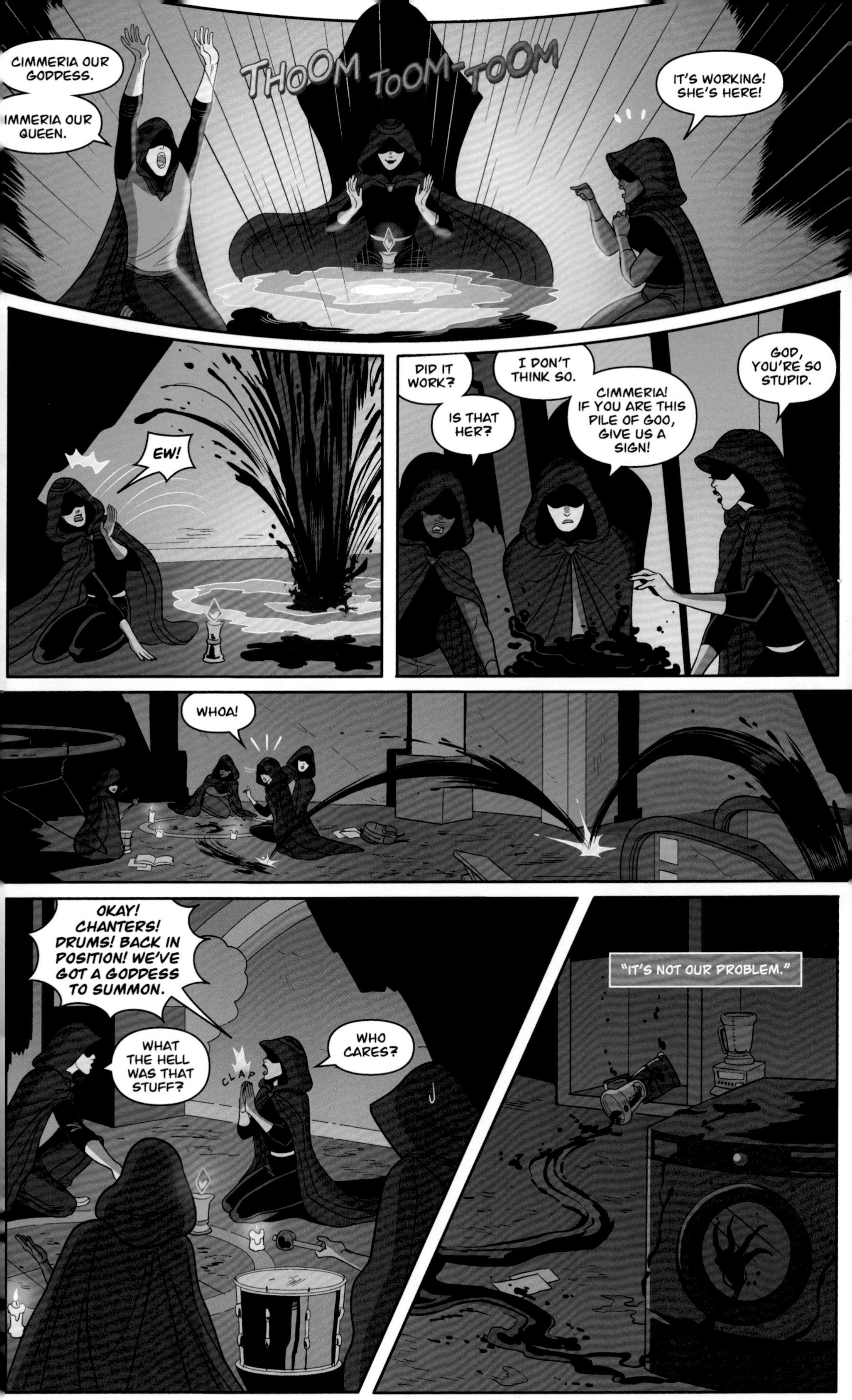
CIMMERIA OUR GODDESS.
IMMERIA OUR QUEEN.
THOOM TOOM-TOOM
IT'S WORKING! SHE'S HERE!
EW!
DID IT WORK?
IS THAT HER?
I DON'T THINK SO.
CIMMERIA! IF YOU ARE THIS PILE OF GOO, GIVE US A SIGN!
GOD, YOU'RE SO STUPID.
WHOA!
OKAY! CHANTERS! DRUMS! BACK IN POSITION! WE'VE GOT A GODDESS TO SUMMON.
WHAT THE HELL WAS THAT STUFF?
CLAP
WHO CARES?
"IT'S NOT OUR PROBLEM."

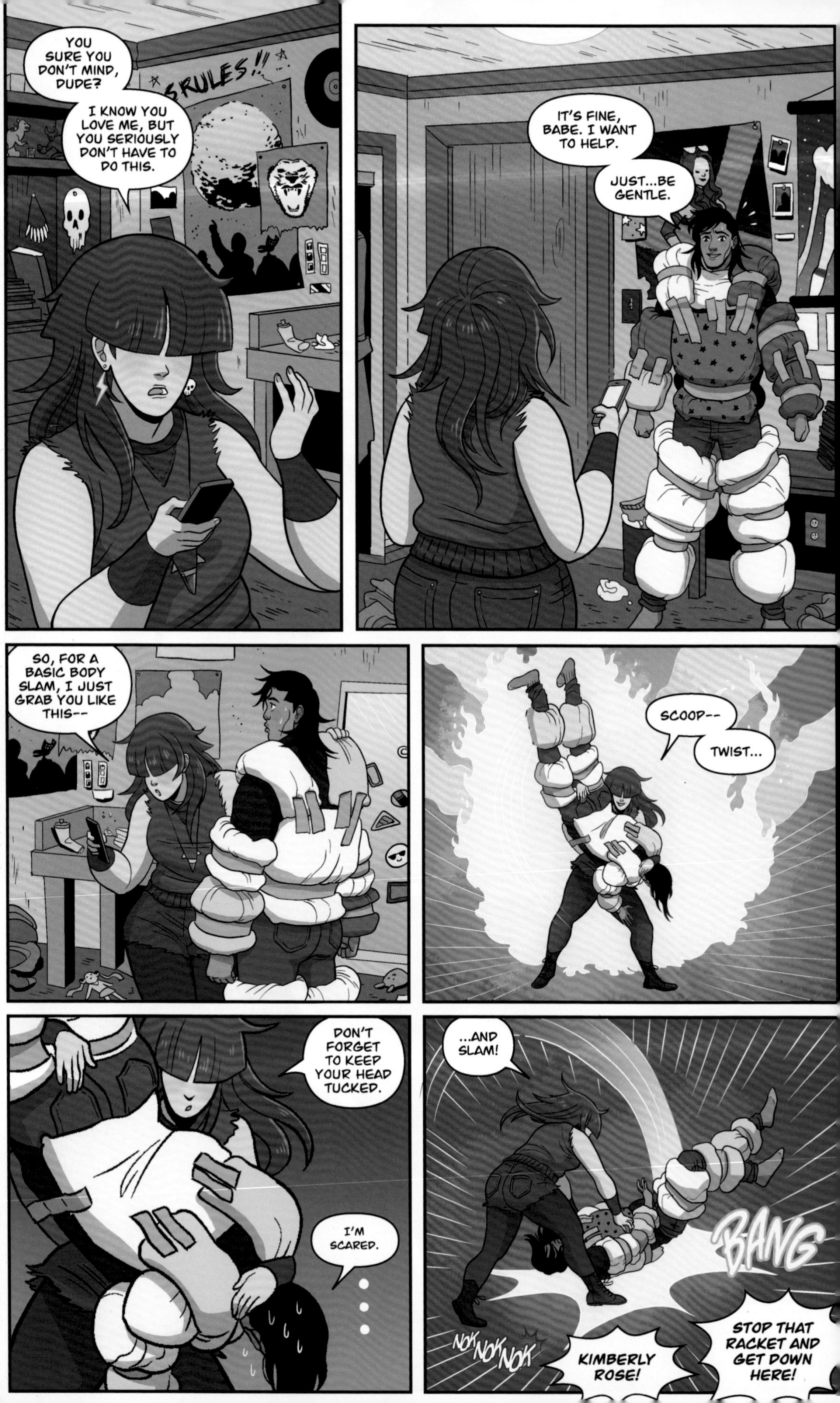

YOU SURE YOU DON'T MIND, DUDE?
I KNOW YOU LOVE ME, BUT YOU SERIOUSLY DON'T HAVE TO DO THIS.
RULES!!
IT'S FINE, BABE. I WANT TO HELP.
JUST...BE GENTLE.
SO, FOR A BASIC BODY SLAM, I JUST GRAB YOU LIKE THIS--
SCOOP--
TWIST...
DON'T FORGET TO KEEP YOUR HEAD TUCKED.
I'M SCARED.
...AND SLAM!
BANG
NOK NOK NOK
KIMBERLY ROSE!
STOP THAT RACKET AND GET DOWN HERE!

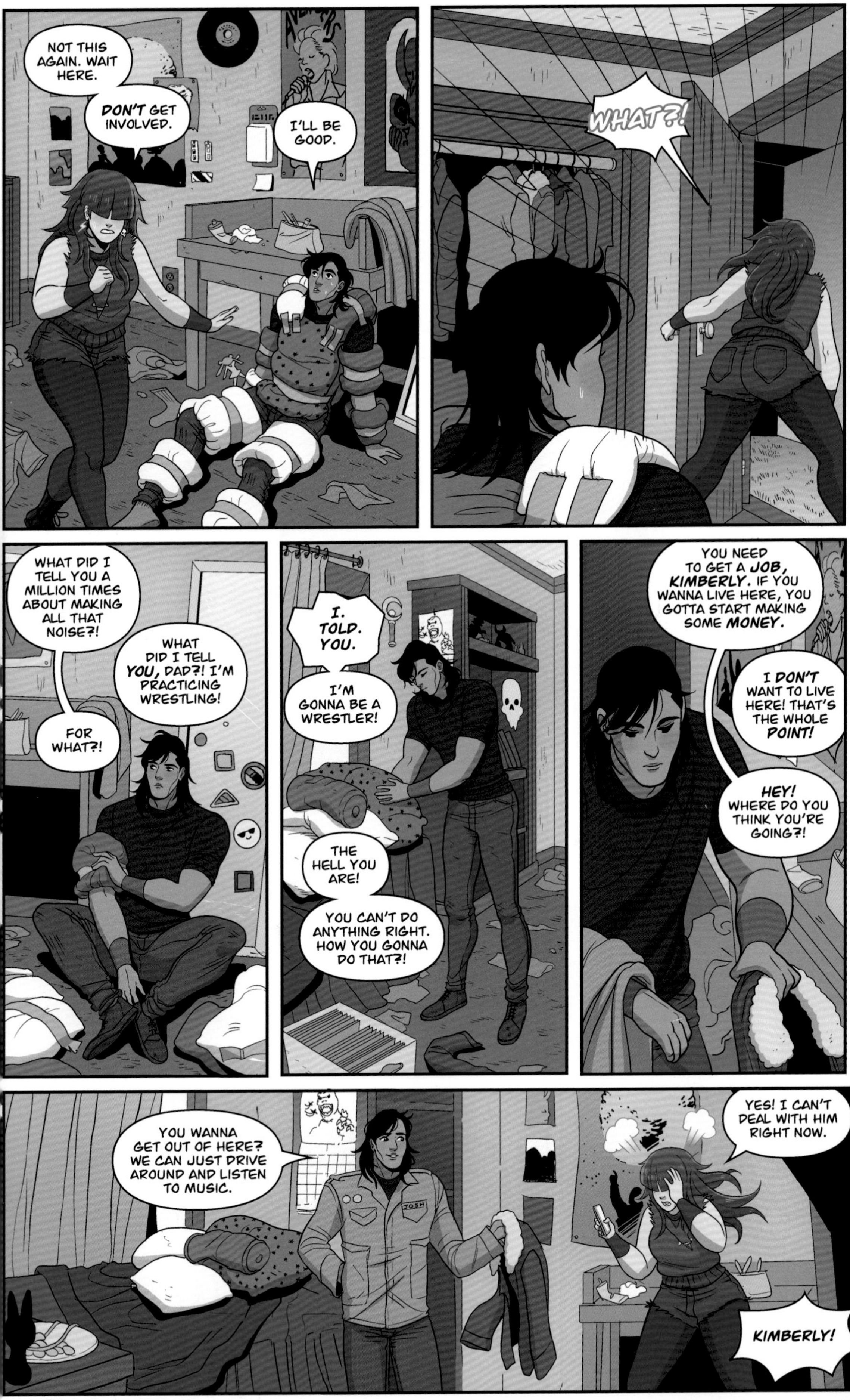
NOT THIS AGAIN. WAIT HERE.
DON'T GET INVOLVED.
I'LL BE GOOD.
WHAT?!
WHAT DID I TELL YOU A MILLION TIMES ABOUT MAKING ALL THAT NOISE?!
WHAT DID I TELL YOU, DAD?! I'M PRACTICING WRESTLING!
FOR WHAT?!
I. TOLD. YOU.
I'M GONNA BE A WRESTLER!
THE HELL YOU ARE!
YOU CAN'T DO ANYTHING RIGHT. HOW YOU GONNA DO THAT?!
YOU NEED TO GET A JOB, KIMBERLY. IF YOU WANNA LIVE HERE, YOU GOTTA START MAKING SOME MONEY.
I DON'T WANT TO LIVE HERE! THAT'S THE WHOLE POINT!
HEY! WHERE DO YOU THINK YOU'RE GOING?!
YOU WANNA GET OUT OF HERE? WE CAN JUST DRIVE AROUND AND LISTEN TO MUSIC.
YES! I CAN'T DEAL WITH HIM RIGHT NOW.
KIMBERLY!

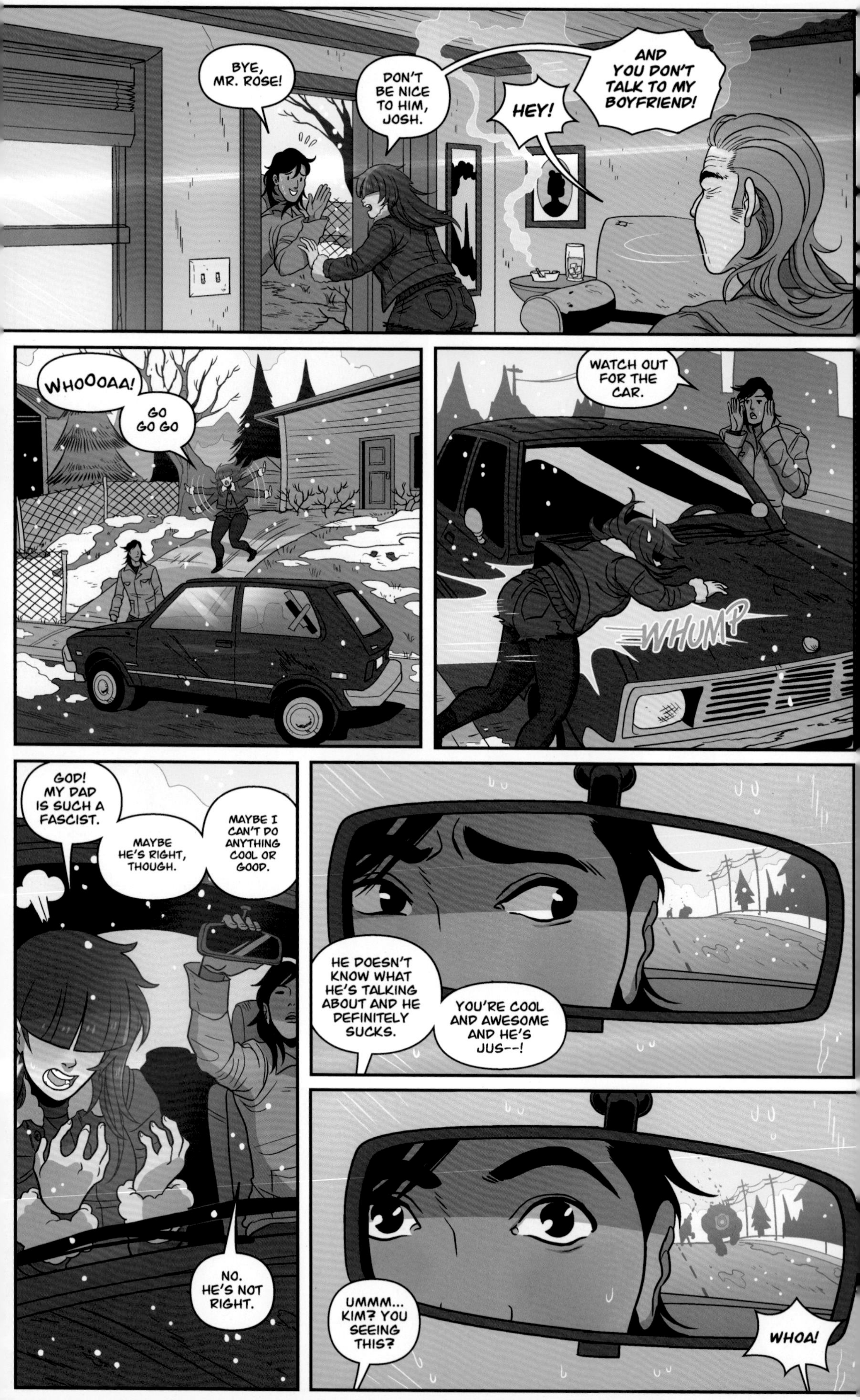
BYE, MR. ROSE!
DON'T BE NICE TO HIM, JOSH.
HEY!
AND YOU DON'T TALK TO MY BOYFRIEND!
WHOOOAA!
GO GO GO
WATCH OUT FOR THE CAR.
WHUMP
GOD! MY DAD IS SUCH A FASCIST.
MAYBE HE'S RIGHT, THOUGH.
MAYBE I CAN'T DO ANYTHING COOL OR GOOD.
NO. HE'S NOT RIGHT.
HE DOESN'T KNOW WHAT HE'S TALKING ABOUT AND HE DEFINITELY SUCKS.
YOU'RE COOL AND AWESOME AND HE'S JUS--!
UMMM... KIM? YOU SEEING THIS?
WHOA!

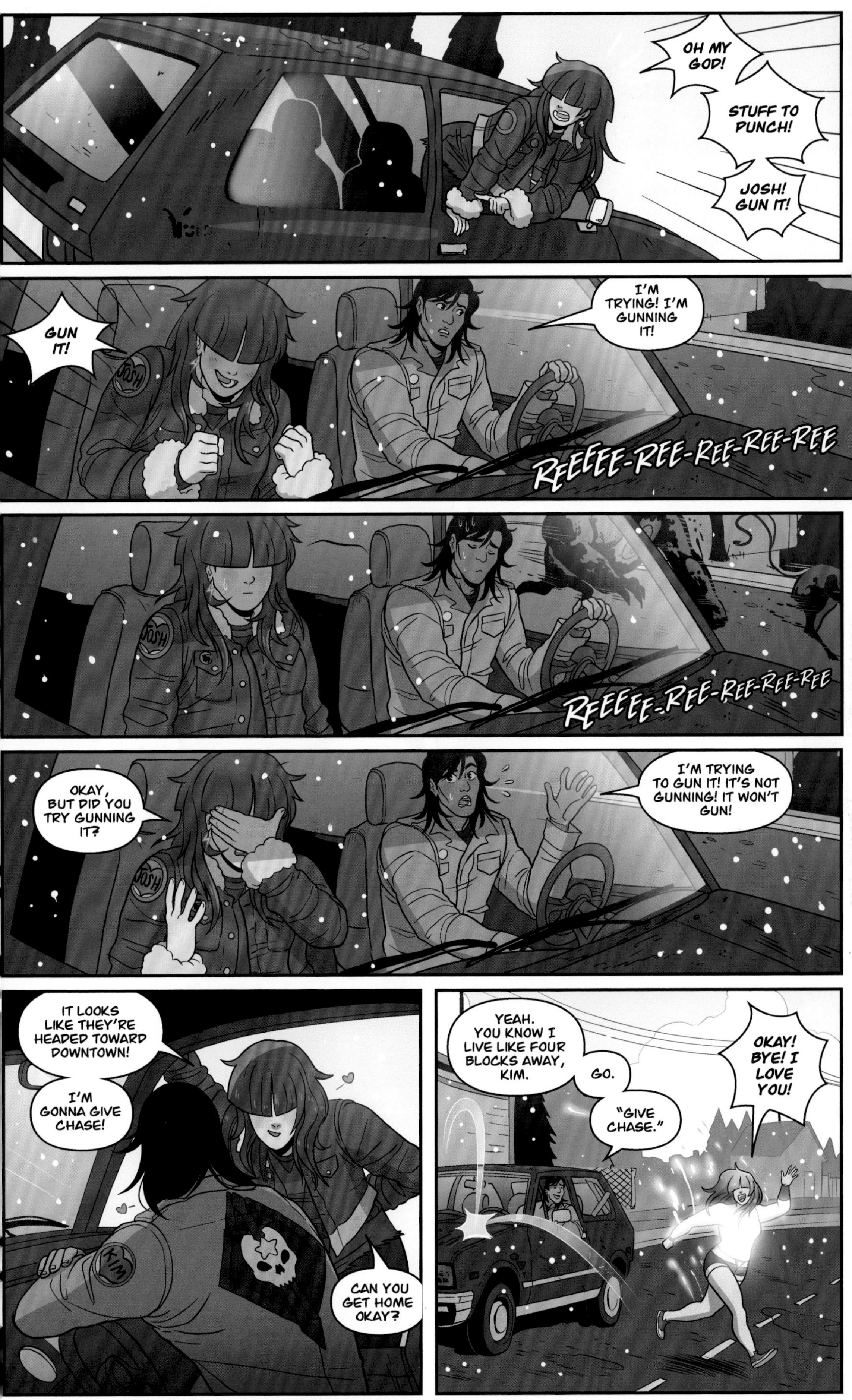
OH MY GOD!
STUFF TO PUNCH!
JOSH! GUN IT!
GUN IT!
I'M TRYING! I'M GUNNING IT!
REEEEE-REE-REE-REE-REE
REEEEE-REE-REE-REE-REE
OKAY, BUT DID YOU TRY GUNNING IT?
I'M TRYING TO GUN IT! IT'S NOT GUNNING! IT WON'T GUN!
IT LOOKS LIKE THEY'RE HEADED TOWARD DOWNTOWN!
I'M GONNA GIVE CHASE!
CAN YOU GET HOME OKAY?
YEAH. YOU KNOW I LIVE LIKE FOUR BLOCKS AWAY, KIM.
GO.
"GIVE CHASE."
OKAY! BYE! I LOVE YOU!

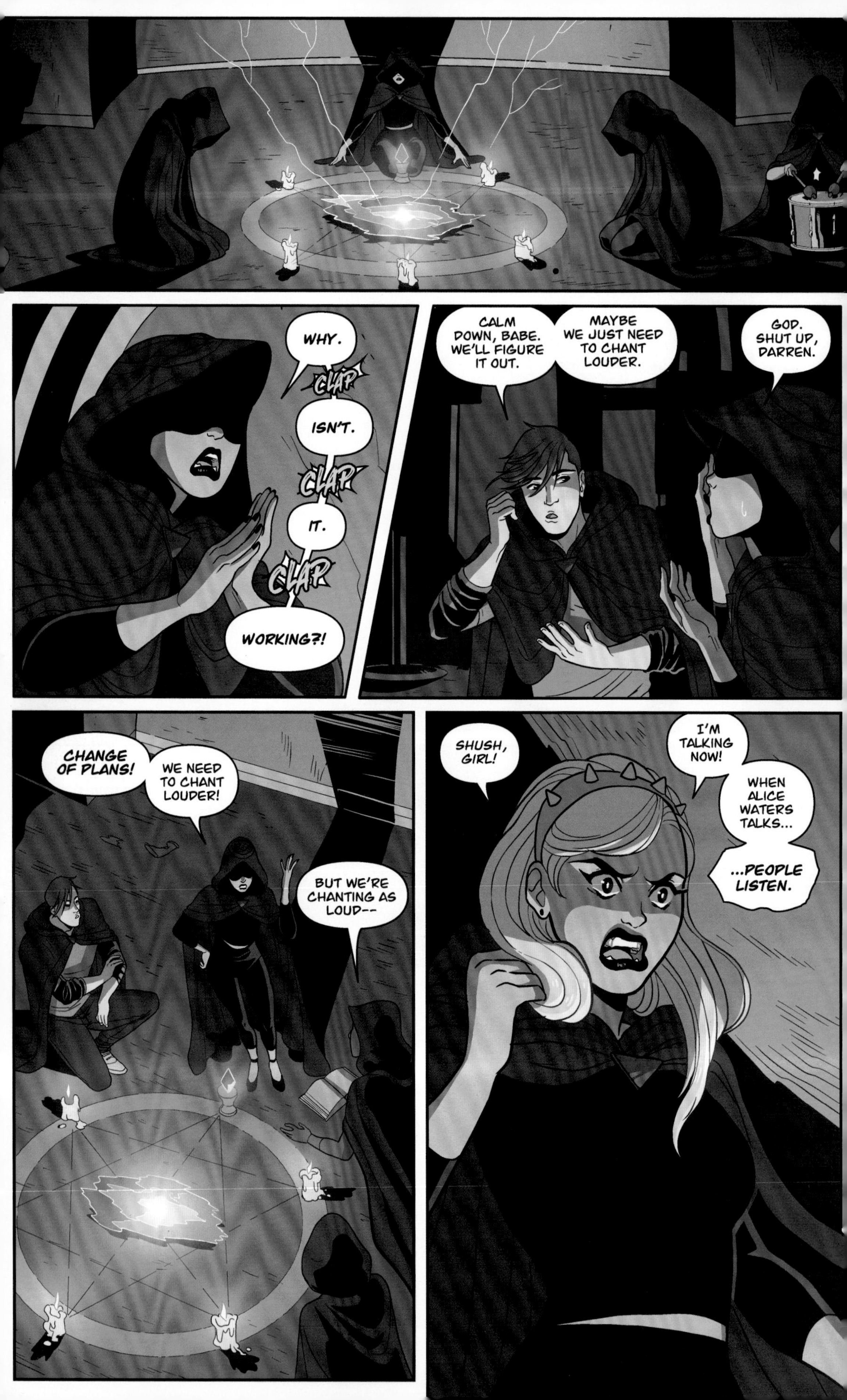
WHY.
CLAP
ISN'T.
CLAP
IT.
CLAP
WORKING?!
CALM DOWN, BABE. WE'LL FIGURE IT OUT.
MAYBE WE JUST NEED TO CHANT LOUDER.
GOD. SHUT UP, DARREN.
CHANGE OF PLANS!
WE NEED TO CHANT LOUDER!
BUT WE'RE CHANTING AS LOUD--
SHUSH, GIRL!
I'M TALKING NOW!
WHEN ALICE WATERS TALKS...
...PEOPLE LISTEN.

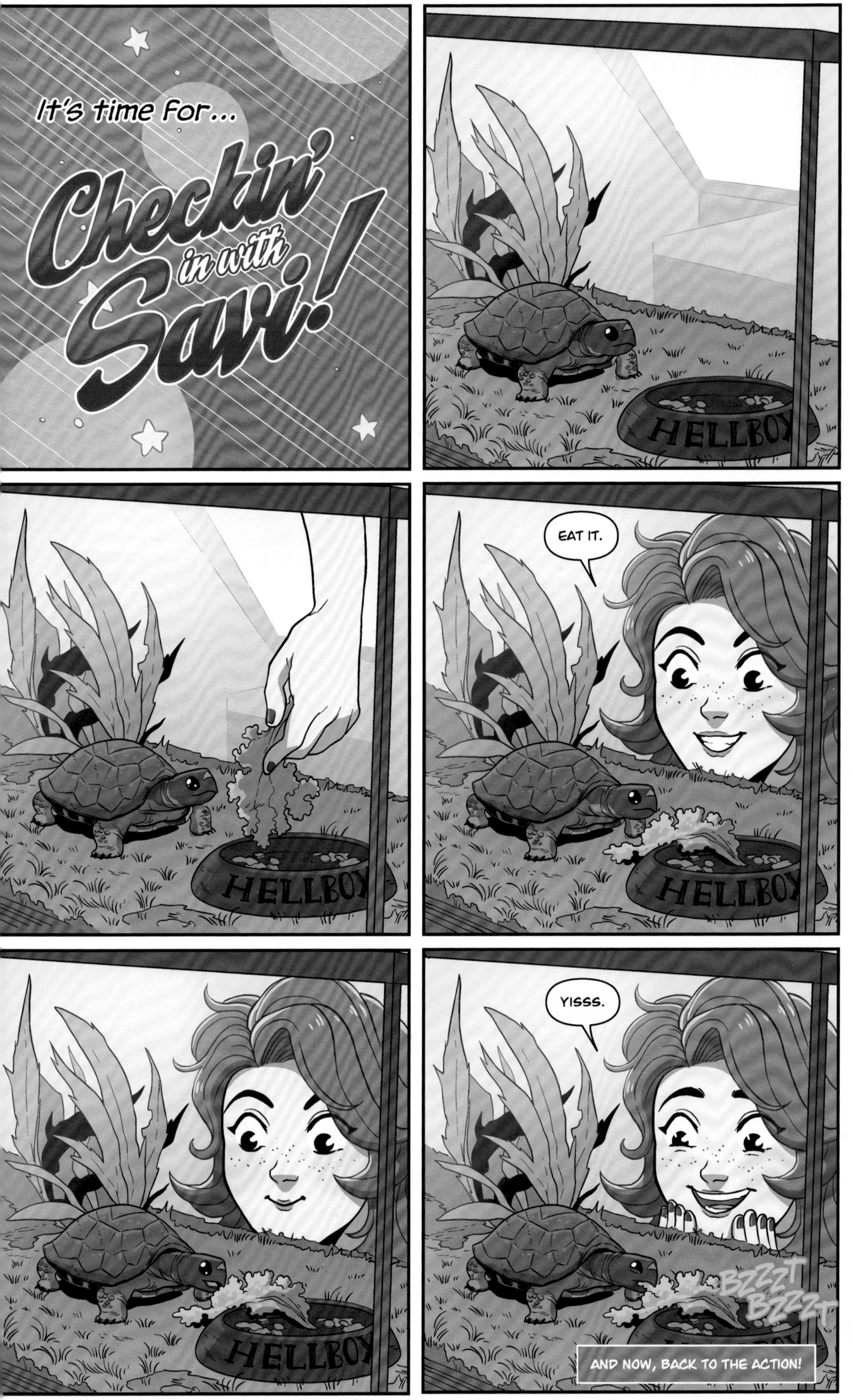
It's time for...
Checkin' in with Savi!
HELLBOY
HELLBOY
EAT IT.
HELLBOY
HELLBOY
YISSS.
BZZZT
BZZZT
AND NOW, BACK TO THE ACTION!

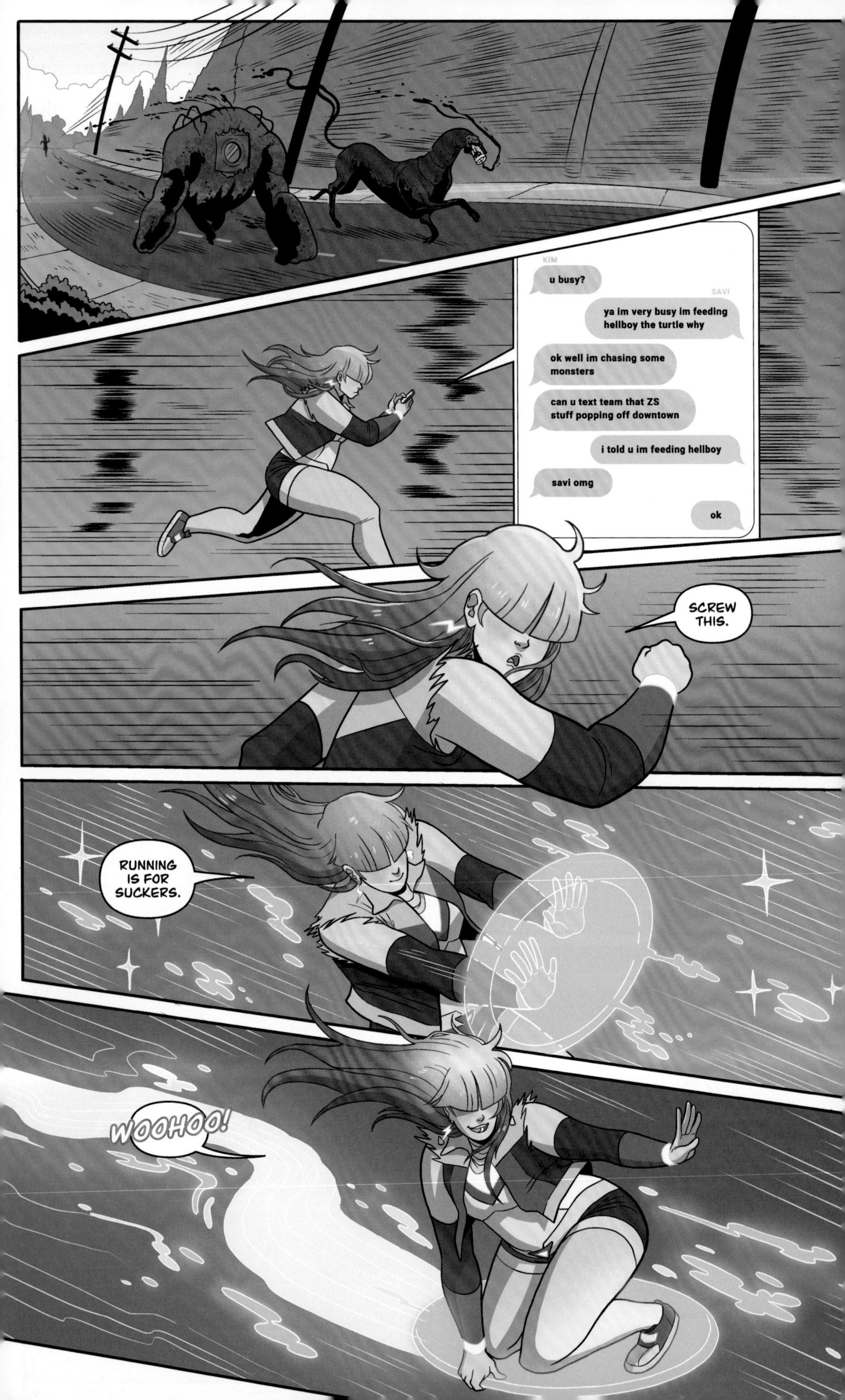
KIM
u busy?
SAVI
ya im very busy im feeding hellboy the turtle why
ok well im chasing some monsters
can u text team that ZS stuff popping off downtown
i told u im feeding hellboy
savi omg
ok
SCREW THIS.
RUNNING IS FOR SUCKERS.
WOOHOO!

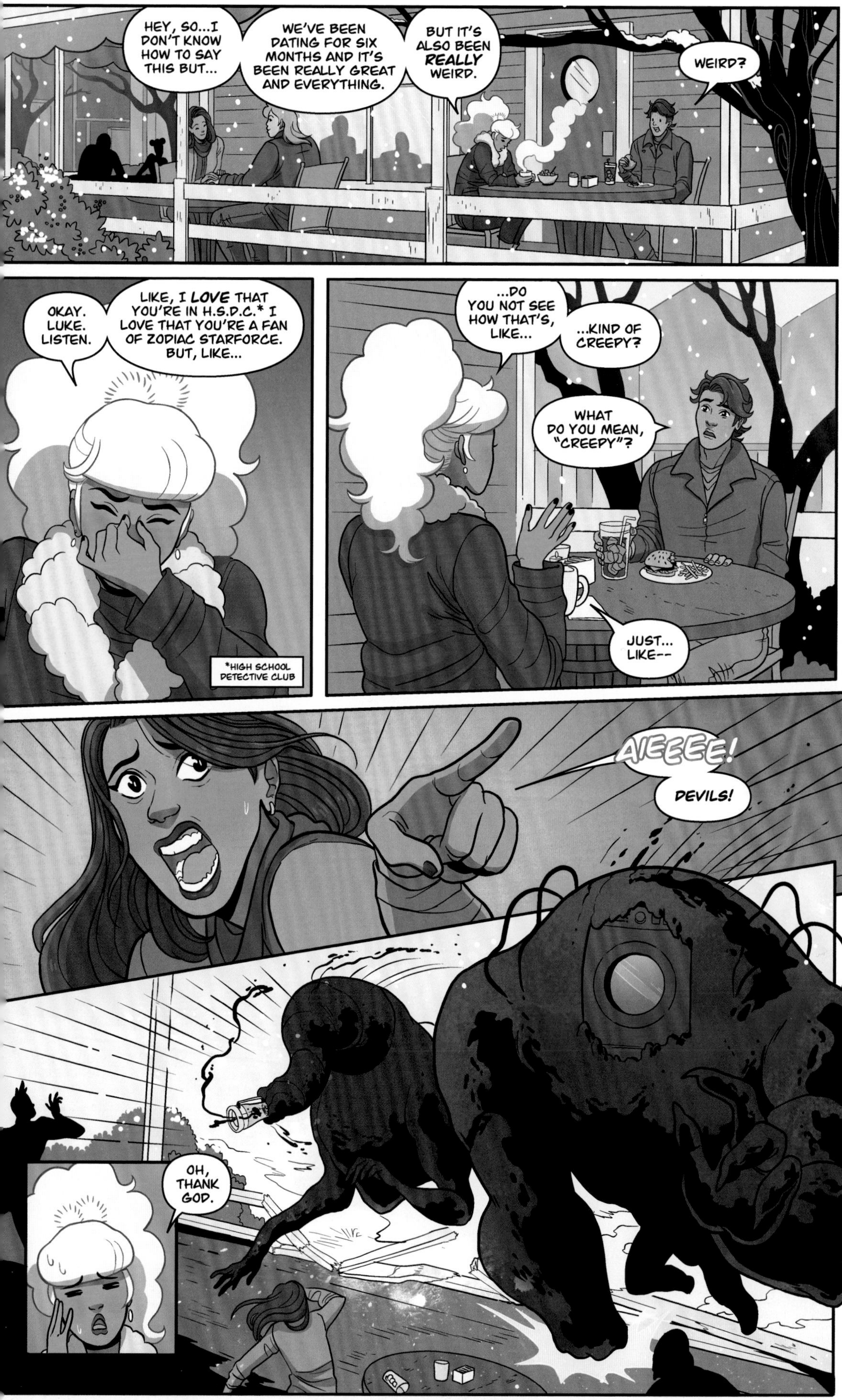
HEY, SO...I DON'T KNOW HOW TO SAY THIS BUT...
WE'VE BEEN DATING FOR SIX MONTHS AND IT'S BEEN REALLY GREAT AND EVERYTHING.
BUT IT'S ALSO BEEN **REALLY** WEIRD.
WEIRD?
OKAY. LUKE. LISTEN.
LIKE, I **LOVE** THAT YOU'RE IN H.S.D.C.* I LOVE THAT YOU'RE A FAN OF ZODIAC STARFORCE. BUT, LIKE...
*HIGH SCHOOL DETECTIVE CLUB
...DO YOU NOT SEE HOW THAT'S, LIKE...
...KIND OF CREEPY?
WHAT DO YOU MEAN, "CREEPY"?
JUST... LIKE--
AIEEEE!
DEVILS!
OH, THANK GOD.

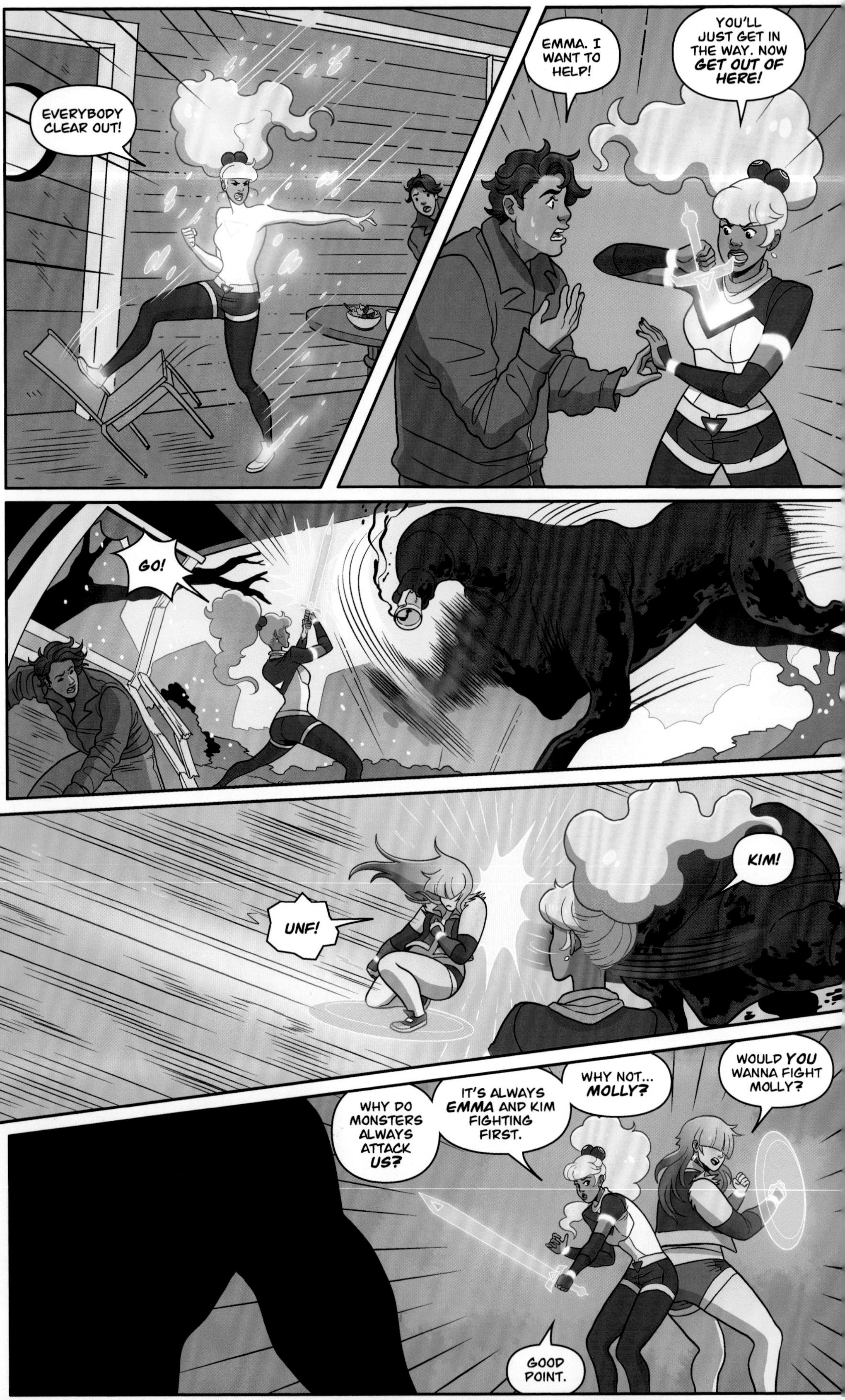
EVERYBODY CLEAR OUT!
EMMA. I WANT TO HELP!
YOU'LL JUST GET IN THE WAY. NOW GET OUT OF HERE!
GO!
KIM!
UNF!
WHY DO MONSTERS ALWAYS ATTACK US?
IT'S ALWAYS EMMA AND KIM FIGHTING FIRST.
WHY NOT... MOLLY?
WOULD YOU WANNA FIGHT MOLLY?
GOOD POINT.

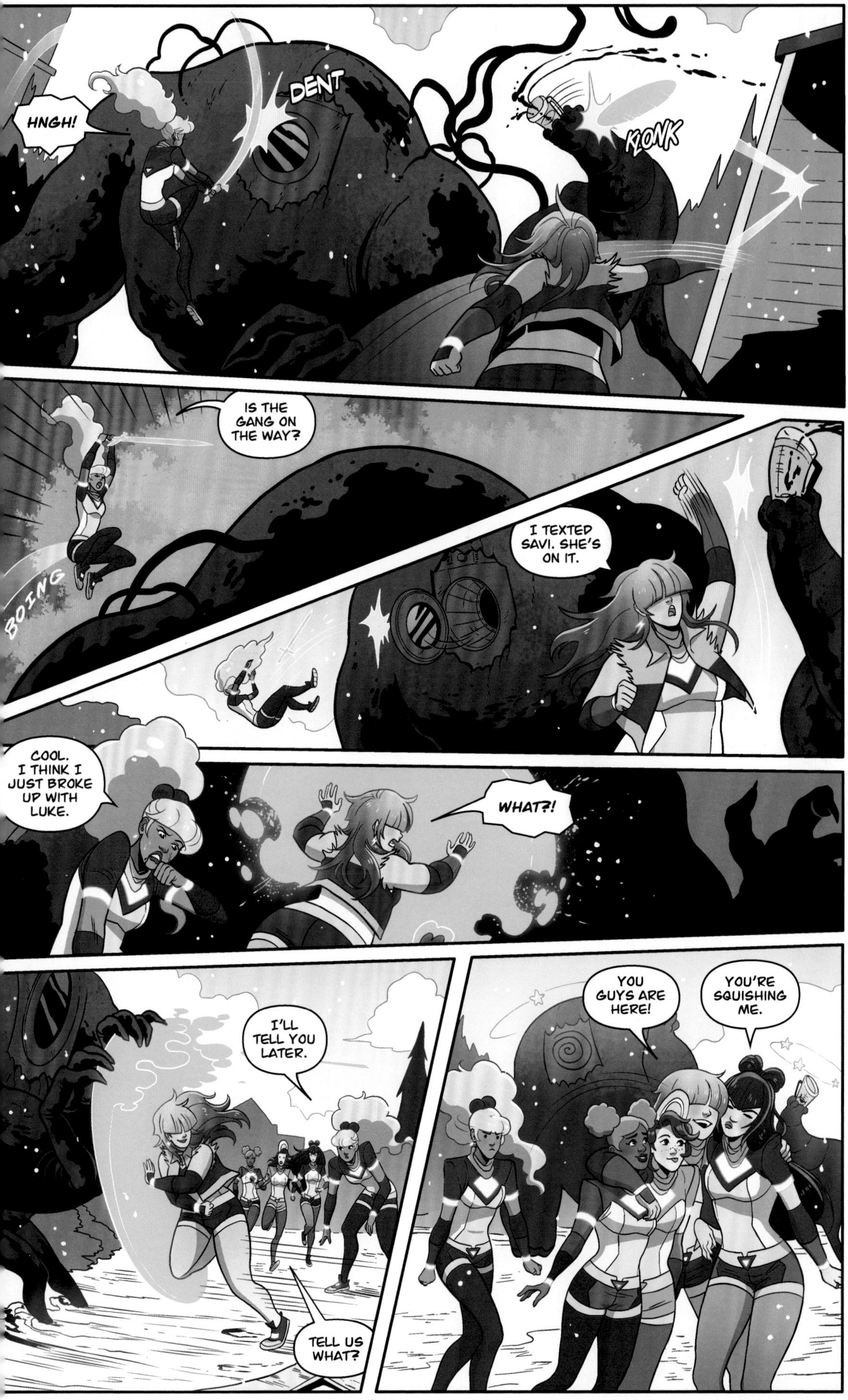
HNGH!
DENT
KLONK
IS THE GANG ON THE WAY?
BOING
I TEXTED SAVI. SHE'S ON IT.
COOL. I THINK I JUST BROKE UP WITH LUKE.
WHAT?!
I'LL TELL YOU LATER.
TELL US WHAT?
YOU GUYS ARE HERE!
YOU'RE SQUISHING ME.

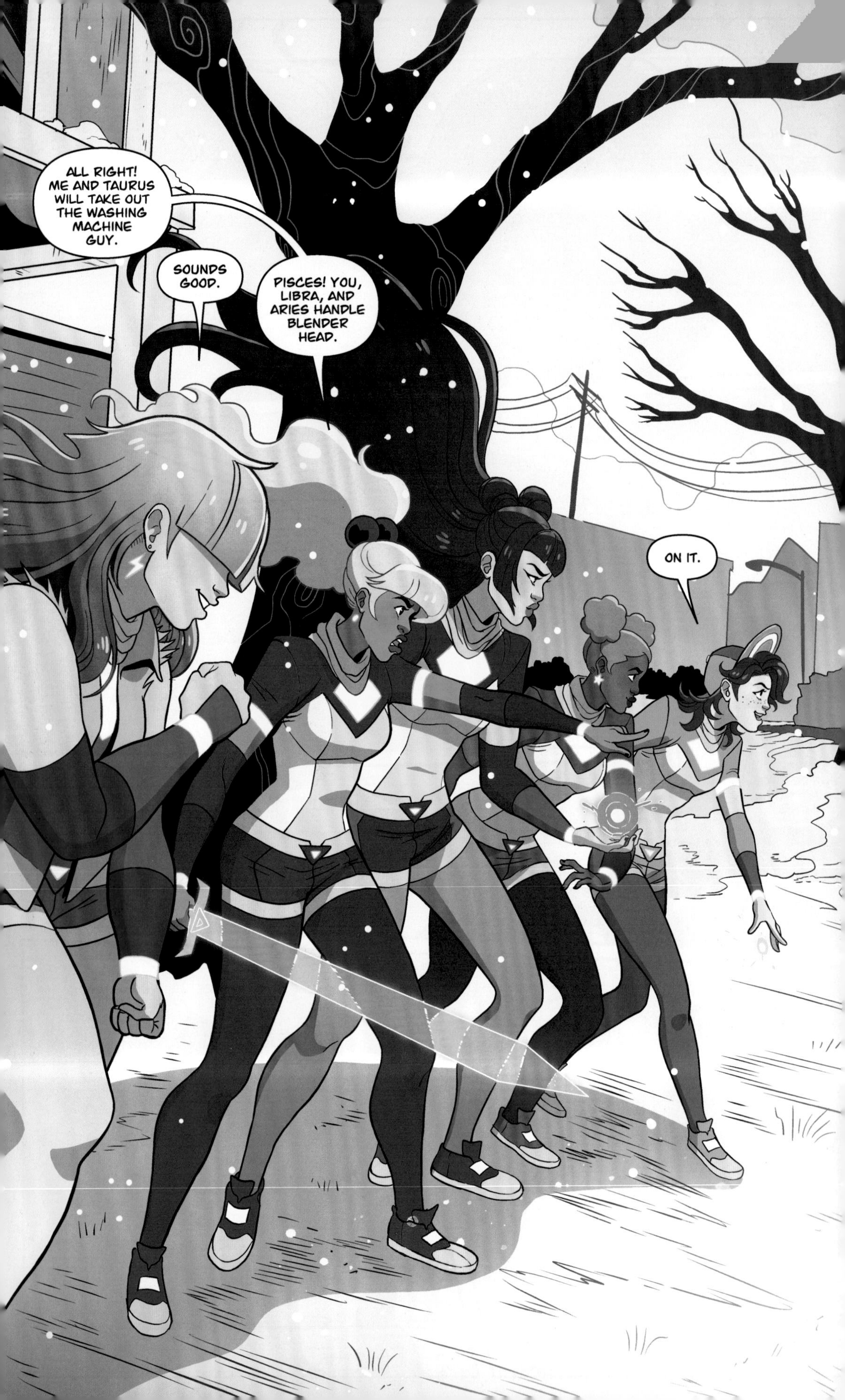
ALL RIGHT! ME AND TAURUS WILL TAKE OUT THE WASHING MACHINE GUY.
SOUNDS GOOD.
PISCES! YOU, LIBRA, AND ARIES HANDLE BLENDER HEAD.
ON IT.

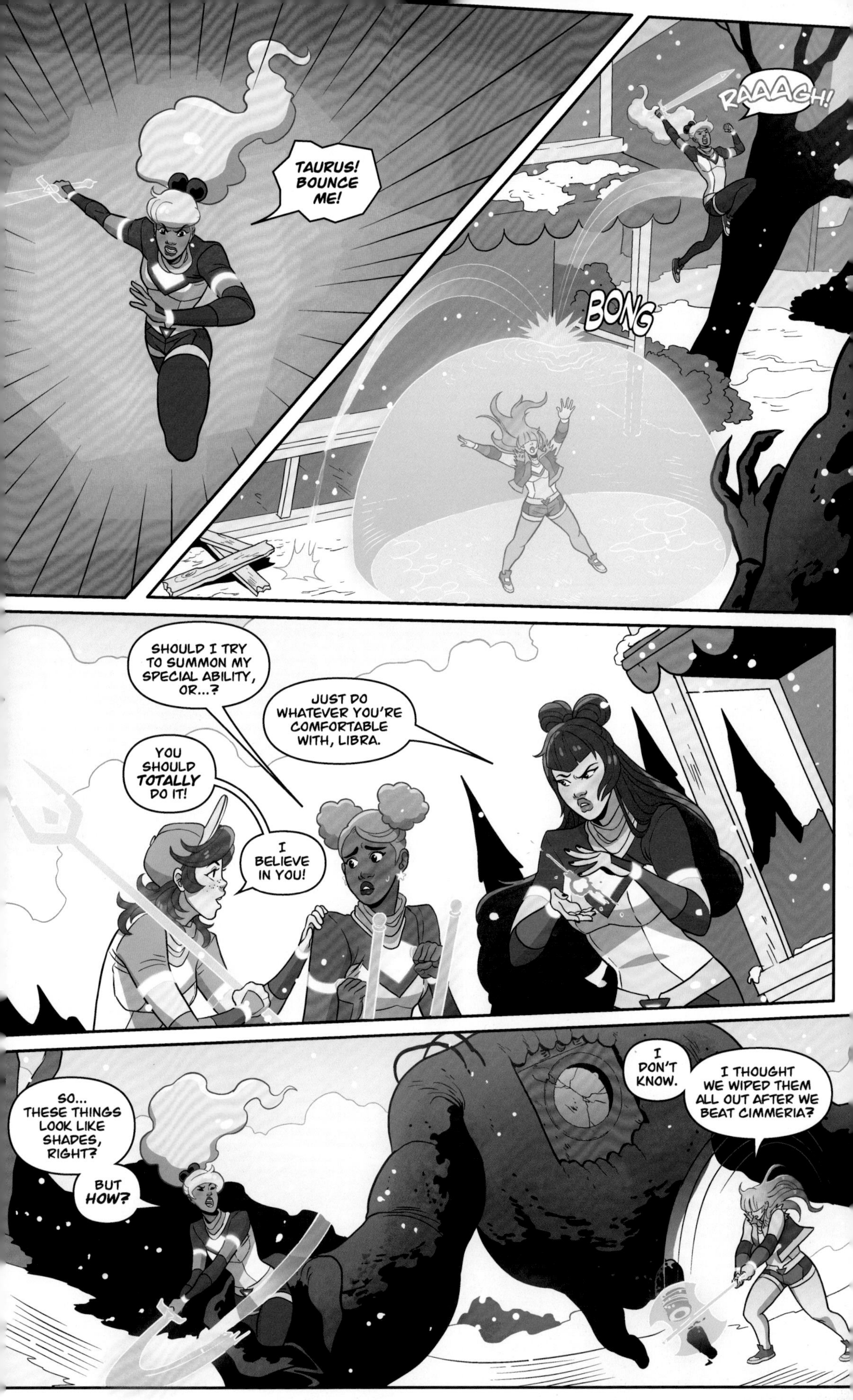

TAURUS! BOUNCE ME!
RAAAGH!
BONG
SHOULD I TRY TO SUMMON MY SPECIAL ABILITY, OR...?
JUST DO WHATEVER YOU'RE COMFORTABLE WITH, LIBRA.
YOU SHOULD TOTALLY DO IT!
I BELIEVE IN YOU!
SO... THESE THINGS LOOK LIKE SHADES, RIGHT?
BUT HOW?
I DON'T KNOW.
I THOUGHT WE WIPED THEM ALL OUT AFTER WE BEAT CIMMERIA?

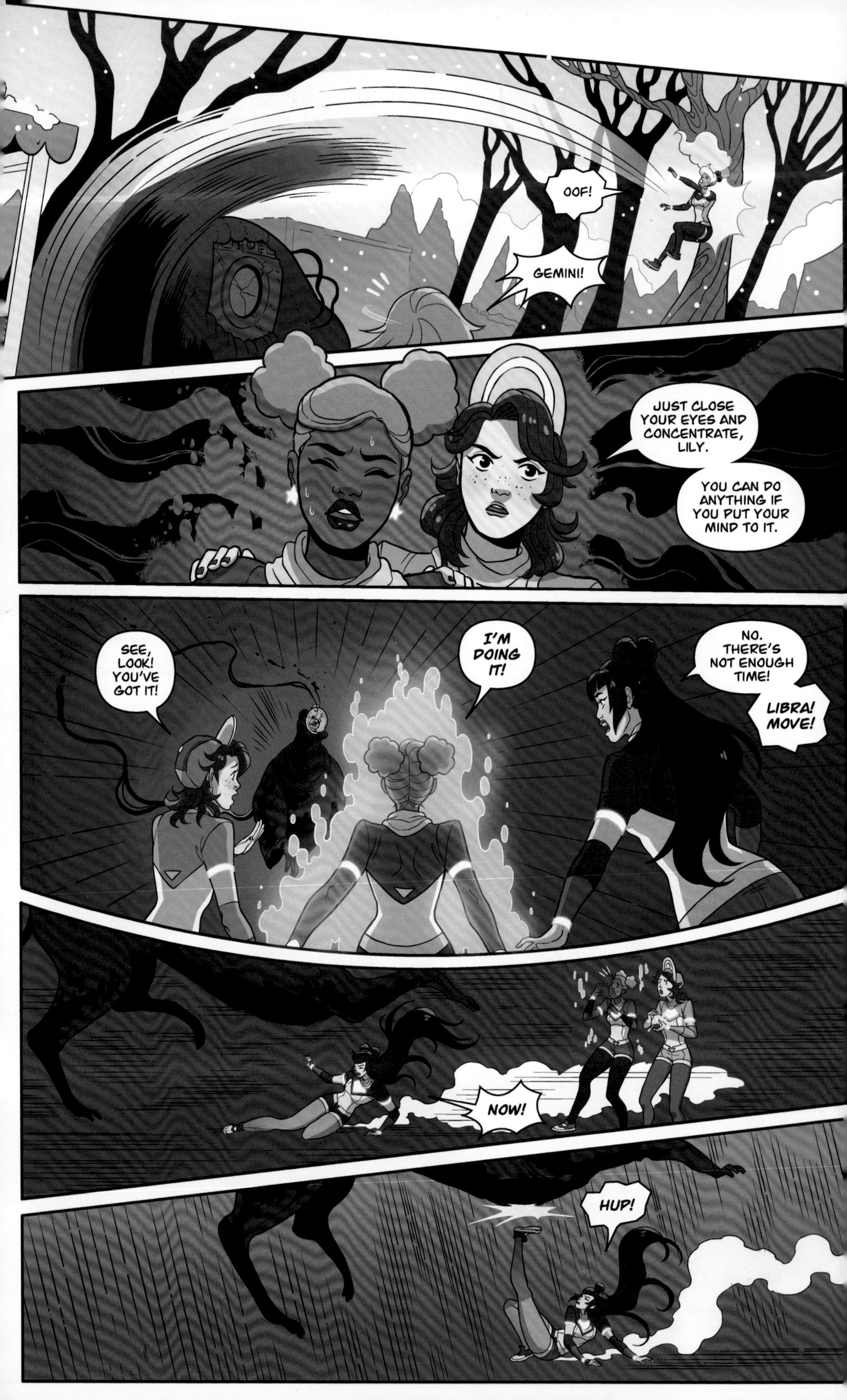
OOF!
GEMINI!
JUST CLOSE YOUR EYES AND CONCENTRATE, LILY.
YOU CAN DO ANYTHING IF YOU PUT YOUR MIND TO IT.
SEE, LOOK! YOU'VE GOT IT!
I'M DOING IT!
NO. THERE'S NOT ENOUGH TIME!
LIBRA! MOVE!
NOW!
HUP!

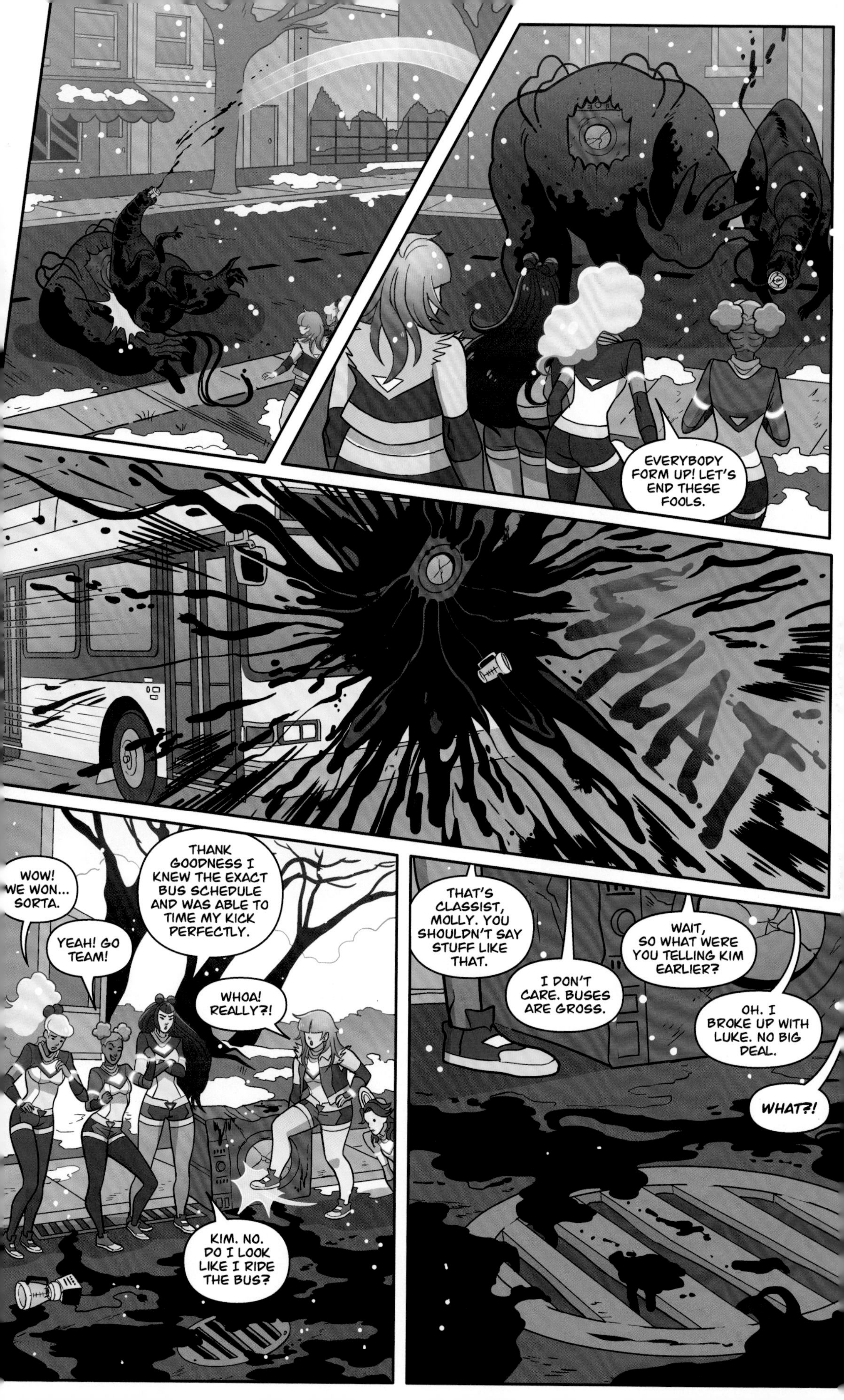
EVERYBODY FORM UP! LET'S END THESE FOOLS.
SPLAT
WOW! WE WON... SORTA.
YEAH! GO TEAM!
THANK GOODNESS I KNEW THE EXACT BUS SCHEDULE AND WAS ABLE TO TIME MY KICK PERFECTLY.
WHOA! REALLY?!
KIM. NO. DO I LOOK LIKE I RIDE THE BUS?
THAT'S CLASSIST, MOLLY. YOU SHOULDN'T SAY STUFF LIKE THAT.
I DON'T CARE. BUSES ARE GROSS.
WAIT, SO WHAT WERE YOU TELLING KIM EARLIER?
OH. I BROKE UP WITH LUKE. NO BIG DEAL.
WHAT?!

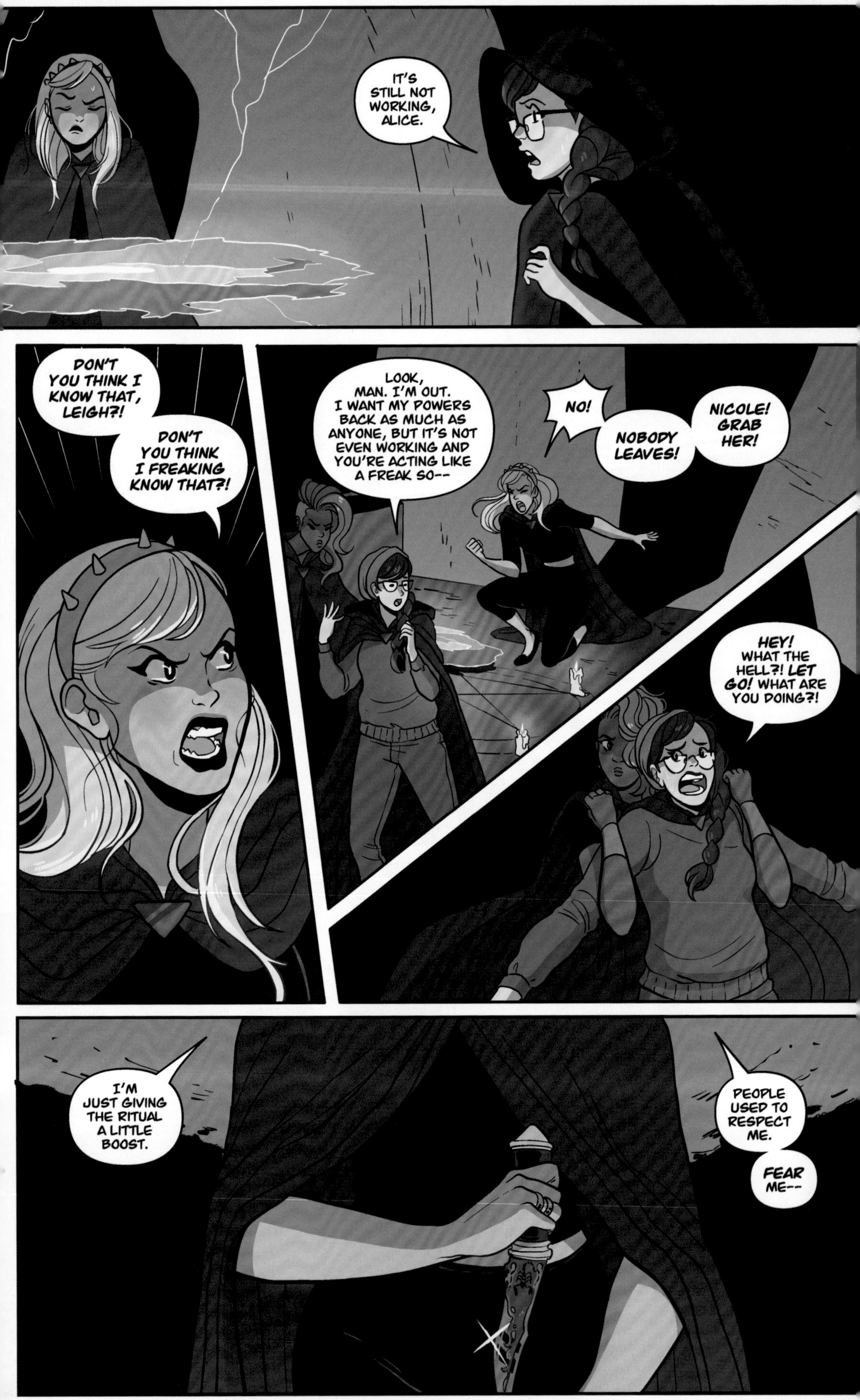
IT'S STILL NOT WORKING, ALICE.
DON'T YOU THINK I KNOW THAT, LEIGH?!
DON'T YOU THINK I FREAKING KNOW THAT?!
LOOK, MAN. I'M OUT. I WANT MY POWERS BACK AS MUCH AS ANYONE, BUT IT'S NOT EVEN WORKING AND YOU'RE ACTING LIKE A FREAK SO--
NO!
NOBODY LEAVES!
NICOLE! GRAB HER!
HEY! WHAT THE HELL?! LET GO! WHAT ARE YOU DOING?!
I'M JUST GIVING THE RITUAL A LITTLE BOOST.
PEOPLE USED TO RESPECT ME.
FEAR ME--

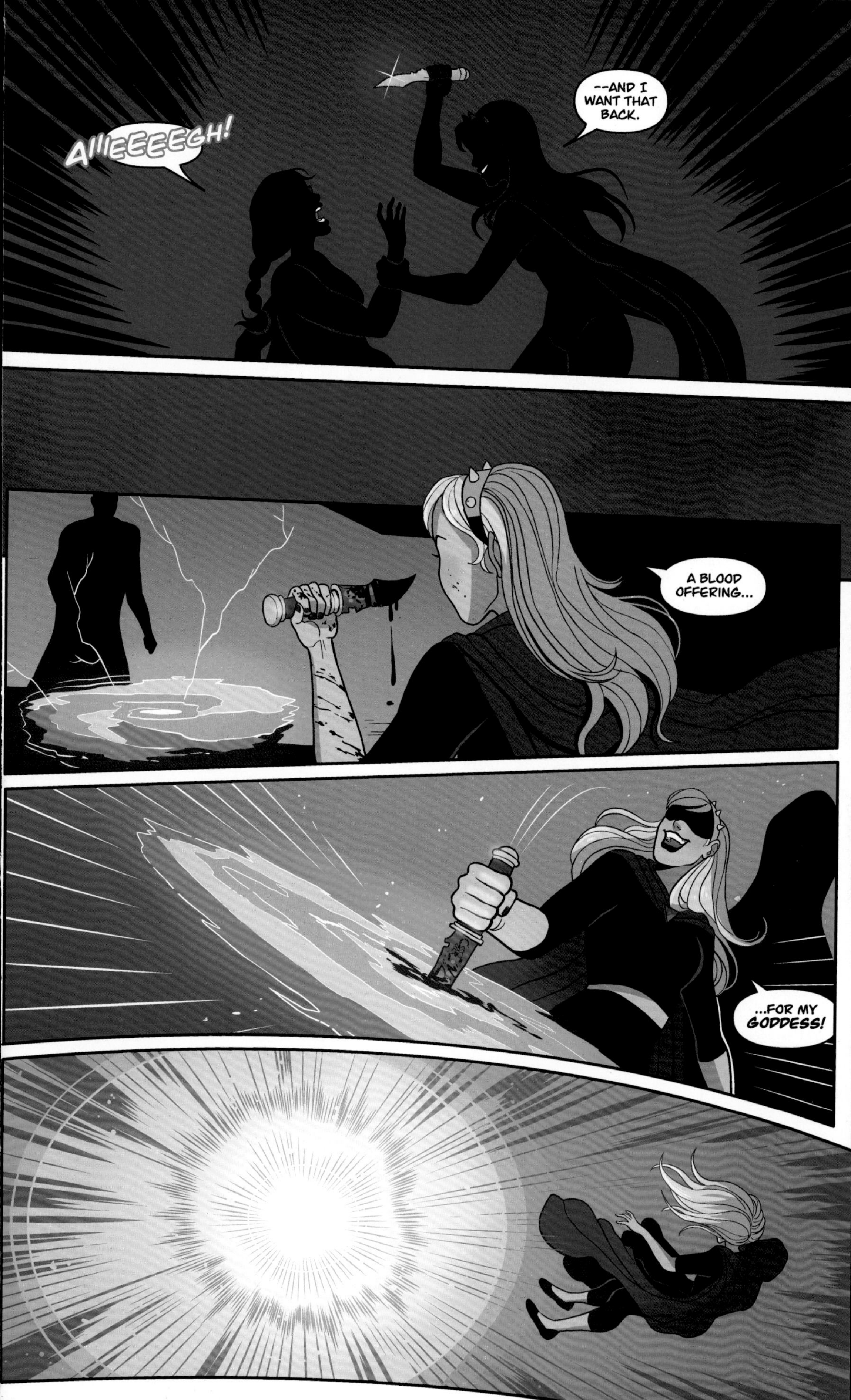
AIIIEEEEEGH!
--AND I WANT THAT BACK.
A BLOOD OFFERING...
...FOR MY GODDESS!

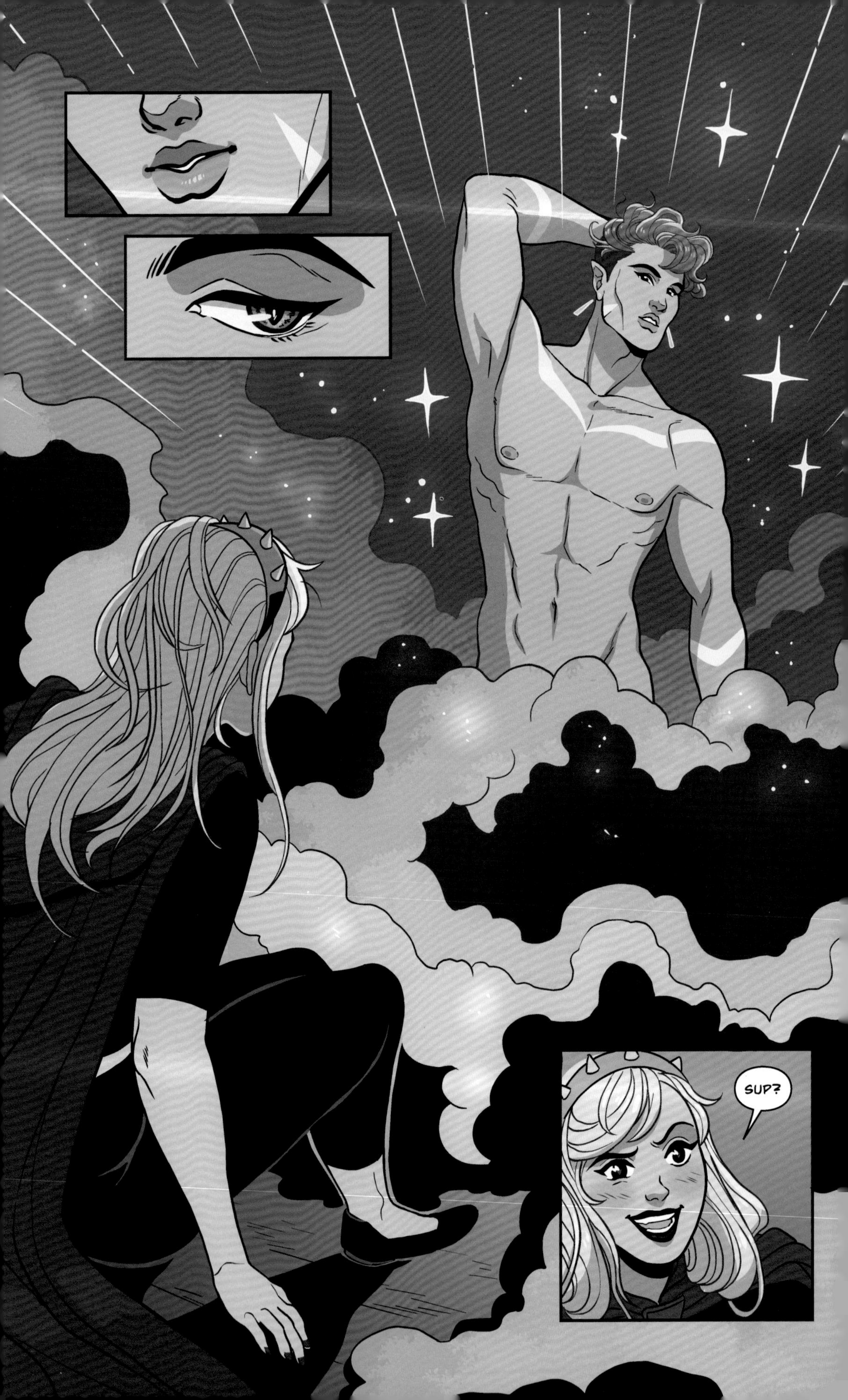
SUP?

CHAPTER TWO

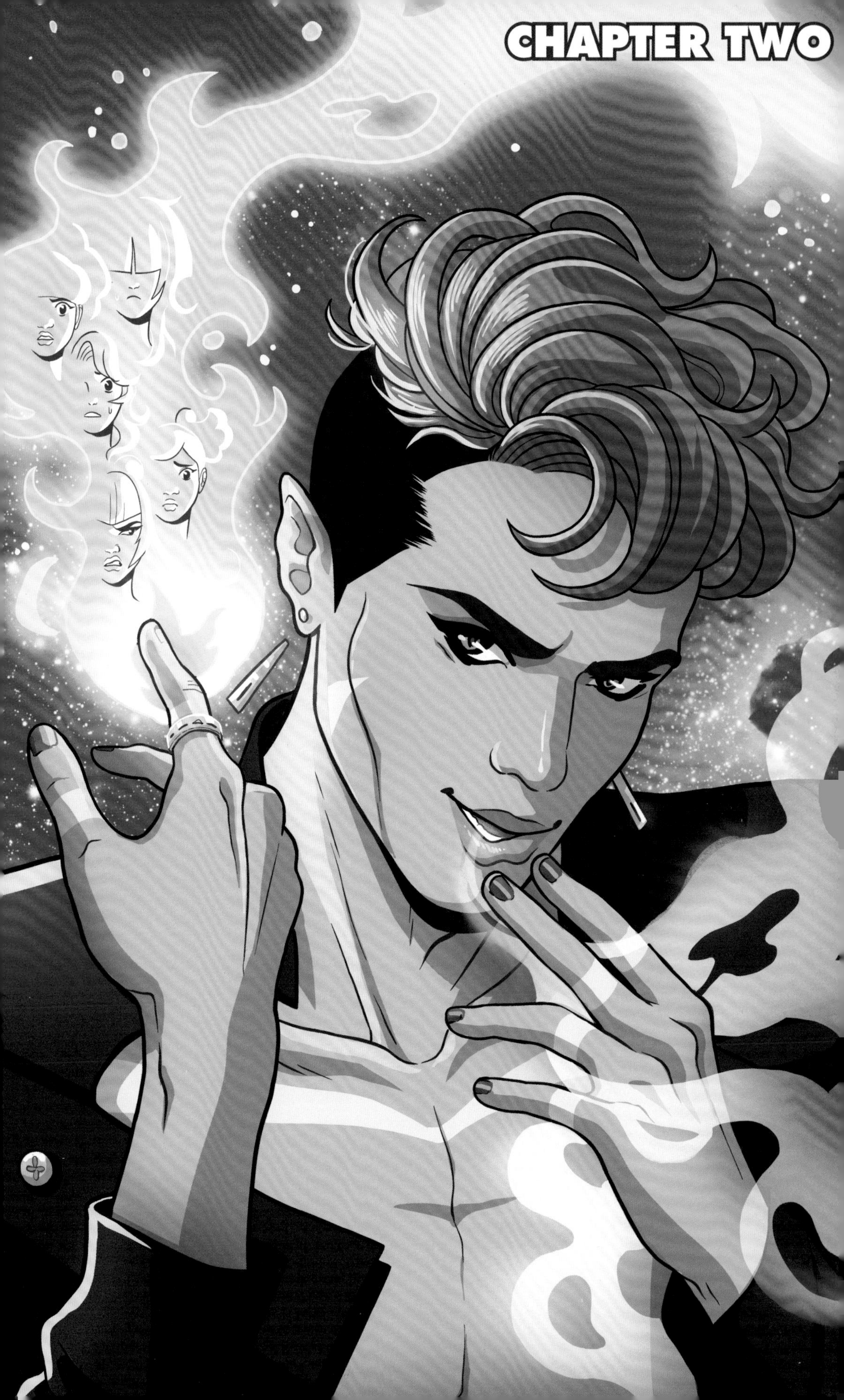

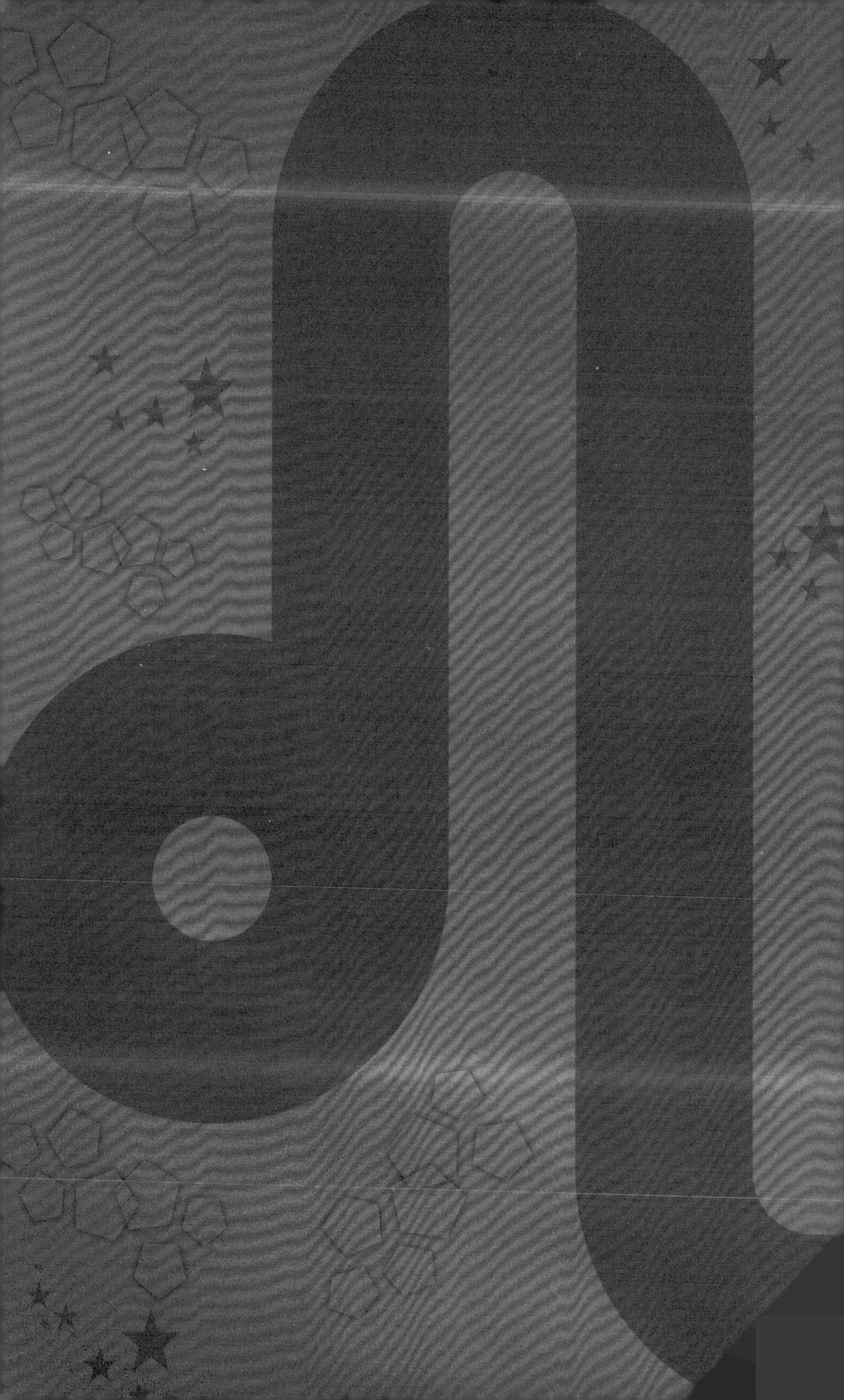

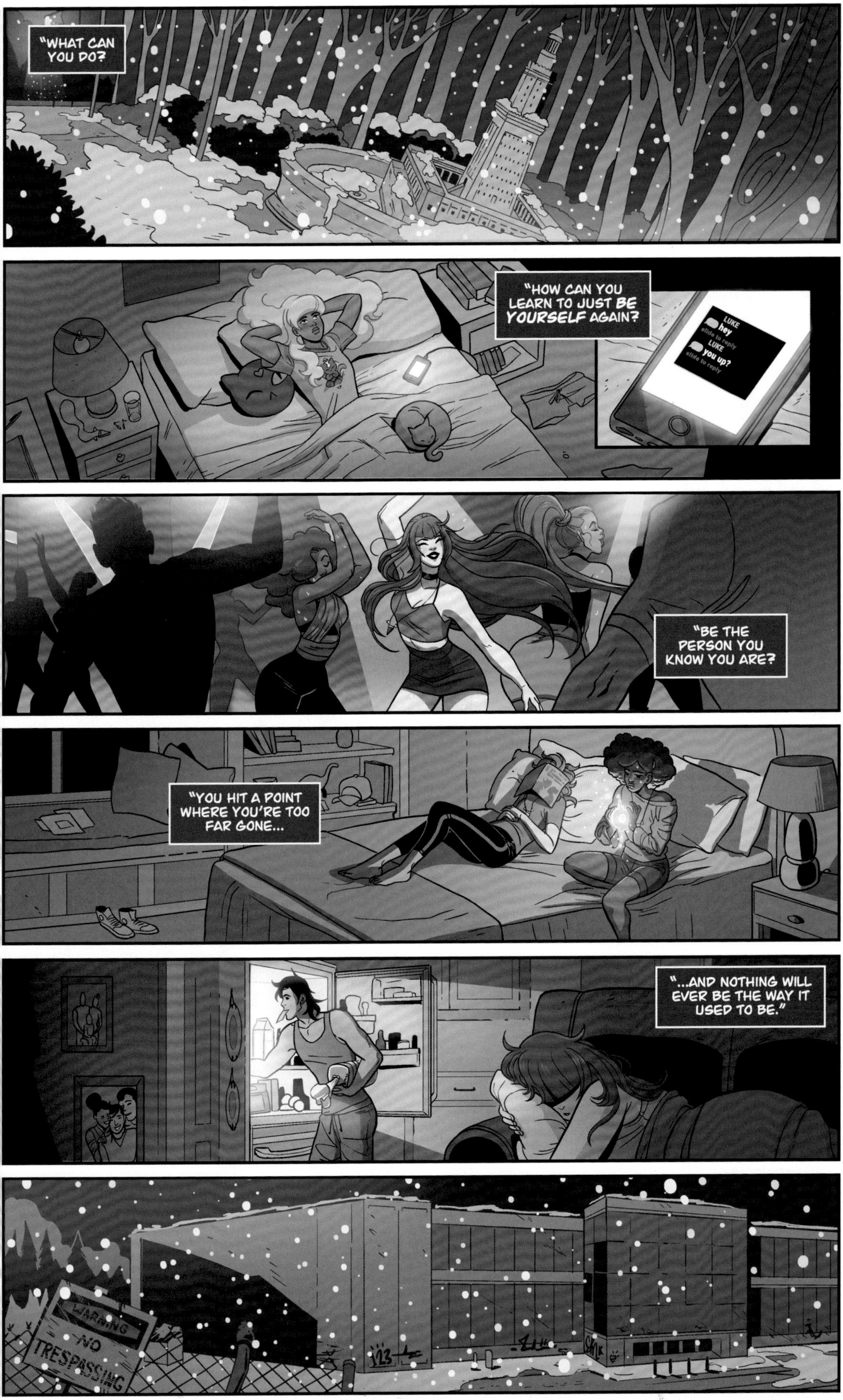
"WHAT CAN YOU DO?
"HOW CAN YOU LEARN TO JUST BE YOURSELF AGAIN?
LUKE
hey
slide to reply
LUKE
you up?
slide to reply
"BE THE PERSON YOU KNOW YOU ARE?
"YOU HIT A POINT WHERE YOU'RE TOO FAR GONE...
"...AND NOTHING WILL EVER BE THE WAY IT USED TO BE."
WARNING
NO
TRESPASSING

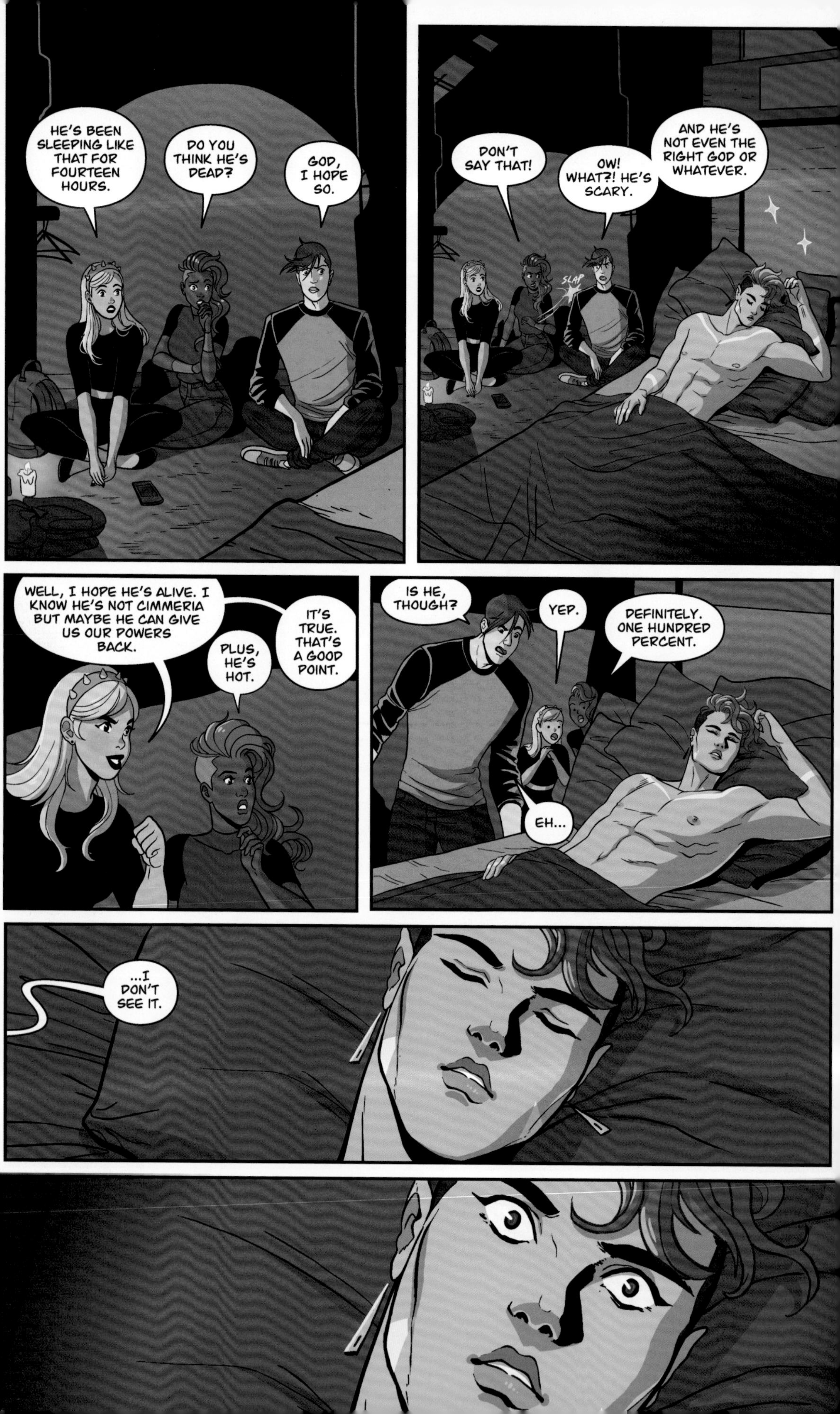
HE'S BEEN SLEEPING LIKE THAT FOR FOURTEEN HOURS.
DO YOU THINK HE'S DEAD?
GOD, I HOPE SO.
DON'T SAY THAT!
SLAP
OW! WHAT?! HE'S SCARY.
AND HE'S NOT EVEN THE RIGHT GOD OR WHATEVER.
WELL, I HOPE HE'S ALIVE. I KNOW HE'S NOT CIMMERIA BUT MAYBE HE CAN GIVE US OUR POWERS BACK.
PLUS, HE'S HOT.
IT'S TRUE. THAT'S A GOOD POINT.
IS HE, THOUGH?
YEP.
DEFINITELY. ONE HUNDRED PERCENT.
EH...
...I DON'T SEE IT.

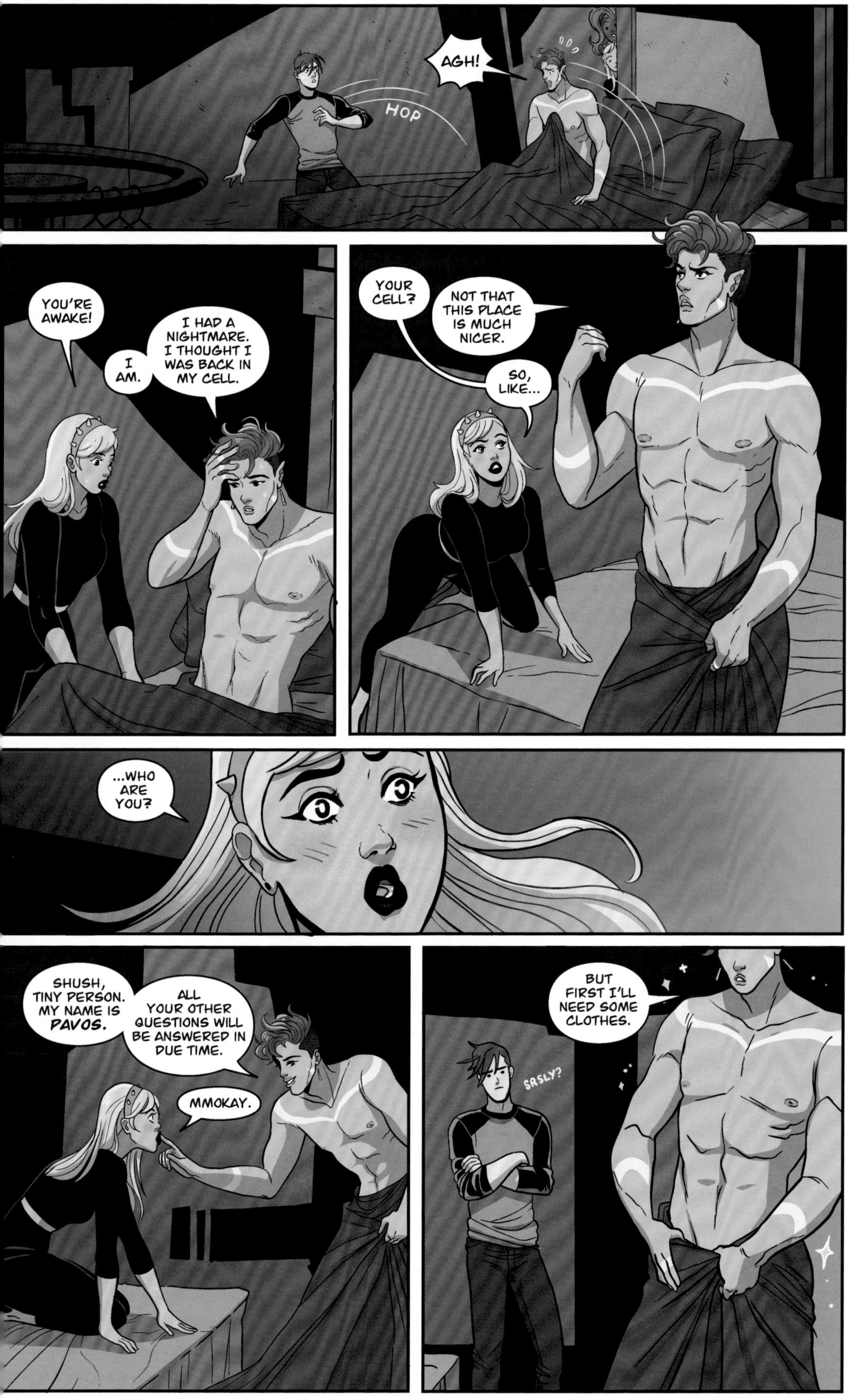

AGH!
HOP
YOU'RE AWAKE!
I AM.
I HAD A NIGHTMARE. I THOUGHT I WAS BACK IN MY CELL.
YOUR CELL?
NOT THAT THIS PLACE IS MUCH NICER.
SO, LIKE...
...WHO ARE YOU?
SHUSH, TINY PERSON. MY NAME IS PAVOS.
ALL YOUR OTHER QUESTIONS WILL BE ANSWERED IN DUE TIME.
MMOKAY.
BUT FIRST I'LL NEED SOME CLOTHES.
SRSLY?

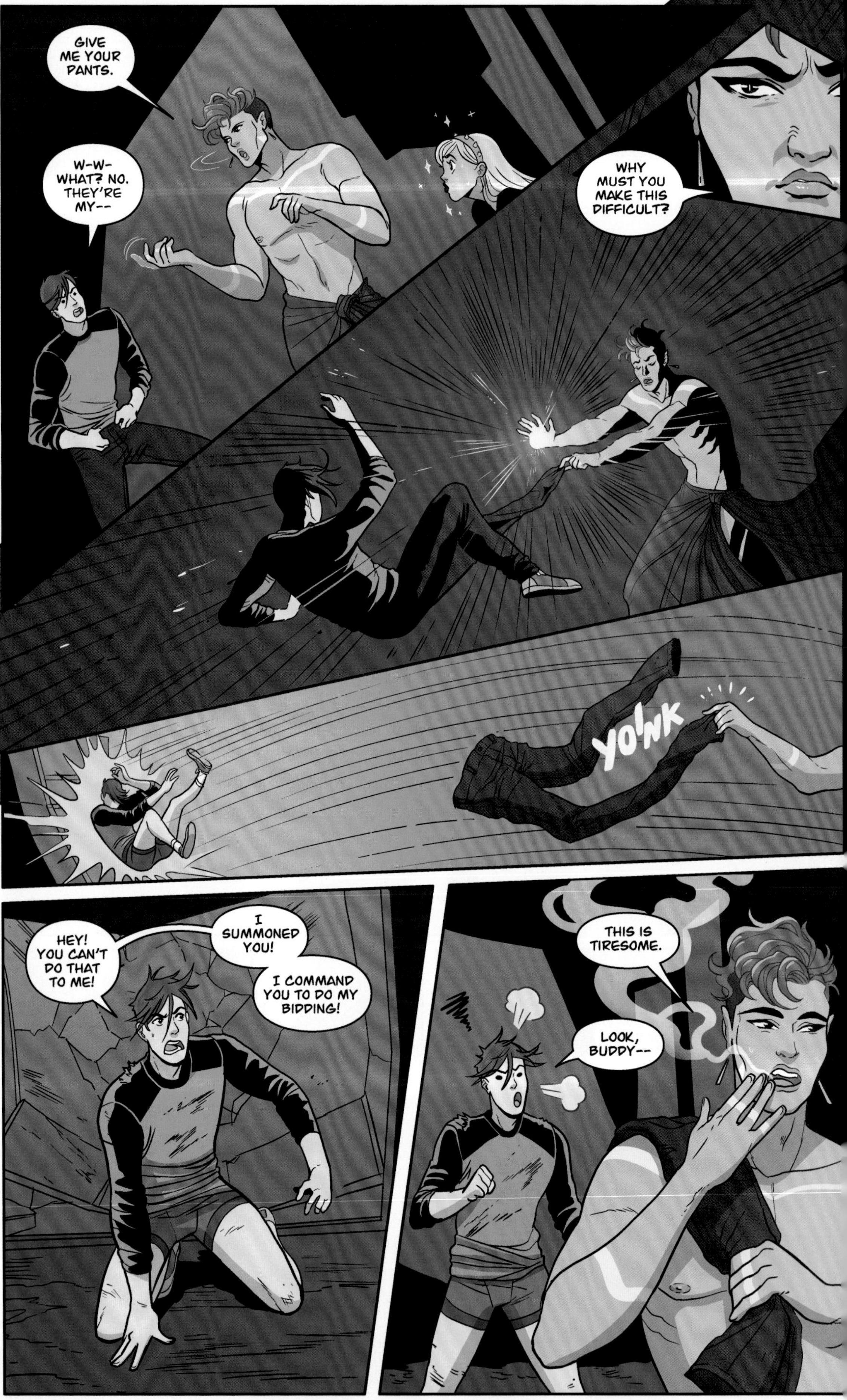
GIVE ME YOUR PANTS.
W-W-WHAT? NO. THEY'RE MY--
WHY MUST YOU MAKE THIS DIFFICULT?
YOINK
HEY! YOU CAN'T DO THAT TO ME!
I SUMMONED YOU!
I COMMAND YOU TO DO MY BIDDING!
THIS IS TIRESOME.
LOOK, BUDDY--

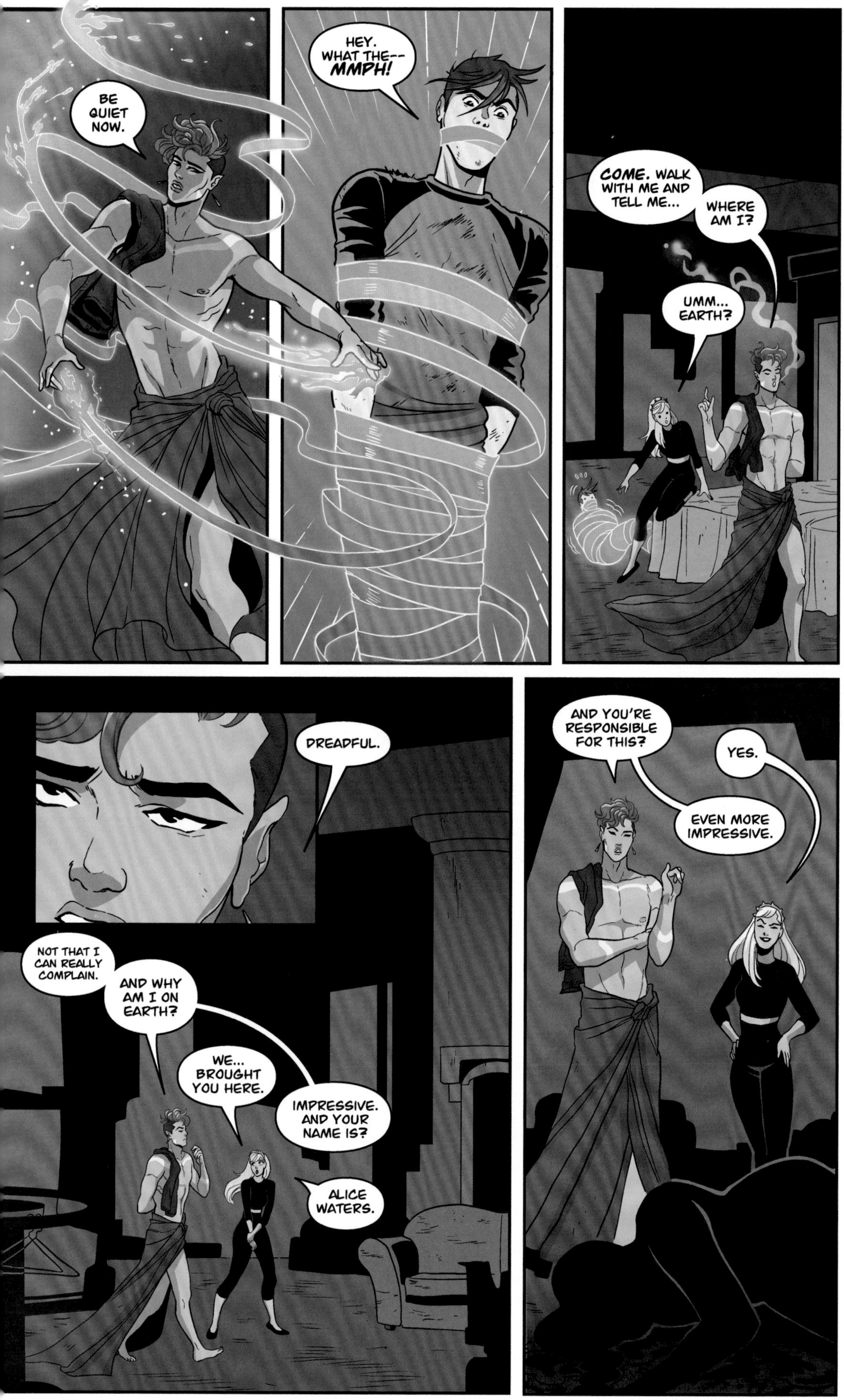
BE QUIET NOW.
HEY. WHAT THE-- MMPH!
COME. WALK WITH ME AND TELL ME...
WHERE AM I?
UMM... EARTH?
DREADFUL.
NOT THAT I CAN REALLY COMPLAIN.
AND WHY AM I ON EARTH?
WE... BROUGHT YOU HERE.
IMPRESSIVE. AND YOUR NAME IS?
ALICE WATERS.
AND YOU'RE RESPONSIBLE FOR THIS?
YES.
EVEN MORE IMPRESSIVE.

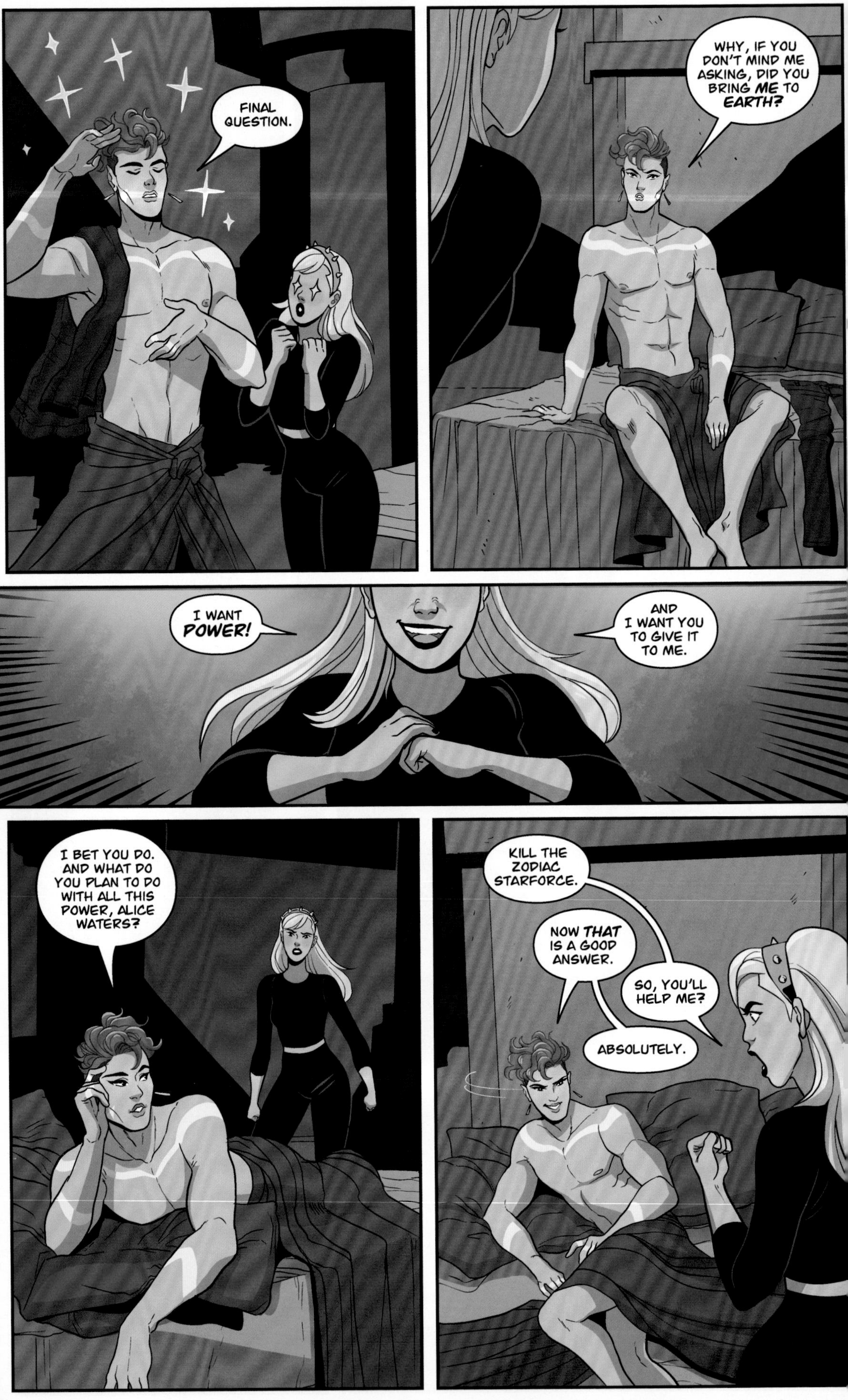

FINAL QUESTION.
WHY, IF YOU DON'T MIND ME ASKING, DID YOU BRING ME TO EARTH?
I WANT POWER!
AND I WANT YOU TO GIVE IT TO ME.
I BET YOU DO. AND WHAT DO YOU PLAN TO DO WITH ALL THIS POWER, ALICE WATERS?
KILL THE ZODIAC STARFORCE.
NOW THAT IS A GOOD ANSWER.
SO, YOU'LL HELP ME?
ABSOLUTELY.

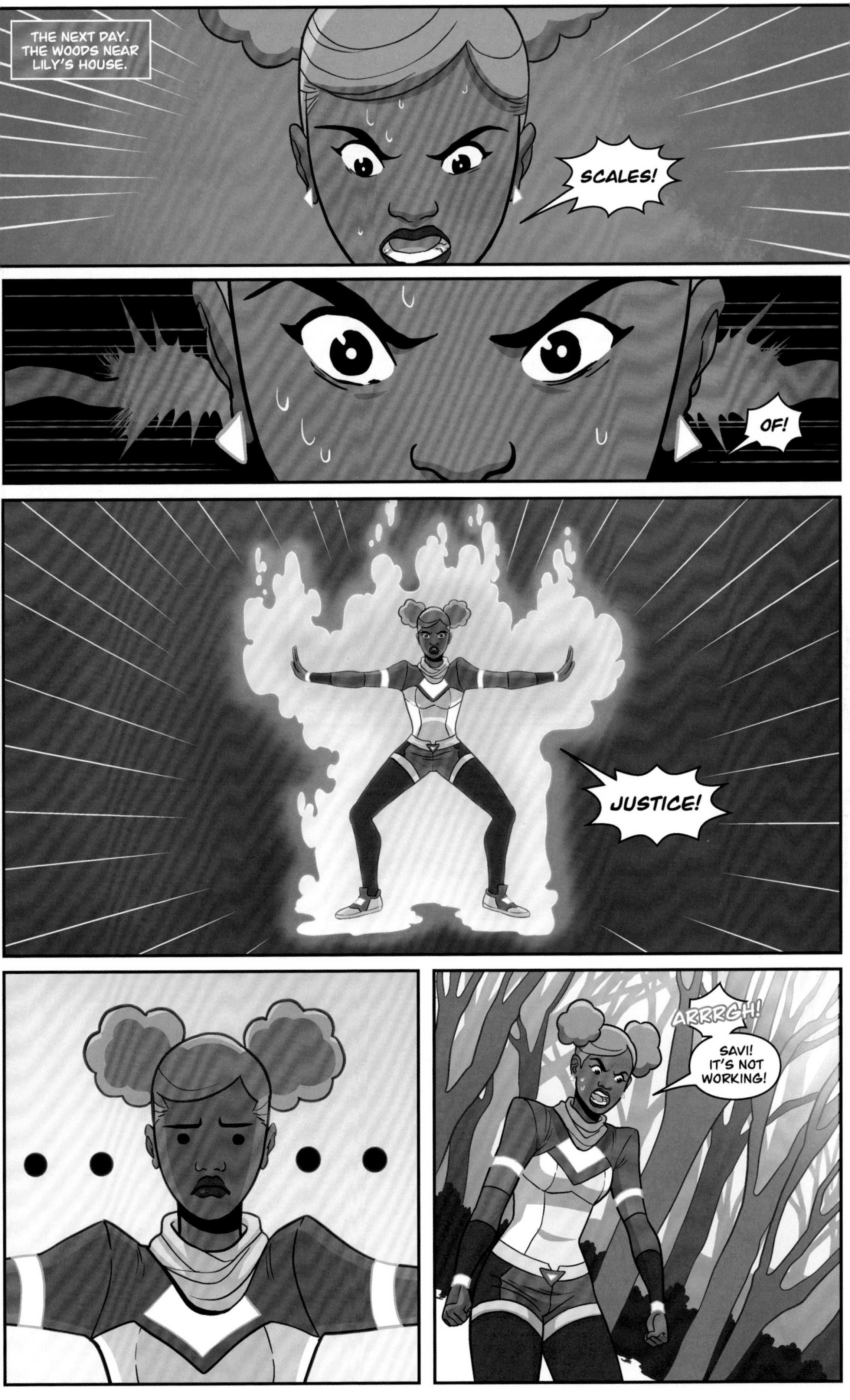
THE NEXT DAY. THE WOODS NEAR LILY'S HOUSE.
SCALES!
OF!
JUSTICE!
. . . .
ARRRGH!
SAVI! IT'S NOT WORKING!

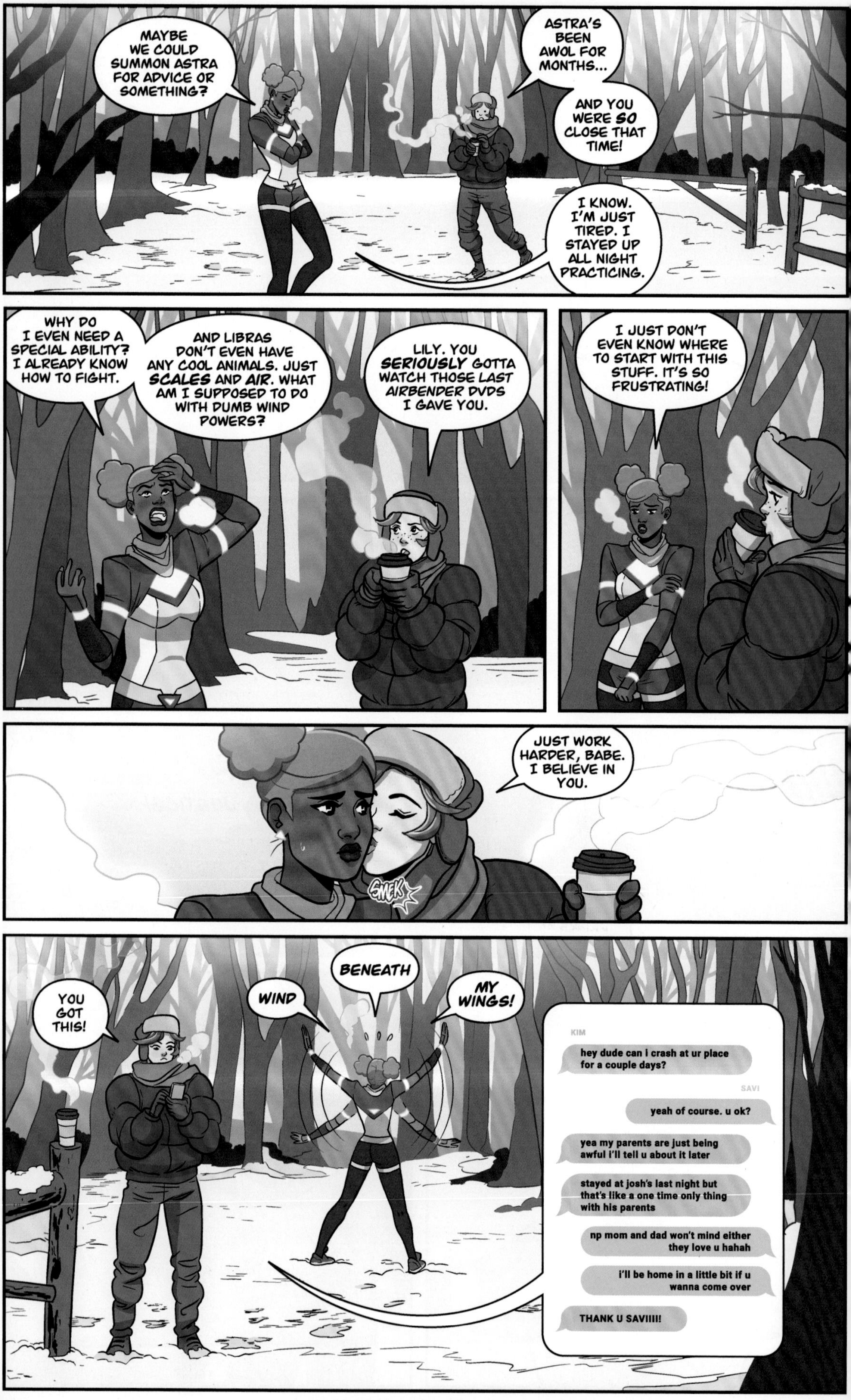
MAYBE WE COULD SUMMON ASTRA FOR ADVICE OR SOMETHING?
ASTRA'S BEEN AWOL FOR MONTHS...
AND YOU WERE SO CLOSE THAT TIME!
I KNOW. I'M JUST TIRED. I STAYED UP ALL NIGHT PRACTICING.
WHY DO I EVEN NEED A SPECIAL ABILITY? I ALREADY KNOW HOW TO FIGHT.
AND LIBRAS DON'T EVEN HAVE ANY COOL ANIMALS. JUST SCALES AND AIR. WHAT AM I SUPPOSED TO DO WITH DUMB WIND POWERS?
LILY. YOU SERIOUSLY GOTTA WATCH THOSE LAST AIRBENDER DVDS I GAVE YOU.
I JUST DON'T EVEN KNOW WHERE TO START WITH THIS STUFF. IT'S SO FRUSTRATING!
JUST WORK HARDER, BABE. I BELIEVE IN YOU.
SMEK
YOU GOT THIS!
WIND
BENEATH
MY WINGS!
KIM
hey dude can i crash at ur place for a couple days?
SAVI
yeah of course. u ok?
yea my parents are just being awful i'll tell u about it later
stayed at josh's last night but that's like a one time only thing with his parents
np mom and dad won't mind either they love u hahah
i'll be home in a little bit if u wanna come over
THANK U SAVIIII!

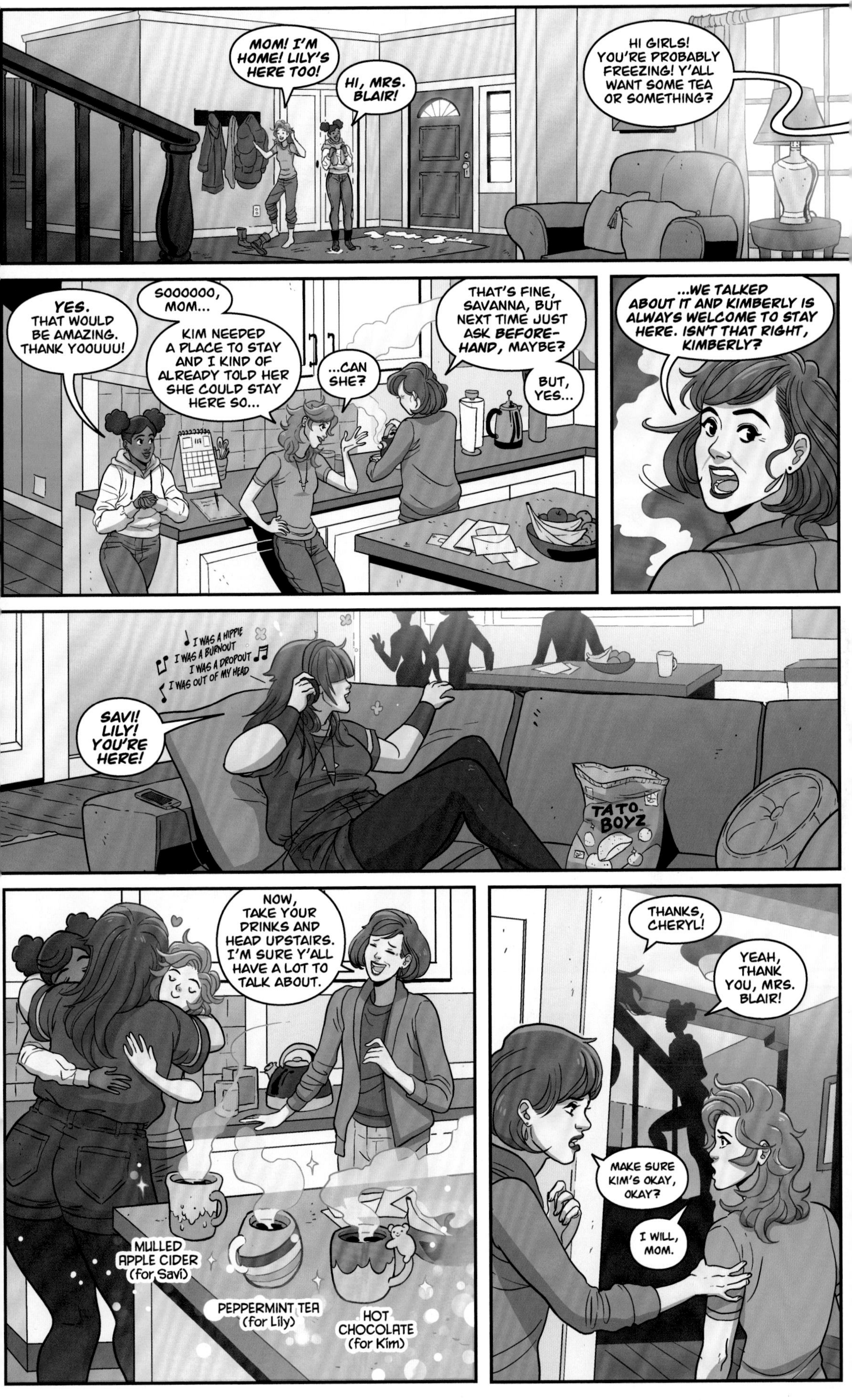
MOM! I'M HOME! LILY'S HERE TOO!
HI, MRS. BLAIR!
HI GIRLS! YOU'RE PROBABLY FREEZING! Y'ALL WANT SOME TEA OR SOMETHING?
YES. THAT WOULD BE AMAZING. THANK YOOUUU!
SOOOOOO, MOM...
KIM NEEDED A PLACE TO STAY AND I KIND OF ALREADY TOLD HER SHE COULD STAY HERE SO...
...CAN SHE?
THAT'S FINE, SAVANNA, BUT NEXT TIME JUST ASK BEFORE-HAND, MAYBE?
BUT, YES...
...WE TALKED ABOUT IT AND KIMBERLY IS ALWAYS WELCOME TO STAY HERE. ISN'T THAT RIGHT, KIMBERLY?
I WAS A HIPPIE
I WAS A BURNOUT
I WAS A DROPOUT
I WAS OUT OF MY HEAD
SAVI! LILY! YOU'RE HERE!
TATO BOYZ
NOW, TAKE YOUR DRINKS AND HEAD UPSTAIRS. I'M SURE Y'ALL HAVE A LOT TO TALK ABOUT.
MULLED APPLE CIDER (for Savi)
PEPPERMINT TEA (for Lily)
HOT CHOCOLATE (for Kim)
THANKS, CHERYL!
YEAH, THANK YOU, MRS. BLAIR!
MAKE SURE KIM'S OKAY, OKAY?
I WILL, MOM.

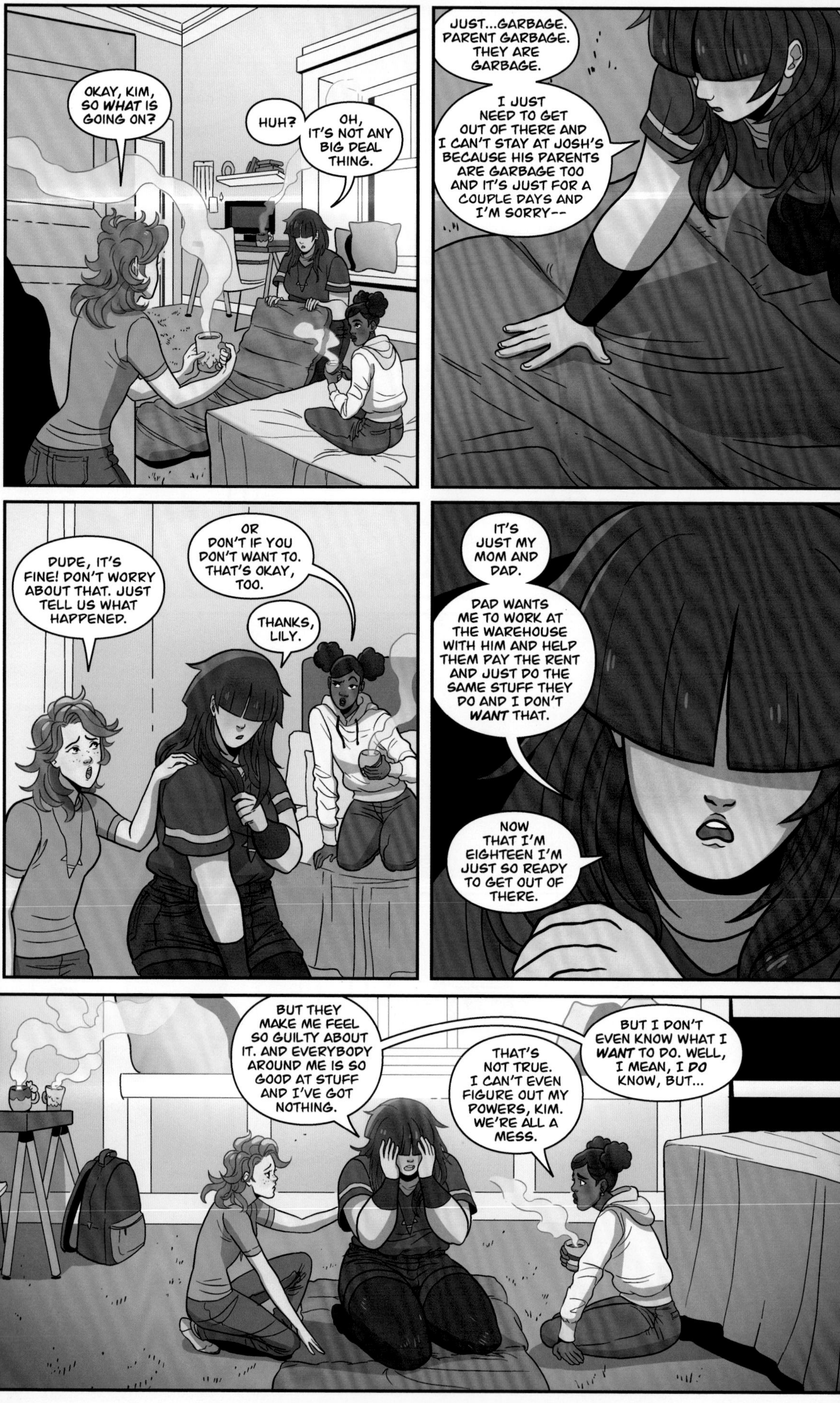
OKAY, KIM, SO WHAT IS GOING ON?
HUH?
OH, IT'S NOT ANY BIG DEAL THING.
JUST...GARBAGE. PARENT GARBAGE. THEY ARE GARBAGE.
I JUST NEED TO GET OUT OF THERE AND I CAN'T STAY AT JOSH'S BECAUSE HIS PARENTS ARE GARBAGE TOO AND IT'S JUST FOR A COUPLE DAYS AND I'M SORRY--
DUDE, IT'S FINE! DON'T WORRY ABOUT THAT. JUST TELL US WHAT HAPPENED.
OR DON'T IF YOU DON'T WANT TO. THAT'S OKAY, TOO.
THANKS, LILY.
IT'S JUST MY MOM AND DAD.
DAD WANTS ME TO WORK AT THE WAREHOUSE WITH HIM AND HELP THEM PAY THE RENT AND JUST DO THE SAME STUFF THEY DO AND I DON'T WANT THAT.
NOW THAT I'M EIGHTEEN I'M JUST SO READY TO GET OUT OF THERE.
BUT THEY MAKE ME FEEL SO GUILTY ABOUT IT. AND EVERYBODY AROUND ME IS SO GOOD AT STUFF AND I'VE GOT NOTHING.
BUT I DON'T EVEN KNOW WHAT I WANT TO DO. WELL, I MEAN, I DO KNOW, BUT...
THAT'S NOT TRUE. I CAN'T EVEN FIGURE OUT MY POWERS, KIM. WE'RE ALL A MESS.

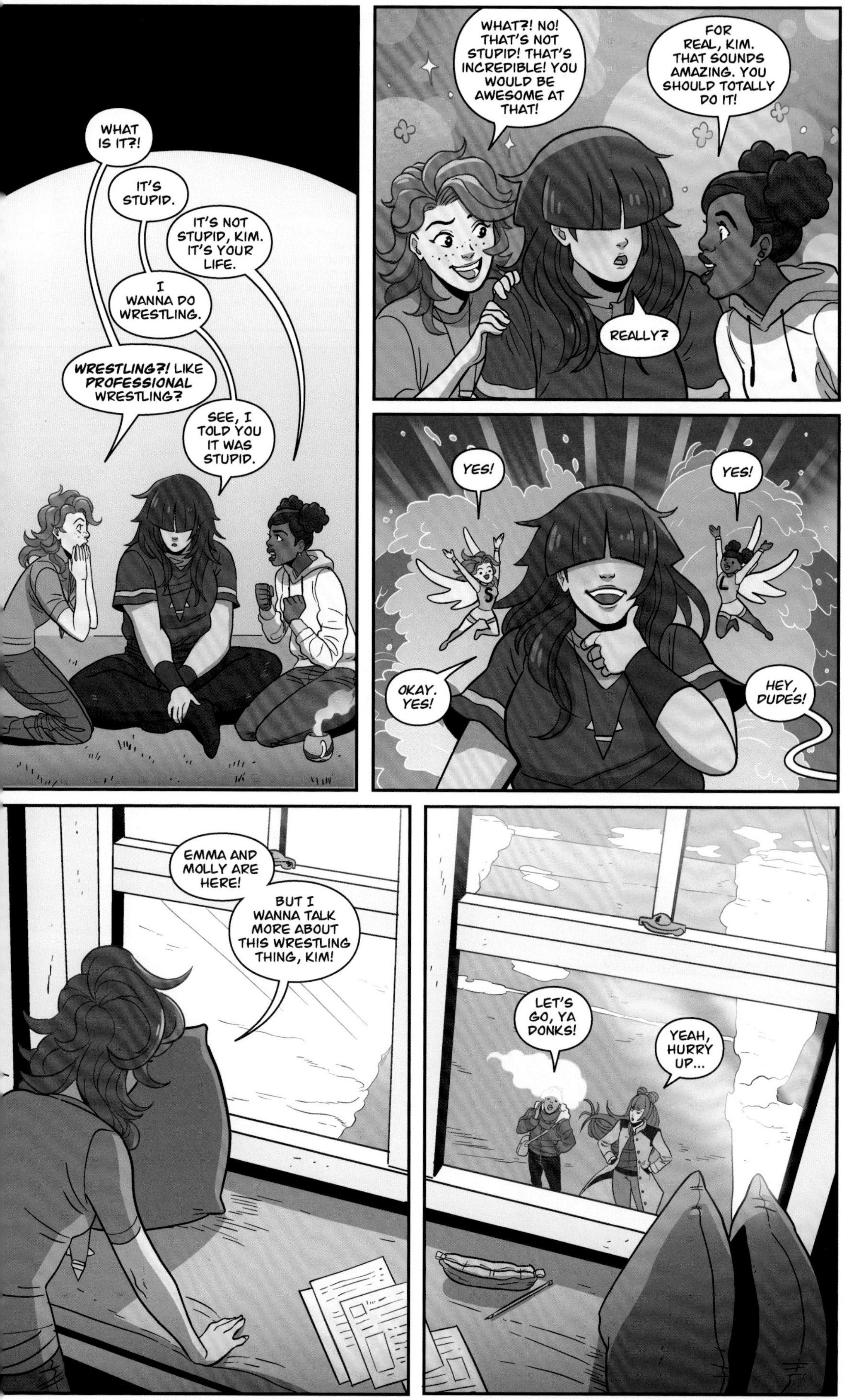
WHAT IS IT?!
IT'S STUPID.
IT'S NOT STUPID, KIM. IT'S YOUR LIFE.
I WANNA DO WRESTLING.
WRESTLING?! LIKE PROFESSIONAL WRESTLING?
SEE, I TOLD YOU IT WAS STUPID.
WHAT?! NO! THAT'S NOT STUPID! THAT'S INCREDIBLE! YOU WOULD BE AWESOME AT THAT!
FOR REAL, KIM. THAT SOUNDS AMAZING. YOU SHOULD TOTALLY DO IT!
REALLY?
YES!
YES!
OKAY. YES!
HEY, DUDES!
EMMA AND MOLLY ARE HERE!
BUT I WANNA TALK MORE ABOUT THIS WRESTLING THING, KIM!
LET'S GO, YA DONKS!
YEAH, HURRY UP...

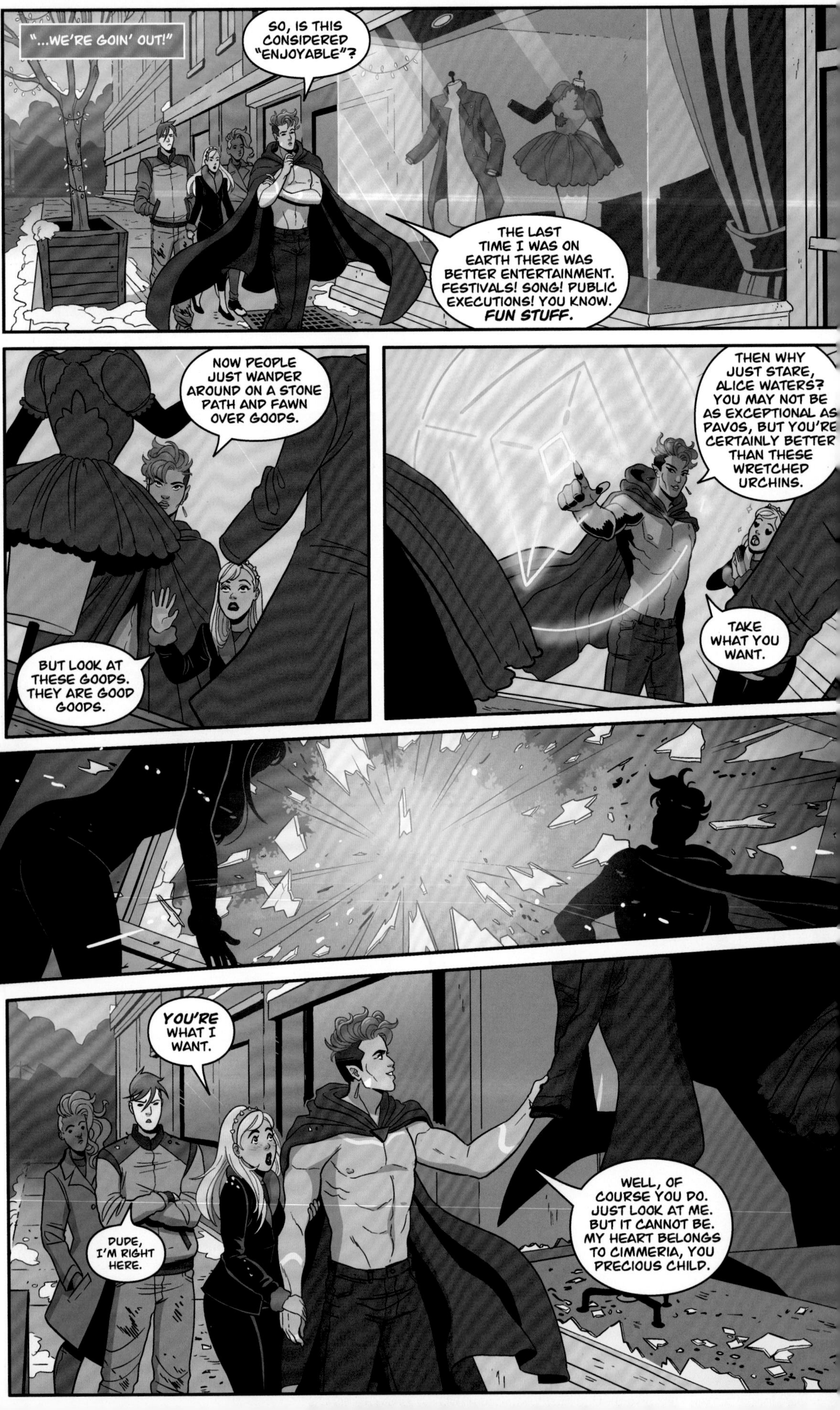
"...WE'RE GOIN' OUT!"
SO, IS THIS CONSIDERED "ENJOYABLE"?
THE LAST TIME I WAS ON EARTH THERE WAS BETTER ENTERTAINMENT. FESTIVALS! SONG! PUBLIC EXECUTIONS! YOU KNOW. FUN STUFF.
NOW PEOPLE JUST WANDER AROUND ON A STONE PATH AND FAWN OVER GOODS.
BUT LOOK AT THESE GOODS. THEY ARE GOOD GOODS.
THEN WHY JUST STARE, ALICE WATERS? YOU MAY NOT BE AS EXCEPTIONAL AS PAVOS, BUT YOU'RE CERTAINLY BETTER THAN THESE WRETCHED URCHINS.
TAKE WHAT YOU WANT.
YOU'RE WHAT I WANT.
WELL, OF COURSE YOU DO. JUST LOOK AT ME. BUT IT CANNOT BE. MY HEART BELONGS TO CIMMERIA, YOU PRECIOUS CHILD.
DUDE, I'M RIGHT HERE.

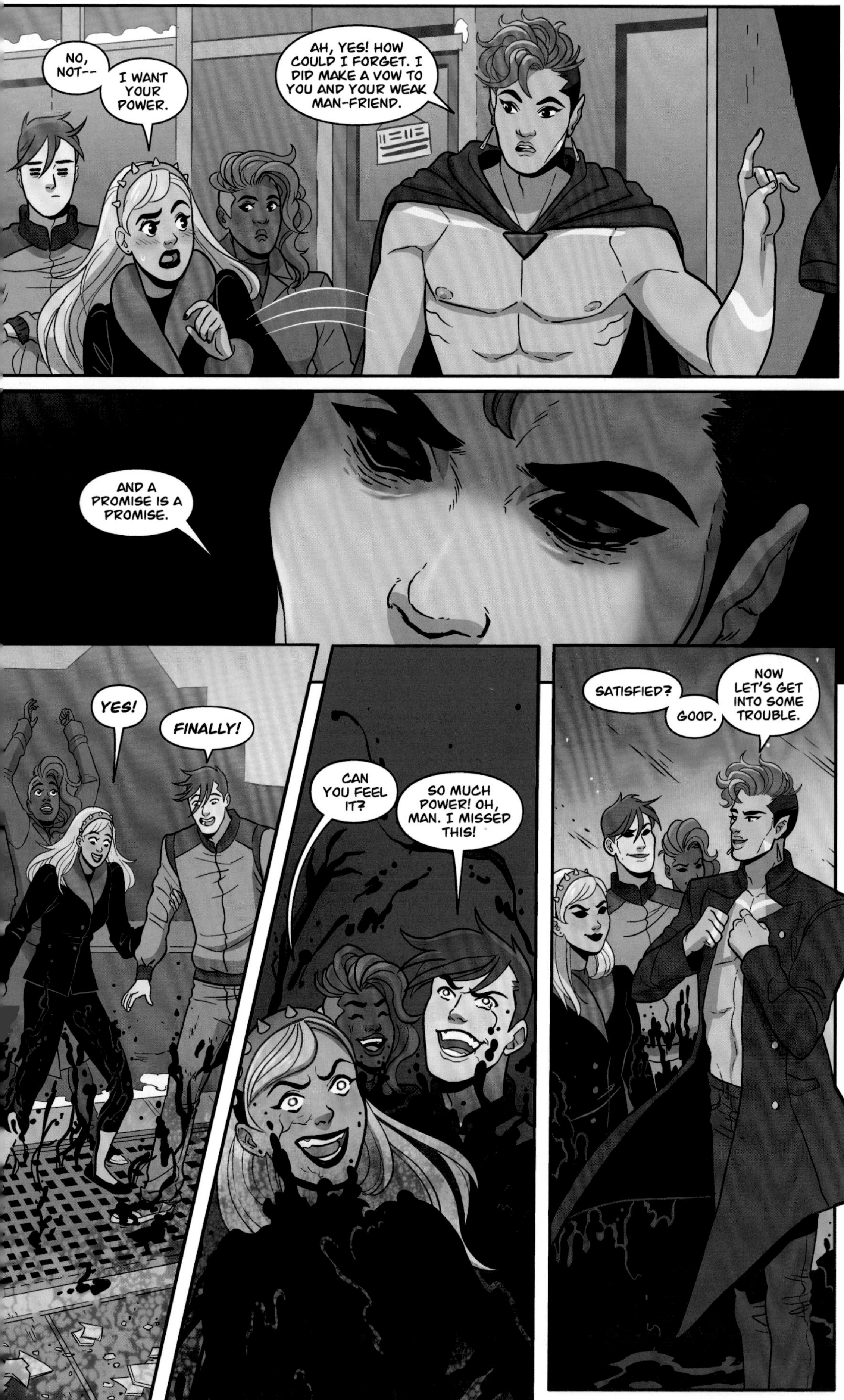
NO, NOT--
I WANT YOUR POWER.
AH, YES! HOW COULD I FORGET. I DID MAKE A VOW TO YOU AND YOUR WEAK MAN-FRIEND.
AND A PROMISE IS A PROMISE.
YES!
FINALLY!
CAN YOU FEEL IT?
SO MUCH POWER! OH, MAN. I MISSED THIS!
SATISFIED?
GOOD.
NOW LET'S GET INTO SOME TROUBLE.

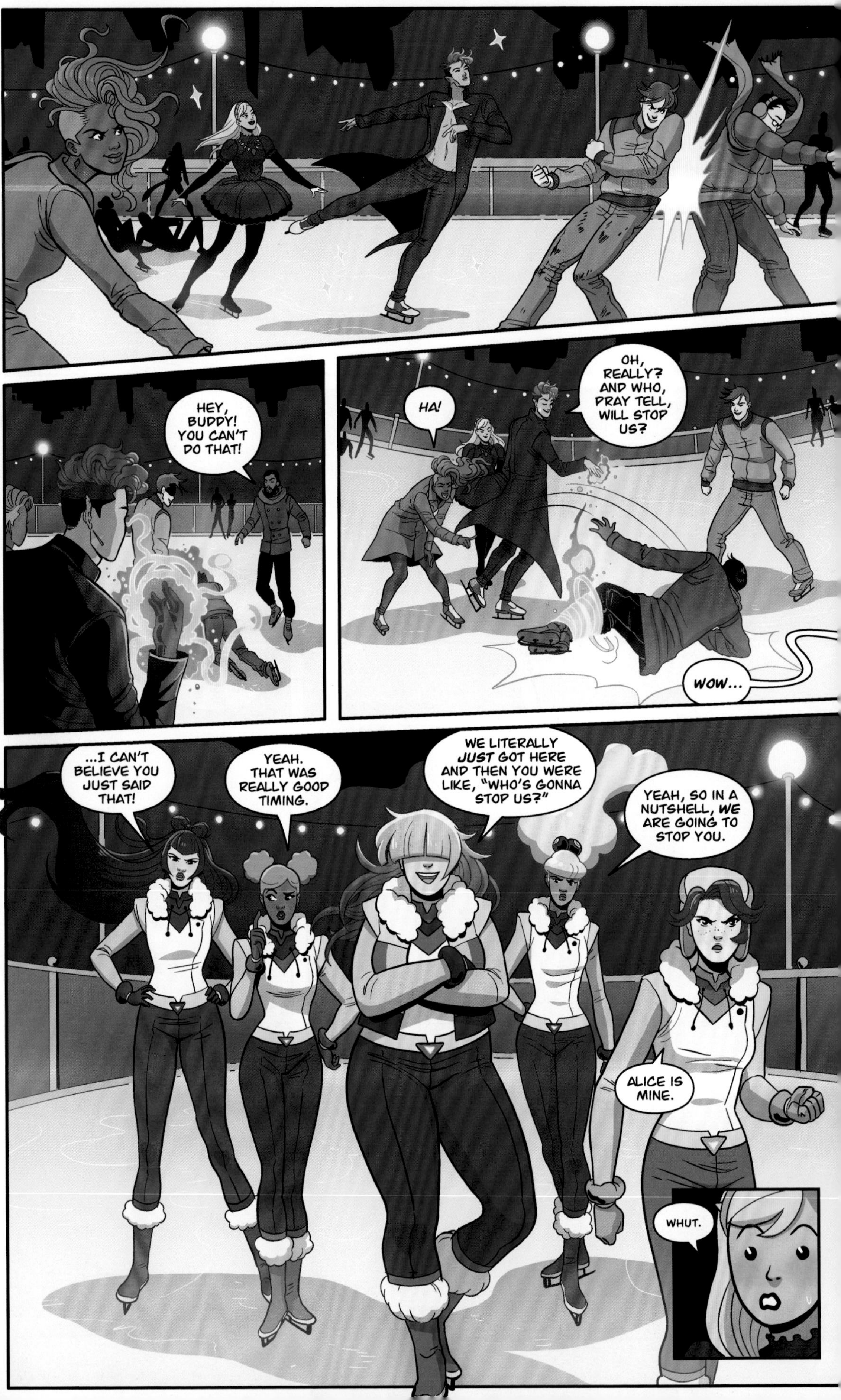
HEY, BUDDY! YOU CAN'T DO THAT!
HA!
OH, REALLY? AND WHO, PRAY TELL, WILL STOP US?
WOW...
...I CAN'T BELIEVE YOU JUST SAID THAT!
YEAH. THAT WAS REALLY GOOD TIMING.
WE LITERALLY JUST GOT HERE AND THEN YOU WERE LIKE, "WHO'S GONNA STOP US?"
YEAH, SO IN A NUTSHELL, WE ARE GOING TO STOP YOU.
ALICE IS MINE.
WHUT.

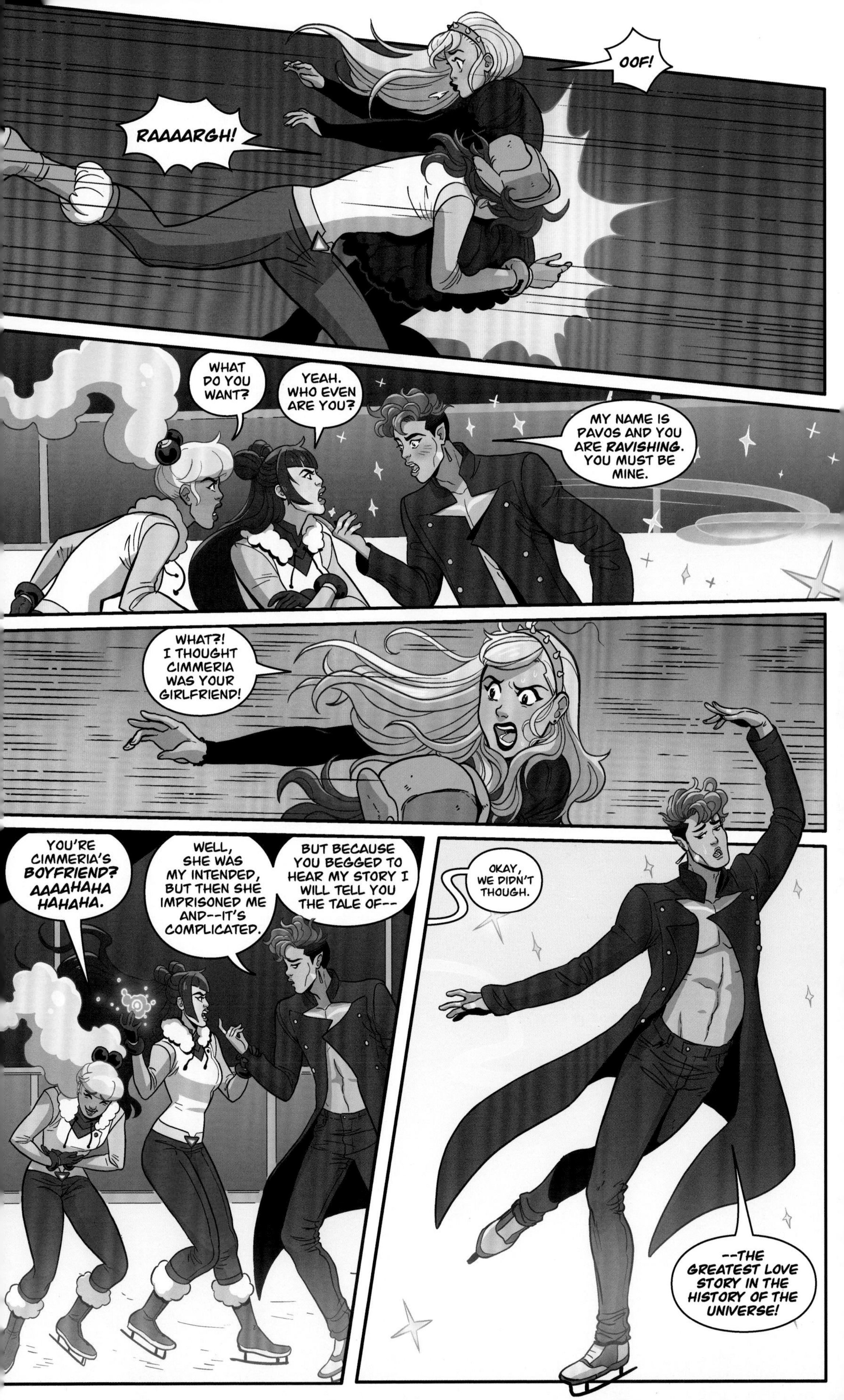
OOF!
RAAAARGH!
WHAT DO YOU WANT?
YEAH. WHO EVEN ARE YOU?
MY NAME IS PAVOS AND YOU ARE RAVISHING. YOU MUST BE MINE.
WHAT?! I THOUGHT CIMMERIA WAS YOUR GIRLFRIEND!
YOU'RE CIMMERIA'S BOYFRIEND? AAAAHAHA HAHAHA.
WELL, SHE WAS MY INTENDED, BUT THEN SHE IMPRISONED ME AND--IT'S COMPLICATED.
BUT BECAUSE YOU BEGGED TO HEAR MY STORY I WILL TELL YOU THE TALE OF--
OKAY, WE DIDN'T THOUGH.
--THE GREATEST LOVE STORY IN THE HISTORY OF THE UNIVERSE!

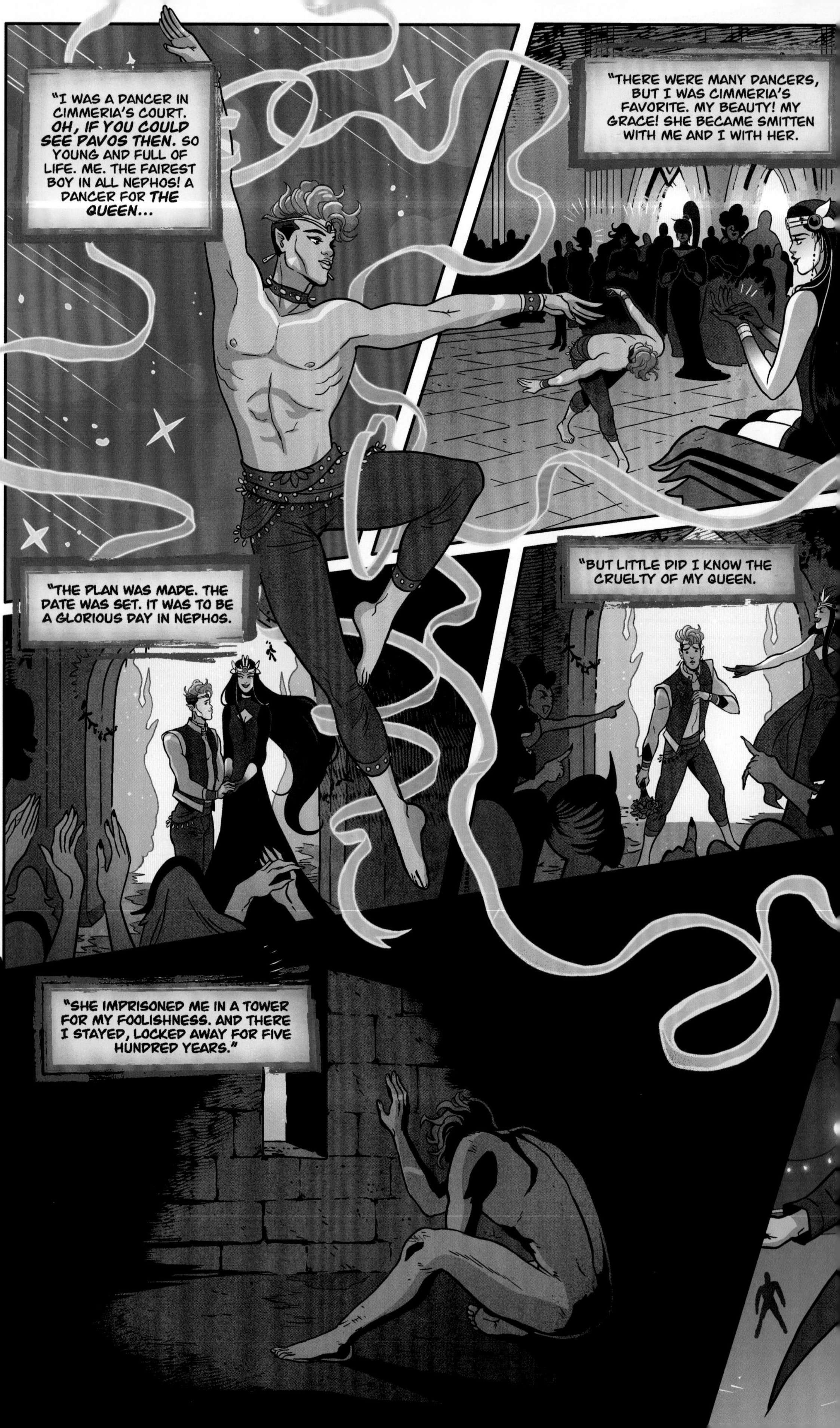
"I WAS A DANCER IN CIMMERIA'S COURT. OH, IF YOU COULD SEE PAVOS THEN. SO YOUNG AND FULL OF LIFE. ME. THE FAIREST BOY IN ALL NEPHOS! A DANCER FOR THE QUEEN...
"THERE WERE MANY DANCERS, BUT I WAS CIMMERIA'S FAVORITE. MY BEAUTY! MY GRACE! SHE BECAME SMITTEN WITH ME AND I WITH HER.
"THE PLAN WAS MADE. THE DATE WAS SET. IT WAS TO BE A GLORIOUS DAY IN NEPHOS.
"BUT LITTLE DID I KNOW THE CRUELTY OF MY QUEEN.
"SHE IMPRISONED ME IN A TOWER FOR MY FOOLISHNESS. AND THERE I STAYED, LOCKED AWAY FOR FIVE HUNDRED YEARS."

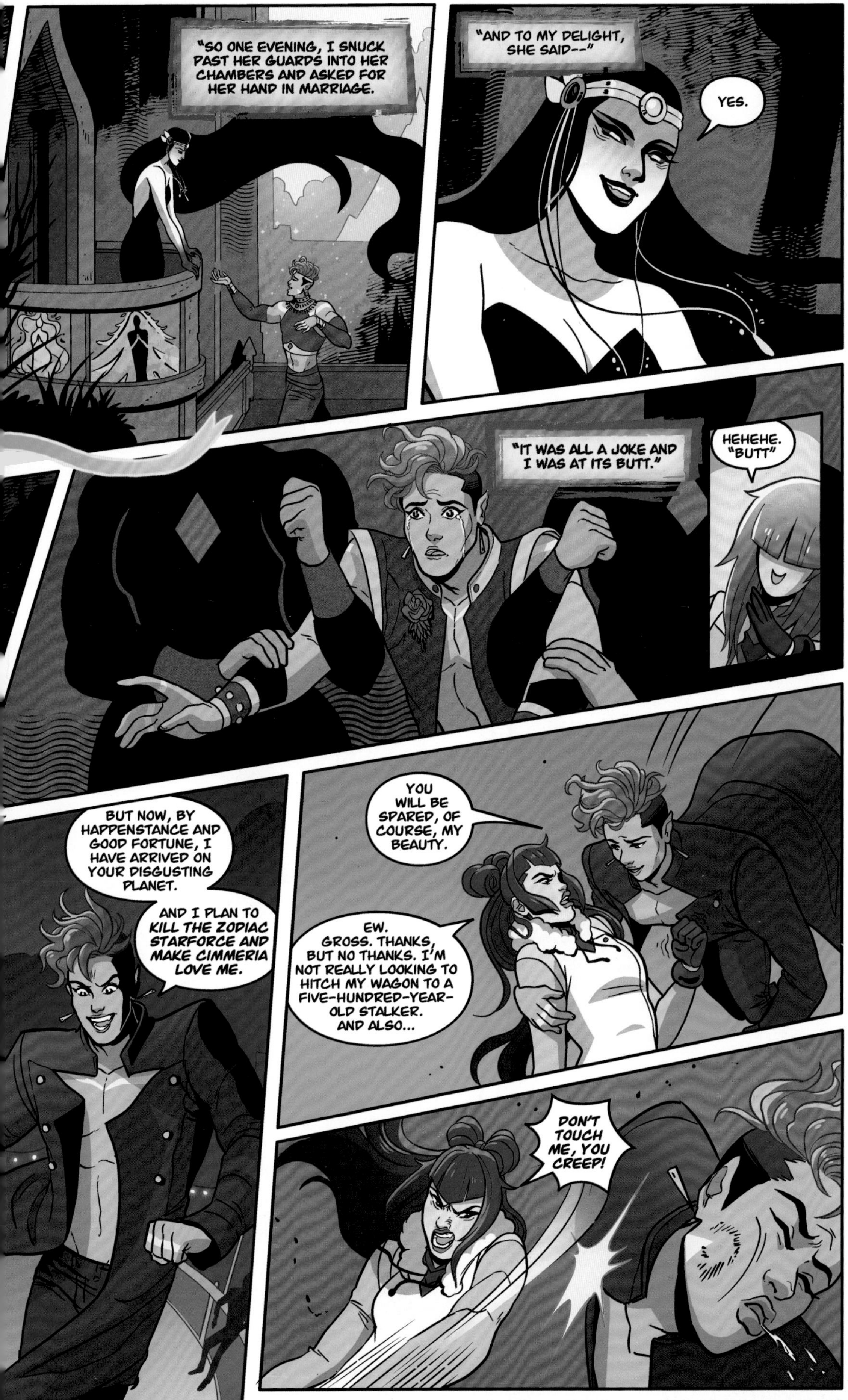
"SO ONE EVENING, I SNUCK PAST HER GUARDS INTO HER CHAMBERS AND ASKED FOR HER HAND IN MARRIAGE.
"AND TO MY DELIGHT, SHE SAID--"
YES.
"IT WAS ALL A JOKE AND I WAS AT ITS BUTT."
HEHEHE. "BUTT"
BUT NOW, BY HAPPENSTANCE AND GOOD FORTUNE, I HAVE ARRIVED ON YOUR DISGUSTING PLANET.
AND I PLAN TO KILL THE ZODIAC STARFORCE AND MAKE CIMMERIA LOVE ME.
YOU WILL BE SPARED, OF COURSE, MY BEAUTY.
EW. GROSS. THANKS, BUT NO THANKS. I'M NOT REALLY LOOKING TO HITCH MY WAGON TO A FIVE-HUNDRED-YEAR-OLD STALKER. AND ALSO...
DON'T TOUCH ME, YOU CREEP!

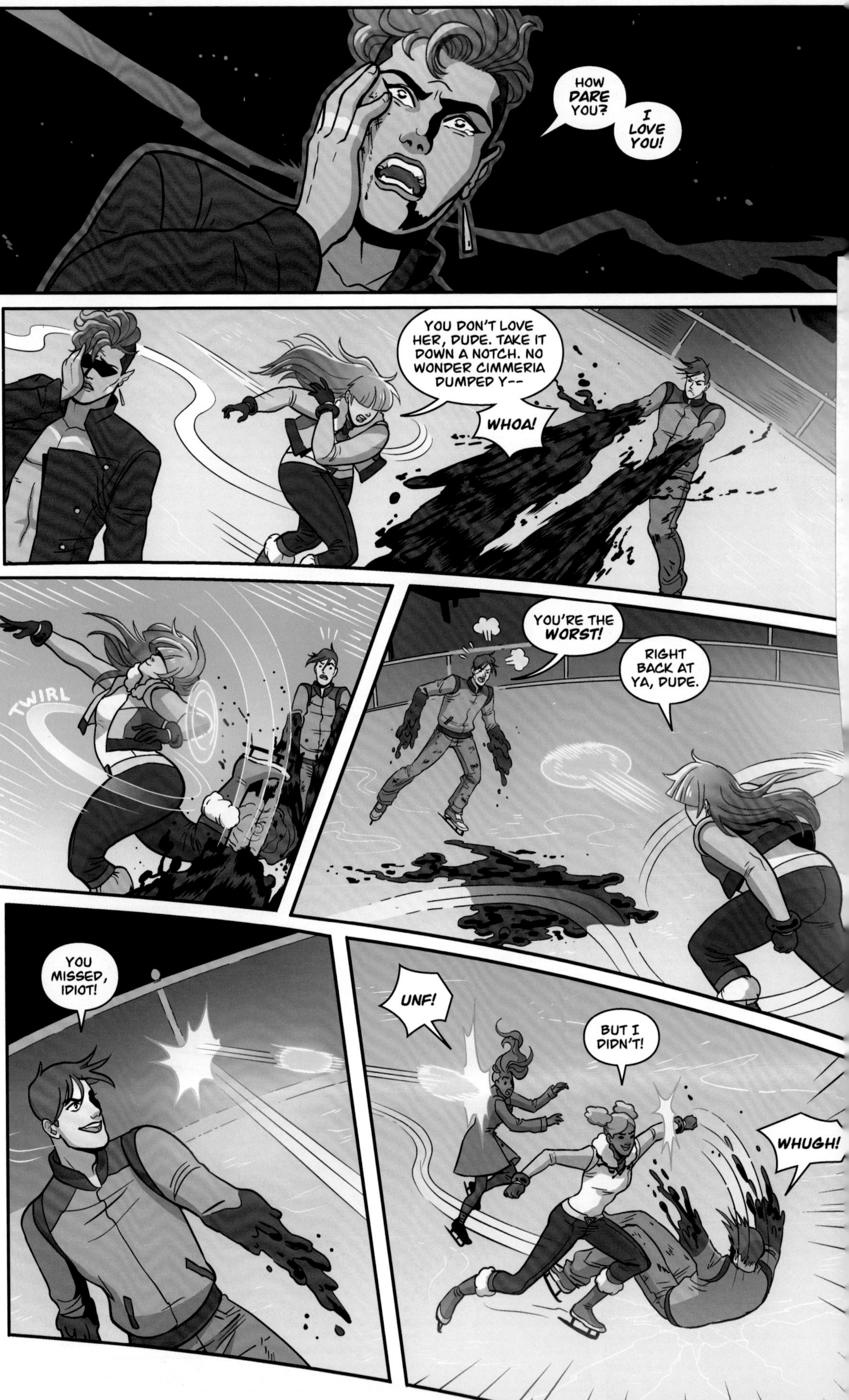
HOW DARE YOU?
I LOVE YOU!
YOU DON'T LOVE HER, DUDE. TAKE IT DOWN A NOTCH. NO WONDER CIMMERIA DUMPED Y--
WHOA!
TWIRL
YOU'RE THE WORST!
RIGHT BACK AT YA, DUDE.
YOU MISSED, IDIOT!
UNF!
BUT I DIDN'T!
WHUGH!

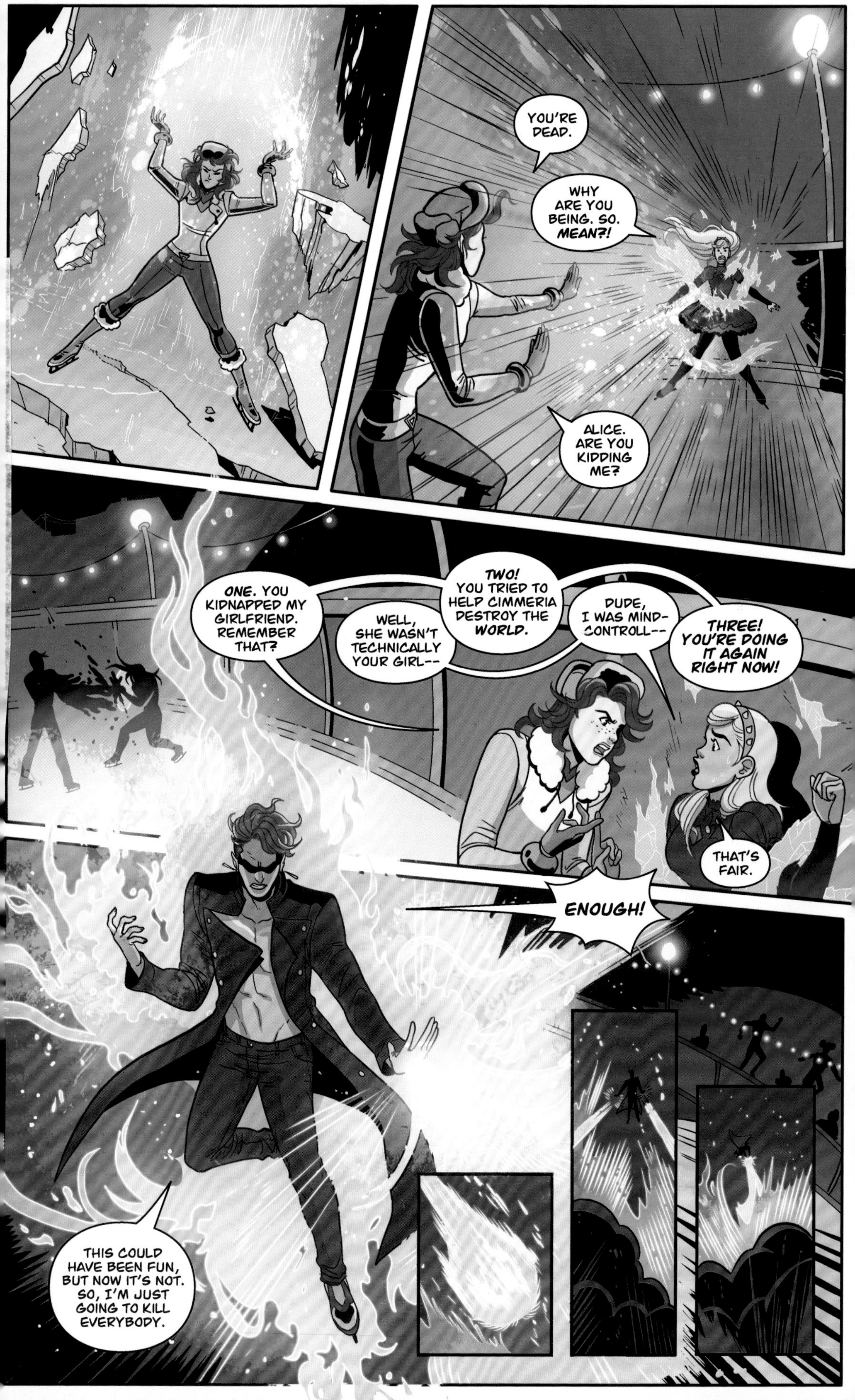
YOU'RE DEAD.
WHY ARE YOU BEING. SO. MEAN?!
ALICE. ARE YOU KIDDING ME?
ONE. YOU KIDNAPPED MY GIRLFRIEND. REMEMBER THAT?
WELL, SHE WASN'T TECHNICALLY YOUR GIRL--
TWO! YOU TRIED TO HELP CIMMERIA DESTROY THE WORLD.
DUDE, I WAS MIND-CONTROLL--
THREE! YOU'RE DOING IT AGAIN RIGHT NOW!
THAT'S FAIR.
ENOUGH!
THIS COULD HAVE BEEN FUN, BUT NOW IT'S NOT. SO, I'M JUST GOING TO KILL EVERYBODY.

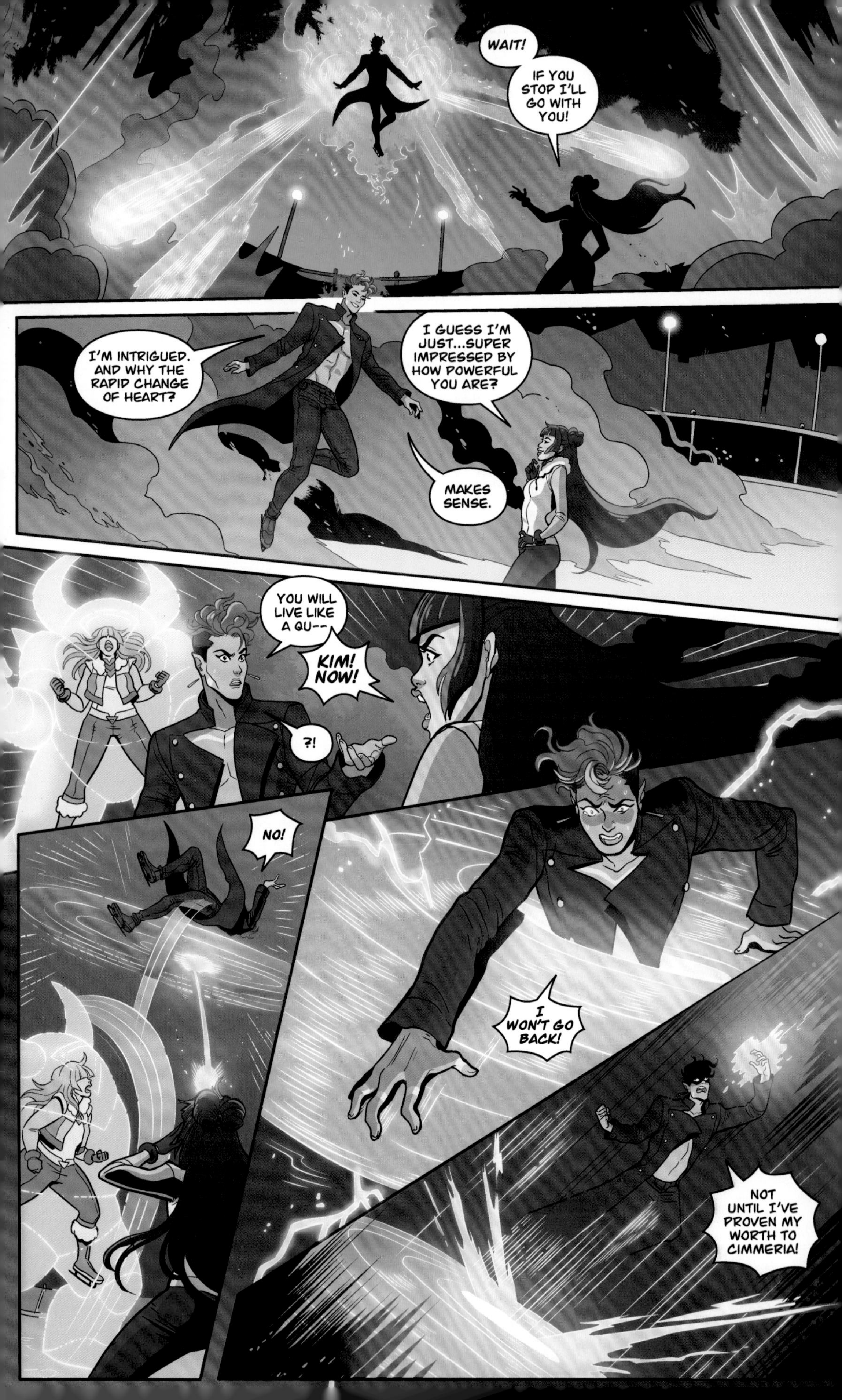
WAIT!
IF YOU STOP I'LL GO WITH YOU!
I'M INTRIGUED. AND WHY THE RAPID CHANGE OF HEART?
I GUESS I'M JUST...SUPER IMPRESSED BY HOW POWERFUL YOU ARE?
MAKES SENSE.
YOU WILL LIVE LIKE A QU--
KIM! NOW!
?!
NO!
I WON'T GO BACK!
NOT UNTIL I'VE PROVEN MY WORTH TO CIMMERIA!

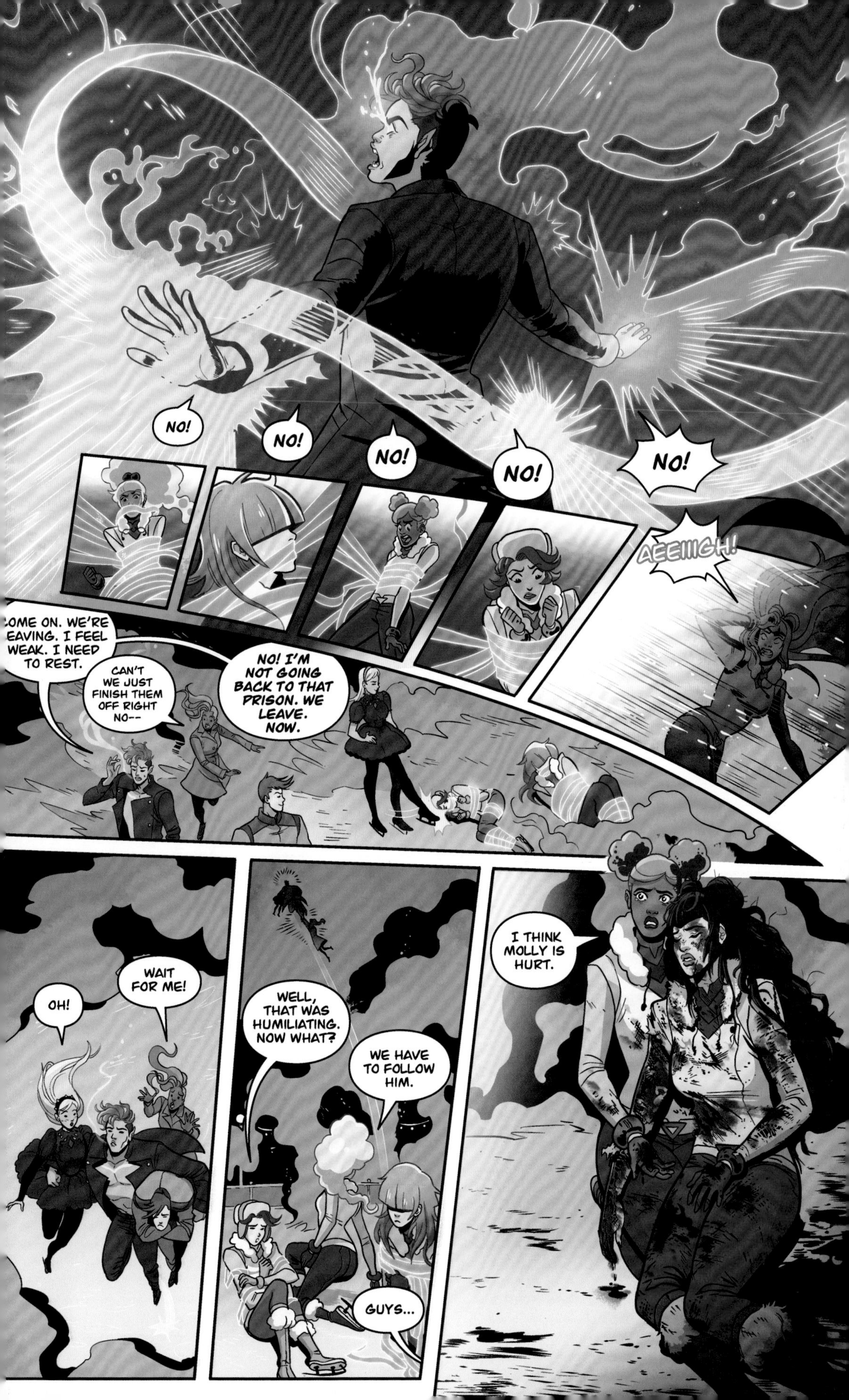
NO!
NO!
NO!
NO!
NO!
AEEIIIGH!
OME ON. WE'RE
EAVING. I FEEL
WEAK. I NEED
TO REST.
CAN'T WE JUST FINISH THEM OFF RIGHT NO--
NO! I'M NOT GOING BACK TO THAT PRISON. WE LEAVE. NOW.
OH!
WAIT FOR ME!
WELL, THAT WAS HUMILIATING. NOW WHAT?
WE HAVE TO FOLLOW HIM.
GUYS...
I THINK MOLLY IS HURT.

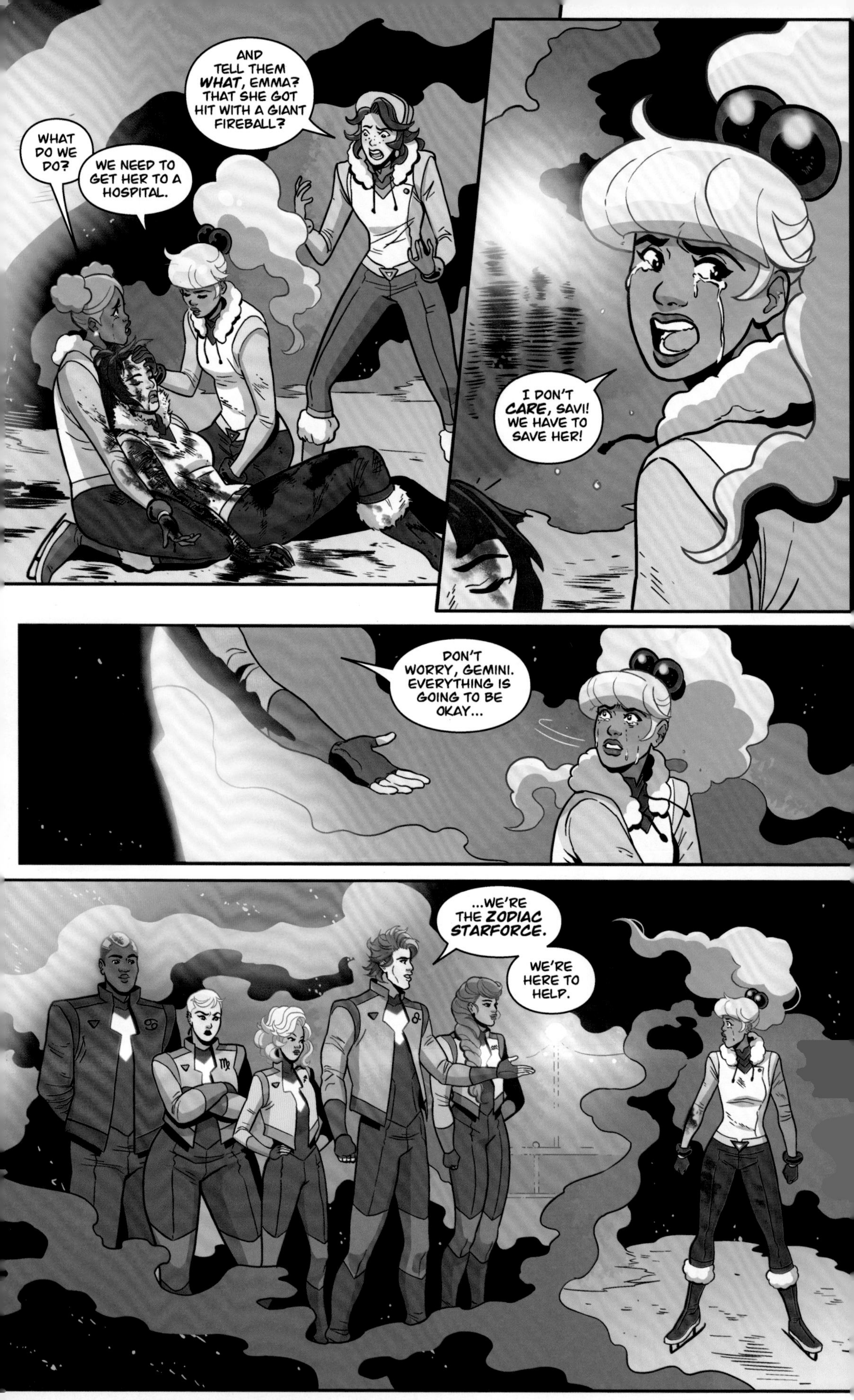

WHAT DO WE DO?
WE NEED TO GET HER TO A HOSPITAL.
AND TELL THEM WHAT, EMMA? THAT SHE GOT HIT WITH A GIANT FIREBALL?
I DON'T CARE, SAVI! WE HAVE TO SAVE HER!
DON'T WORRY, GEMINI. EVERYTHING IS GOING TO BE OKAY...
...WE'RE THE ZODIAC STARFORCE.
WE'RE HERE TO HELP.

CHAPTER THREE

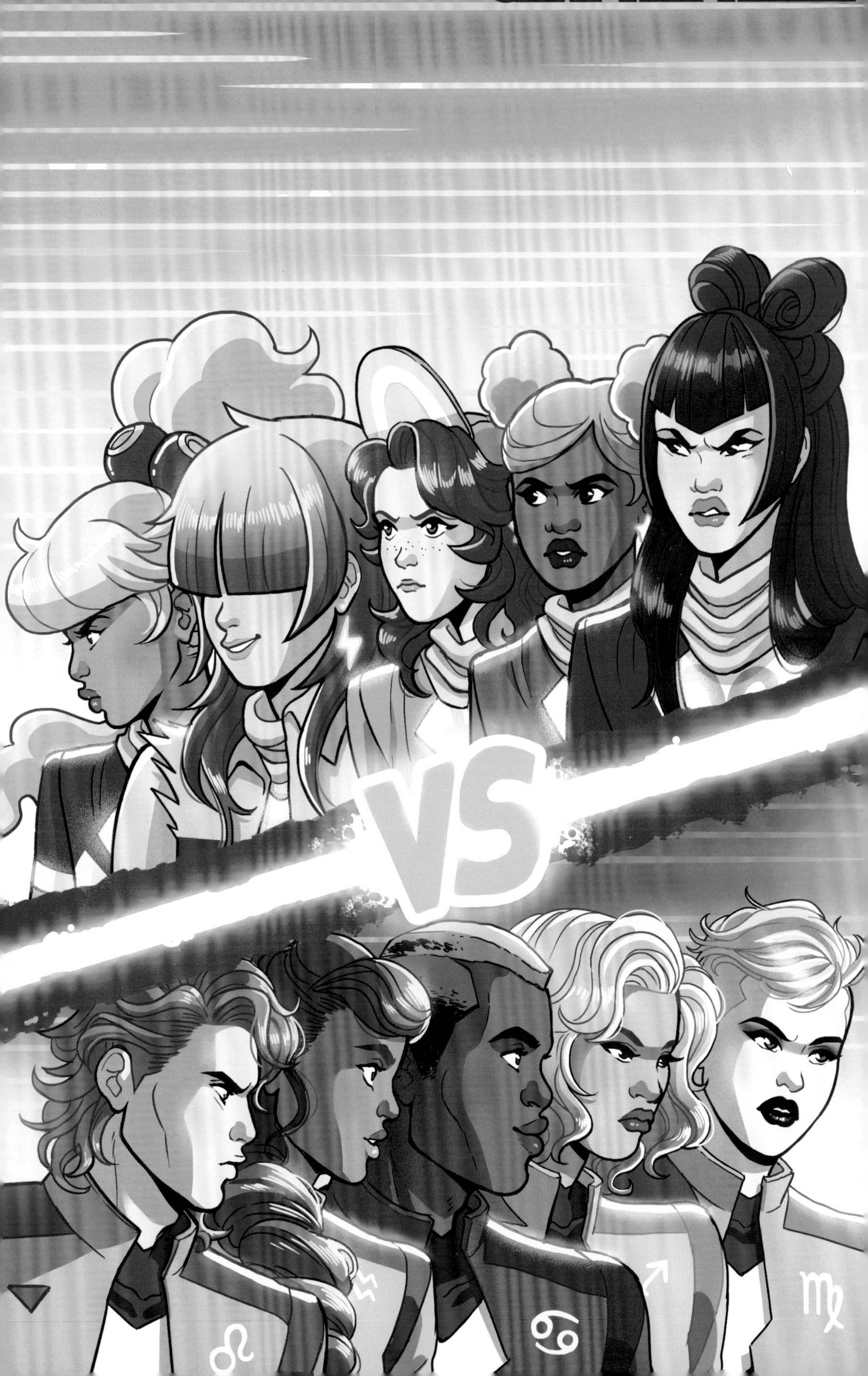
VS

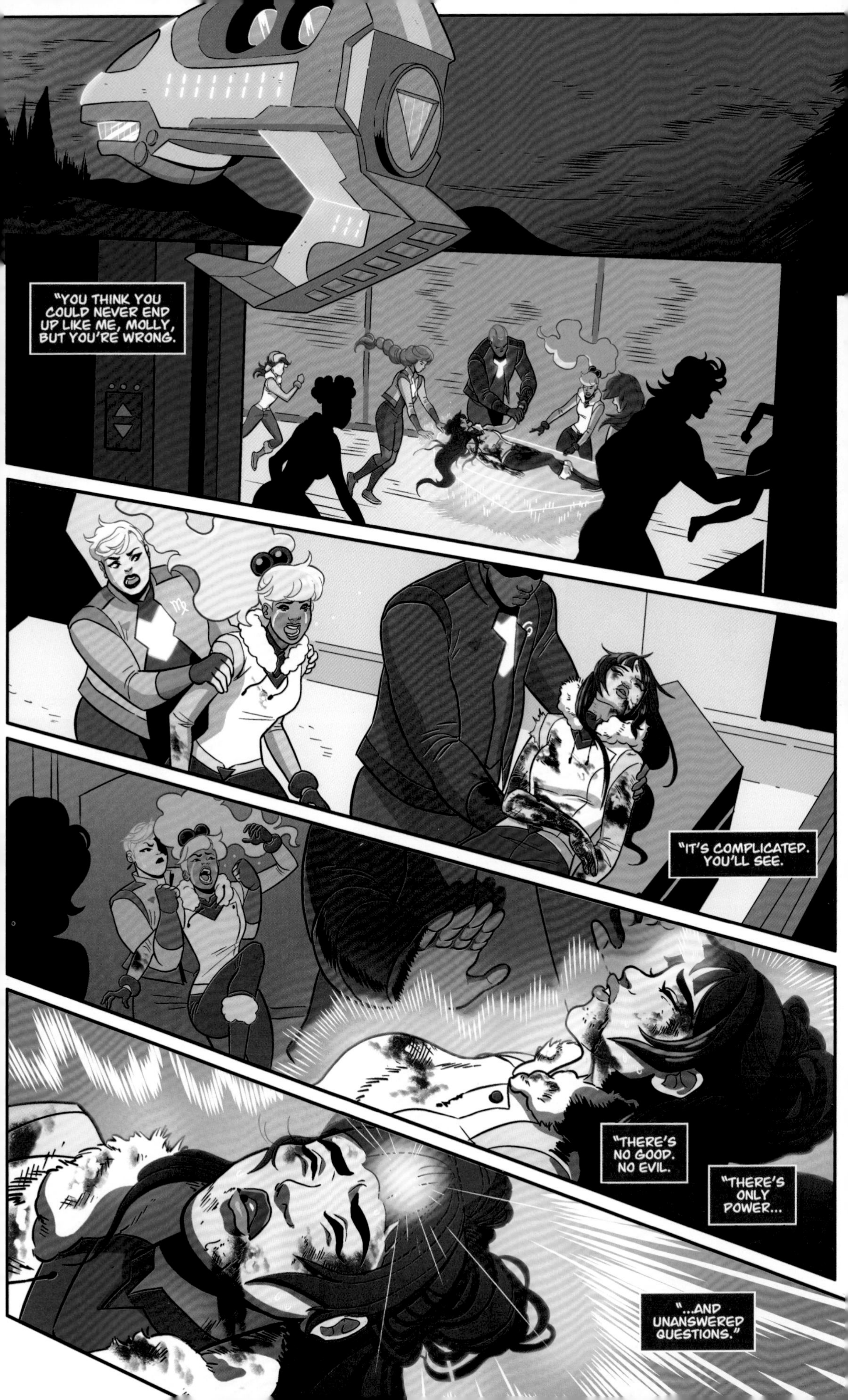
"YOU THINK YOU COULD NEVER END UP LIKE ME, MOLLY, BUT YOU'RE WRONG.
"IT'S COMPLICATED. YOU'LL SEE.
"THERE'S NO GOOD. NO EVIL.
"THERE'S ONLY POWER...
"...AND UNANSWERED QUESTIONS."

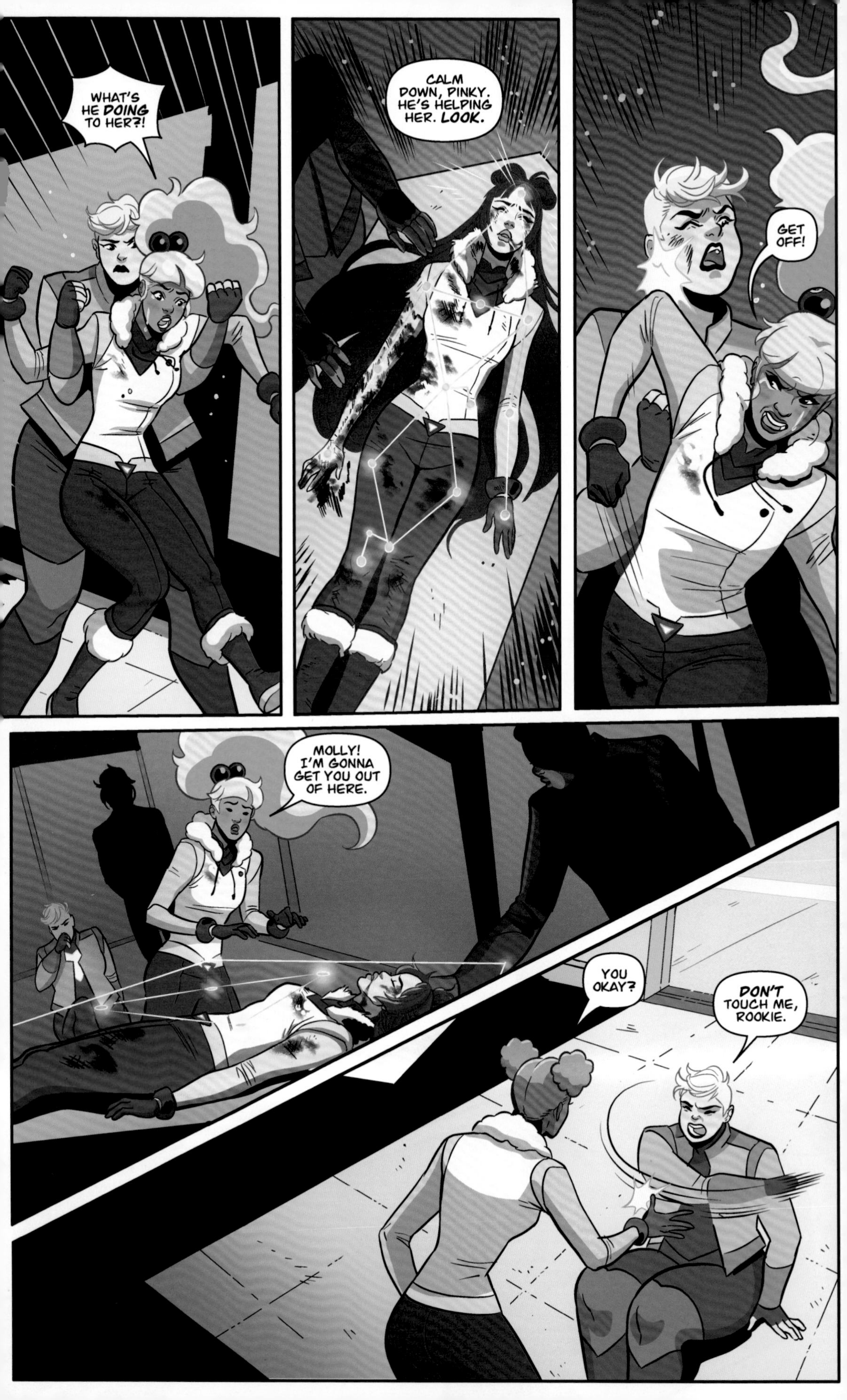
WHAT'S HE DOING TO HER?!
CALM DOWN, PINKY. HE'S HELPING HER. LOOK.
GET OFF!
MOLLY! I'M GONNA GET YOU OUT OF HERE.
YOU OKAY?
DON'T TOUCH ME, ROOKIE.

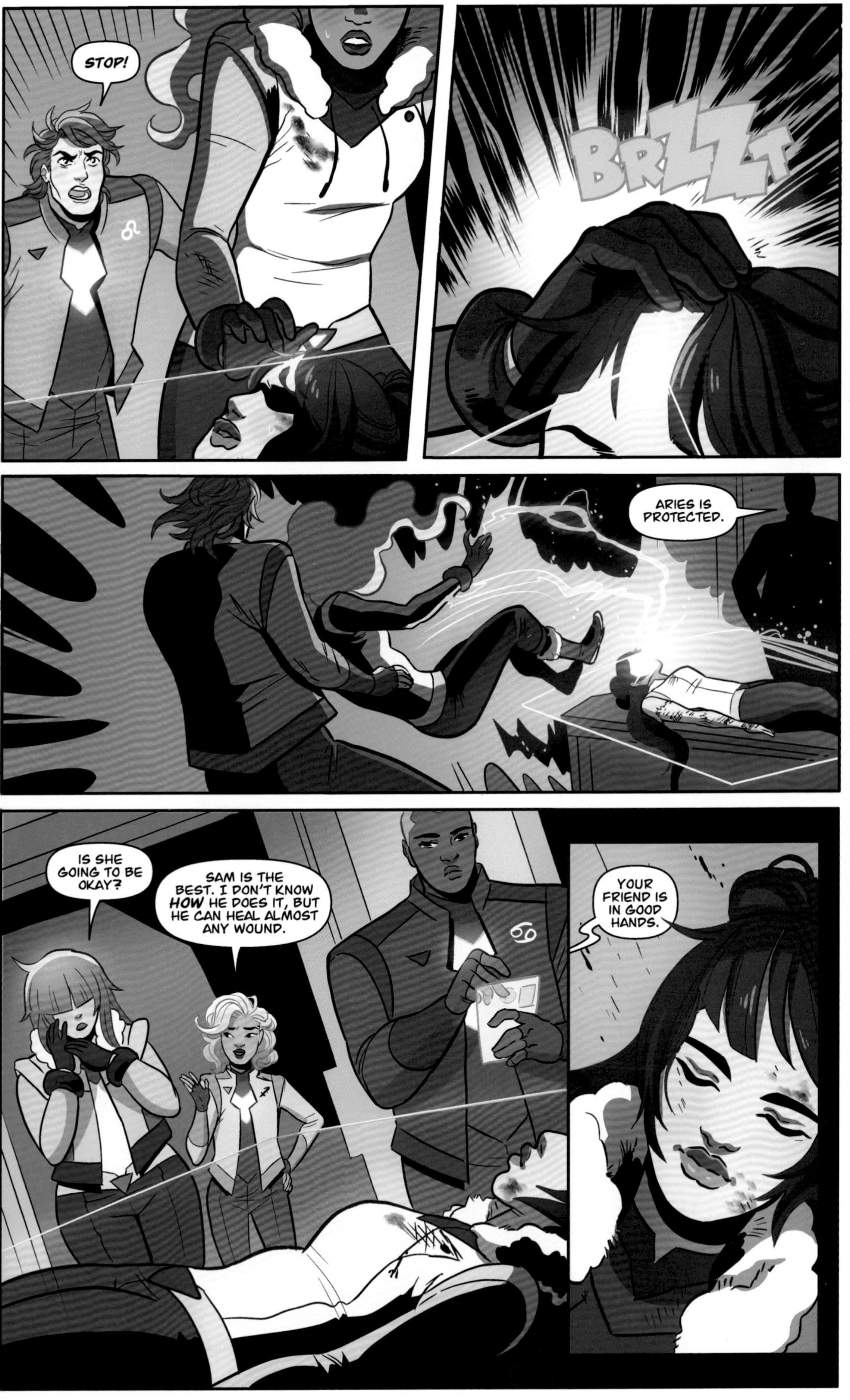
STOP!
BRZZt
ARIES IS PROTECTED.
IS SHE GOING TO BE OKAY?
SAM IS THE BEST. I DON'T KNOW HOW HE DOES IT, BUT HE CAN HEAL ALMOST ANY WOUND.
YOUR FRIEND IS IN GOOD HANDS.

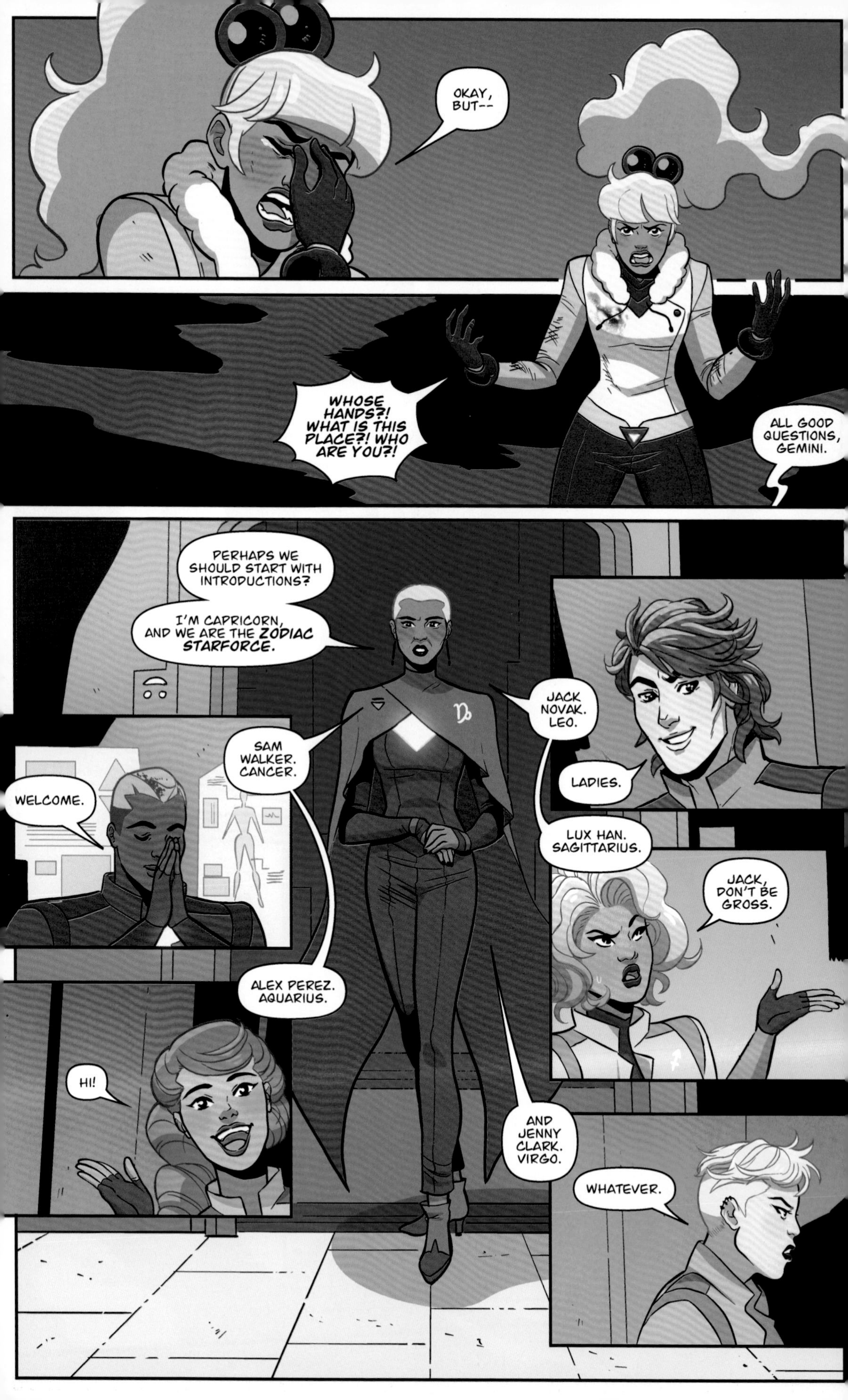
OKAY, BUT--
WHOSE HANDS?! WHAT IS THIS PLACE?! WHO ARE YOU?!
ALL GOOD QUESTIONS, GEMINI.
PERHAPS WE SHOULD START WITH INTRODUCTIONS?
I'M CAPRICORN, AND WE ARE THE ZODIAC STARFORCE.
JACK NOVAK. LEO.
LADIES.
SAM WALKER. CANCER.
WELCOME.
LUX HAN. SAGITTARIUS.
JACK, DON'T BE GROSS.
ALEX PEREZ. AQUARIUS.
HI!
AND JENNY CLARK. VIRGO.
WHATEVER.

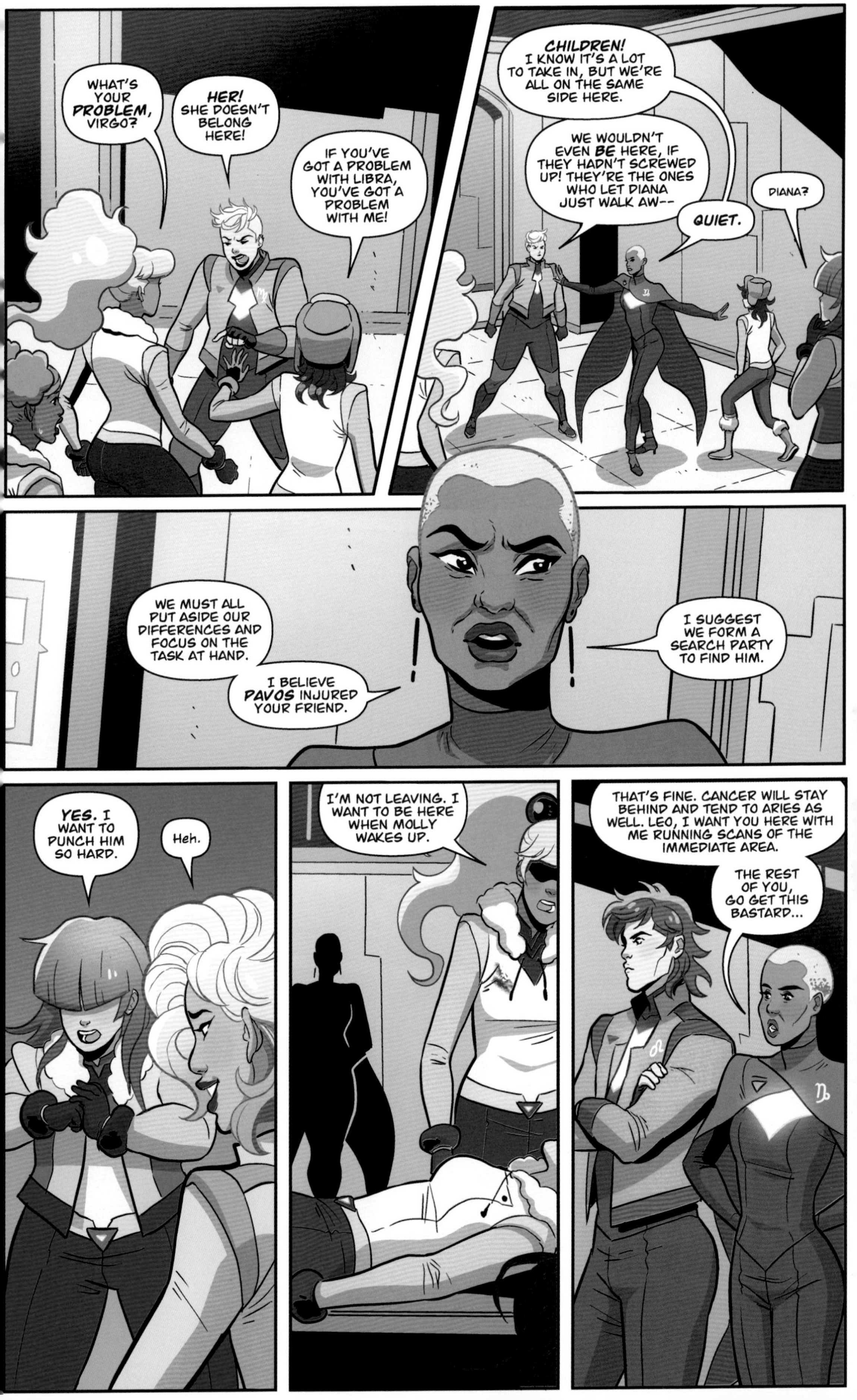

WHAT'S YOUR PROBLEM, VIRGO?
HER! SHE DOESN'T BELONG HERE!
IF YOU'VE GOT A PROBLEM WITH LIBRA, YOU'VE GOT A PROBLEM WITH ME!
CHILDREN! I KNOW IT'S A LOT TO TAKE IN, BUT WE'RE ALL ON THE SAME SIDE HERE.
WE WOULDN'T EVEN BE HERE, IF THEY HADN'T SCREWED UP! THEY'RE THE ONES WHO LET DIANA JUST WALK AW--
QUIET.
DIANA?
WE MUST ALL PUT ASIDE OUR DIFFERENCES AND FOCUS ON THE TASK AT HAND.
I BELIEVE PAVOS INJURED YOUR FRIEND.
I SUGGEST WE FORM A SEARCH PARTY TO FIND HIM.
YES. I WANT TO PUNCH HIM SO HARD.
Heh.
I'M NOT LEAVING. I WANT TO BE HERE WHEN MOLLY WAKES UP.
THAT'S FINE. CANCER WILL STAY BEHIND AND TEND TO ARIES AS WELL. LEO, I WANT YOU HERE WITH ME RUNNING SCANS OF THE IMMEDIATE AREA.
THE REST OF YOU, GO GET THIS BASTARD...

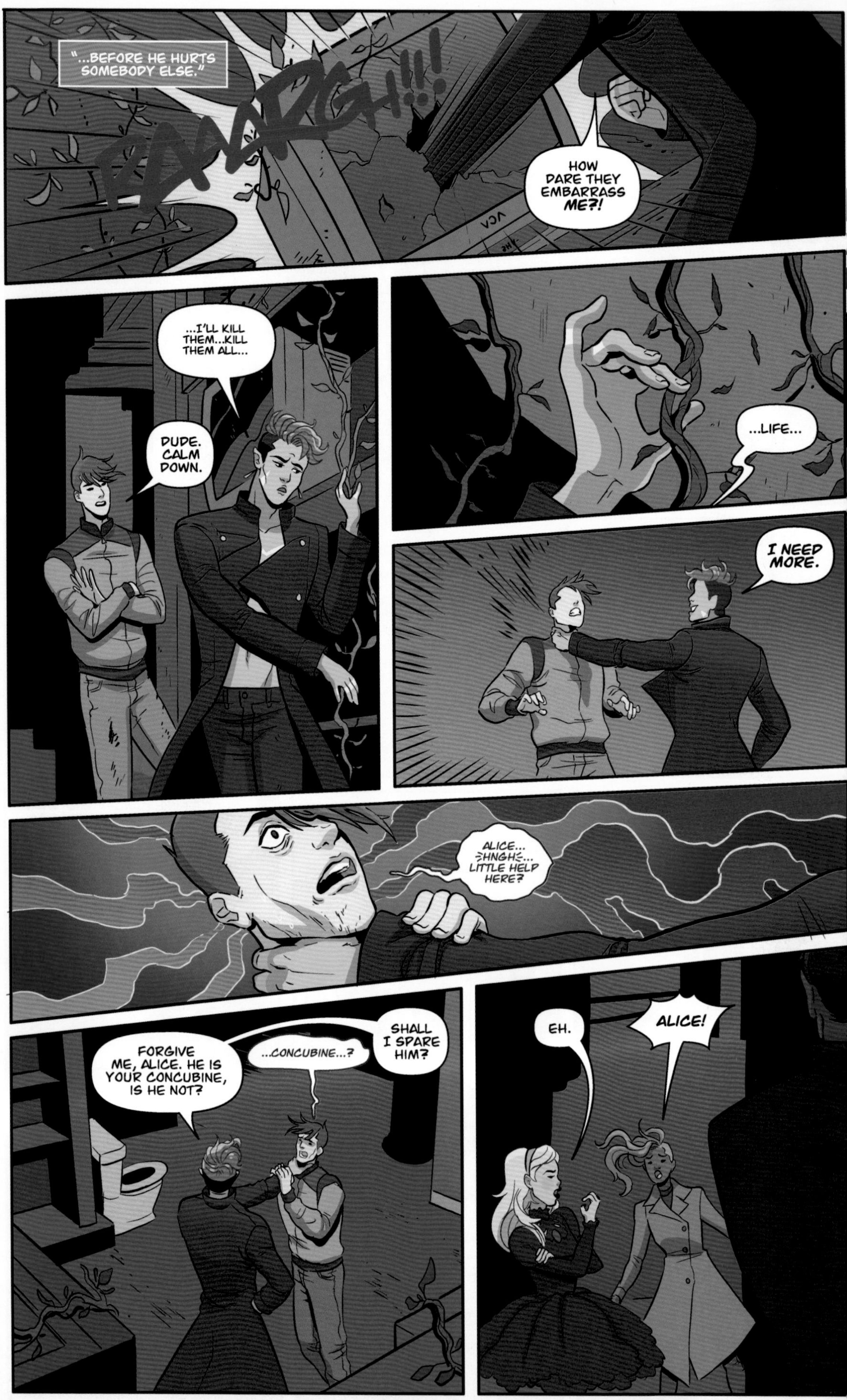
"...BEFORE HE HURTS SOMEBODY ELSE."
RAAARGH!!!
HOW DARE THEY EMBARRASS ME?!
...I'LL KILL THEM...KILL THEM ALL...
DUDE. CALM DOWN.
...LIFE...
I NEED MORE.
ALICE... HNGH... LITTLE HELP HERE?
FORGIVE ME, ALICE. HE IS YOUR CONCUBINE, IS HE NOT?
SHALL I SPARE HIM?
...CONCUBINE...?
EH.
ALICE!

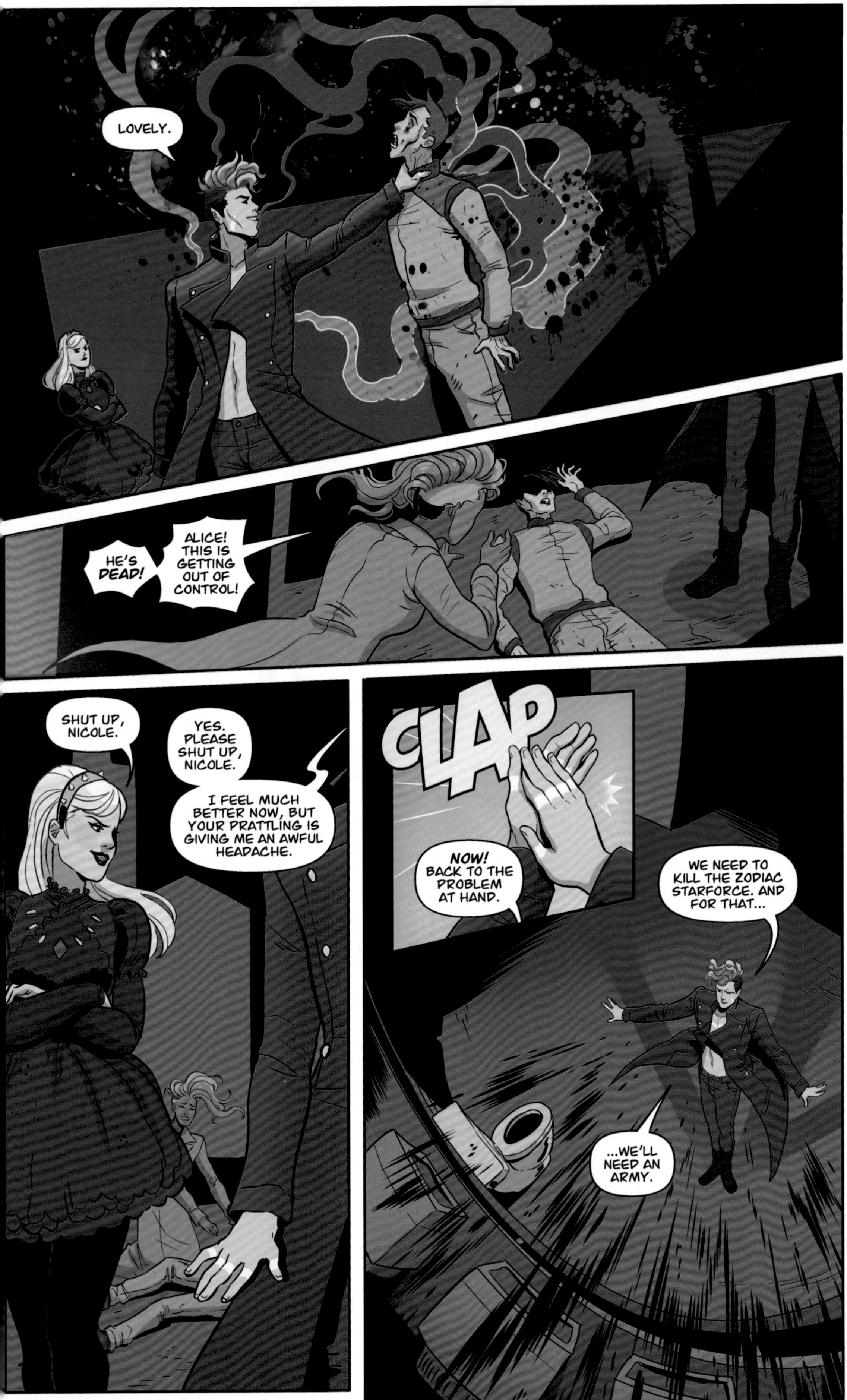
LOVELY.
HE'S *DEAD!*
ALICE! THIS IS GETTING OUT OF CONTROL!
SHUT UP, NICOLE.
YES. PLEASE SHUT UP, NICOLE.
I FEEL MUCH BETTER NOW, BUT YOUR PRATTLING IS GIVING ME AN AWFUL HEADACHE.
CLAP
NOW! BACK TO THE PROBLEM AT HAND.
WE NEED TO KILL THE ZODIAC STARFORCE. AND FOR THAT...
...WE'LL NEED AN ARMY.

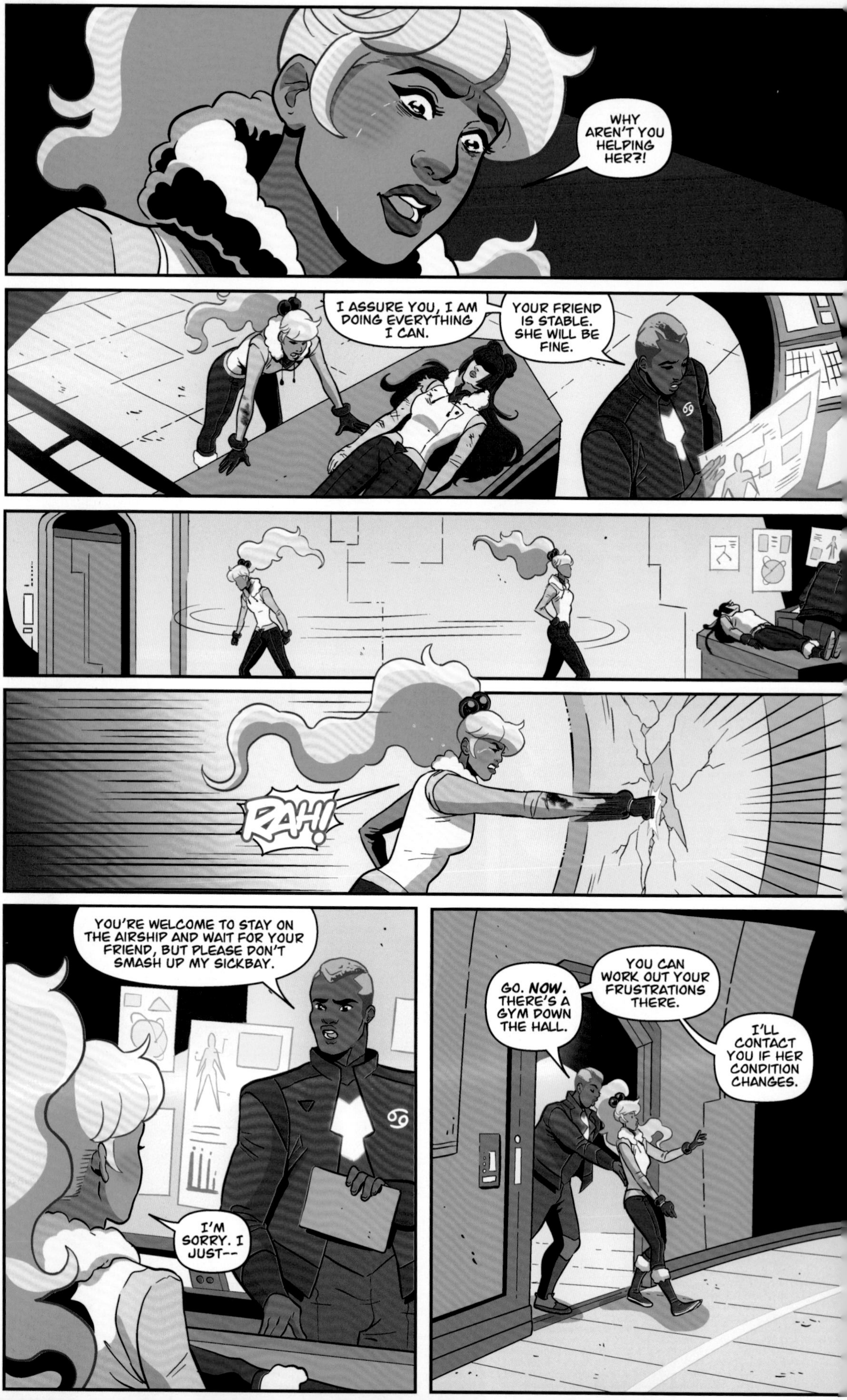
WHY AREN'T YOU HELPING HER?!
I ASSURE YOU, I AM DOING EVERYTHING I CAN.
YOUR FRIEND IS STABLE. SHE WILL BE FINE.
RAH!
YOU'RE WELCOME TO STAY ON THE AIRSHIP AND WAIT FOR YOUR FRIEND, BUT PLEASE DON'T SMASH UP MY SICKBAY.
I'M SORRY. I JUST--
GO. NOW. THERE'S A GYM DOWN THE HALL.
YOU CAN WORK OUT YOUR FRUSTRATIONS THERE.
I'LL CONTACT YOU IF HER CONDITION CHANGES.

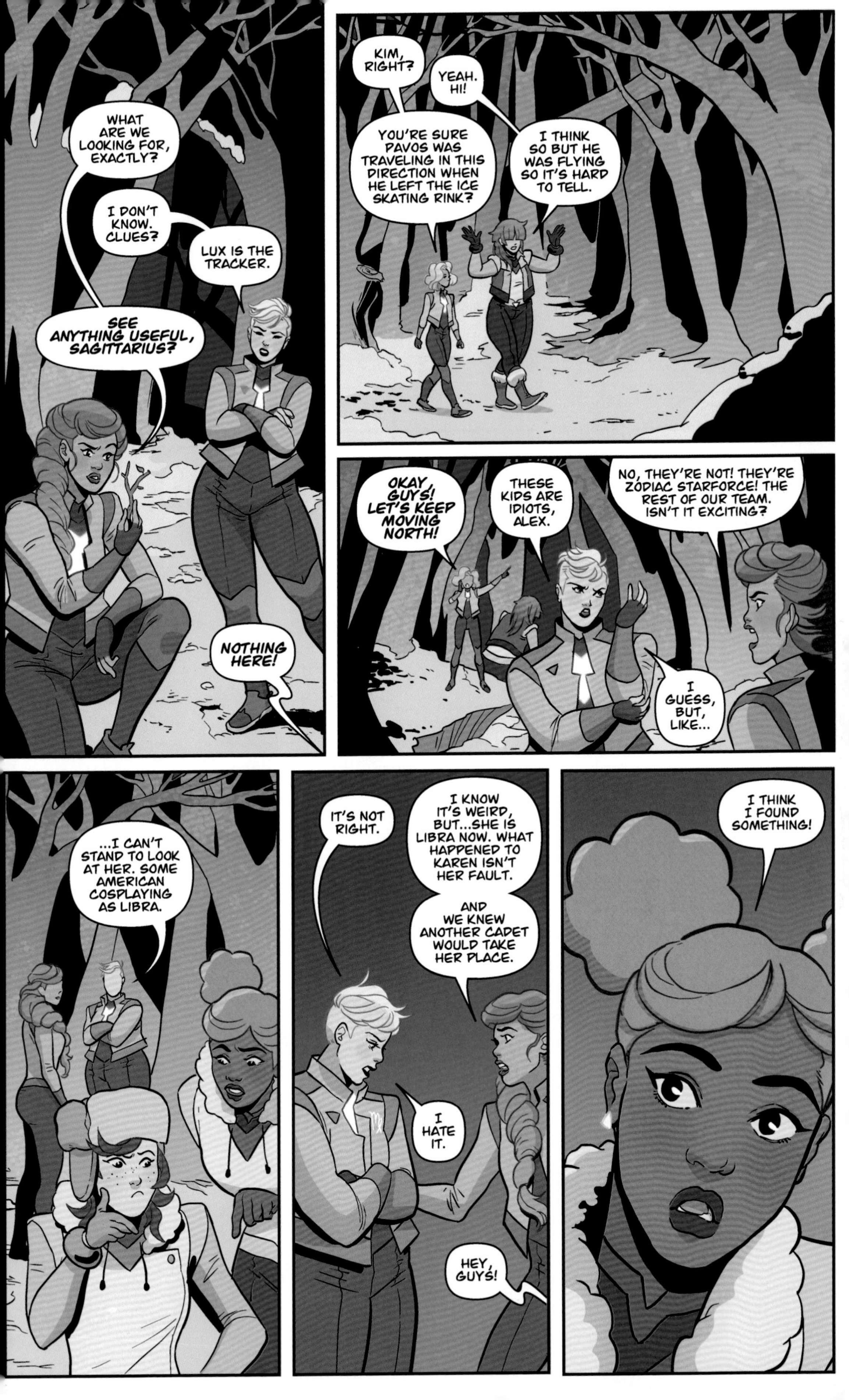
WHAT ARE WE LOOKING FOR, EXACTLY?
I DON'T KNOW. CLUES?
LUX IS THE TRACKER.
SEE ANYTHING USEFUL, SAGITTARIUS?
NOTHING HERE!
KIM, RIGHT?
YEAH. HI!
YOU'RE SURE PAVOS WAS TRAVELING IN THIS DIRECTION WHEN HE LEFT THE ICE SKATING RINK?
I THINK SO BUT HE WAS FLYING SO IT'S HARD TO TELL.
OKAY, GUYS! LET'S KEEP MOVING NORTH!
THESE KIDS ARE IDIOTS, ALEX.
NO, THEY'RE NOT! THEY'RE ZODIAC STARFORCE! THE REST OF OUR TEAM. ISN'T IT EXCITING?
I GUESS, BUT, LIKE...
...I CAN'T STAND TO LOOK AT HER. SOME AMERICAN COSPLAYING AS LIBRA.
IT'S NOT RIGHT.
I KNOW IT'S WEIRD, BUT...SHE IS LIBRA NOW. WHAT HAPPENED TO KAREN ISN'T HER FAULT.
AND WE KNEW ANOTHER CADET WOULD TAKE HER PLACE.
I HATE IT.
HEY, GUYS!
I THINK I FOUND SOMETHING!

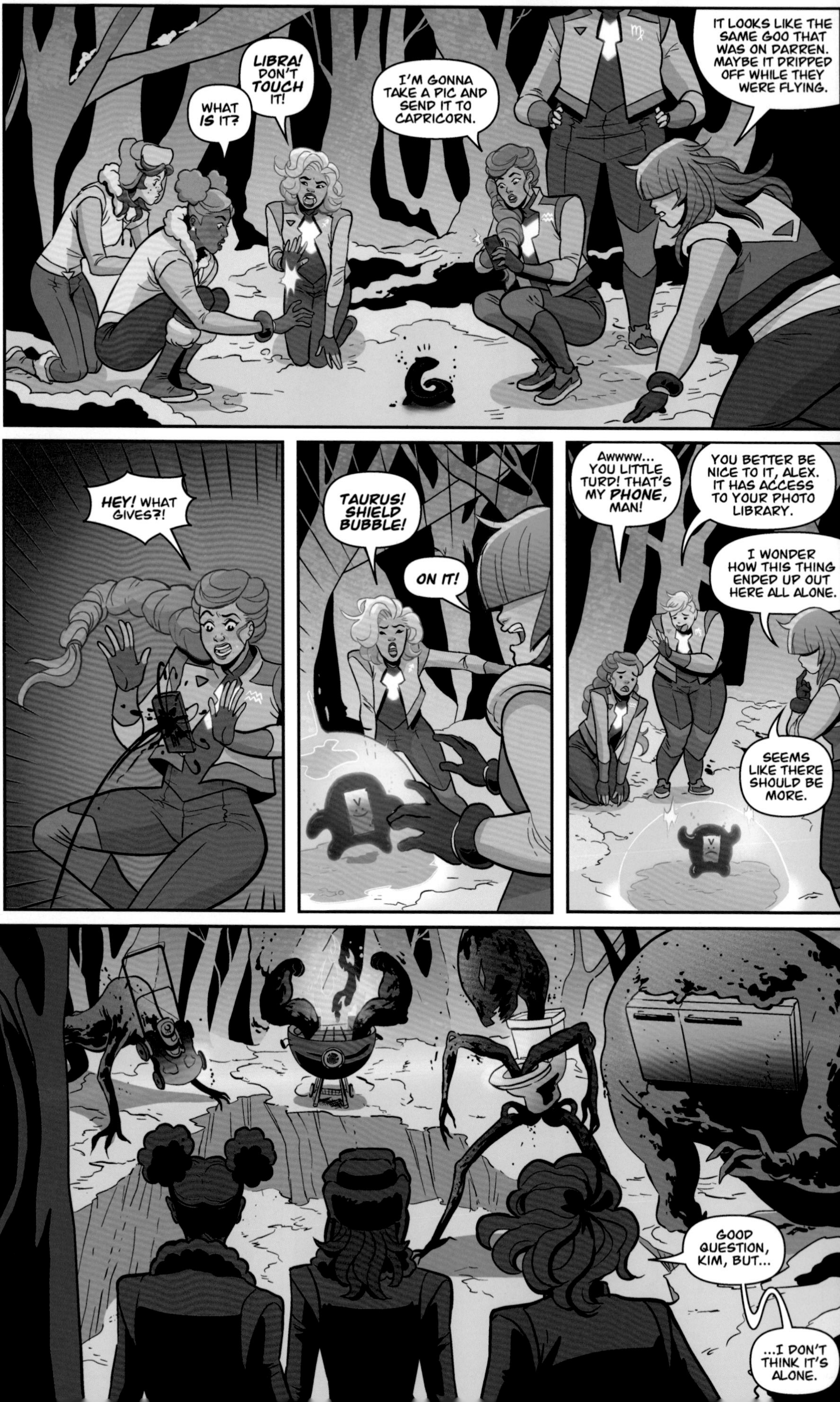
WHAT IS IT?
LIBRA! DON'T TOUCH IT!
I'M GONNA TAKE A PIC AND SEND IT TO CAPRICORN.
IT LOOKS LIKE THE SAME GOO THAT WAS ON DARREN. MAYBE IT DRIPPED OFF WHILE THEY WERE FLYING.
HEY! WHAT GIVES?!
TAURUS! SHIELD BUBBLE!
ON IT!
AWWWW... YOU LITTLE TURD! THAT'S MY PHONE, MAN!
YOU BETTER BE NICE TO IT, ALEX. IT HAS ACCESS TO YOUR PHOTO LIBRARY.
I WONDER HOW THIS THING ENDED UP OUT HERE ALL ALONE.
SEEMS LIKE THERE SHOULD BE MORE.
GOOD QUESTION, KIM, BUT...
...I DON'T THINK IT'S ALONE.

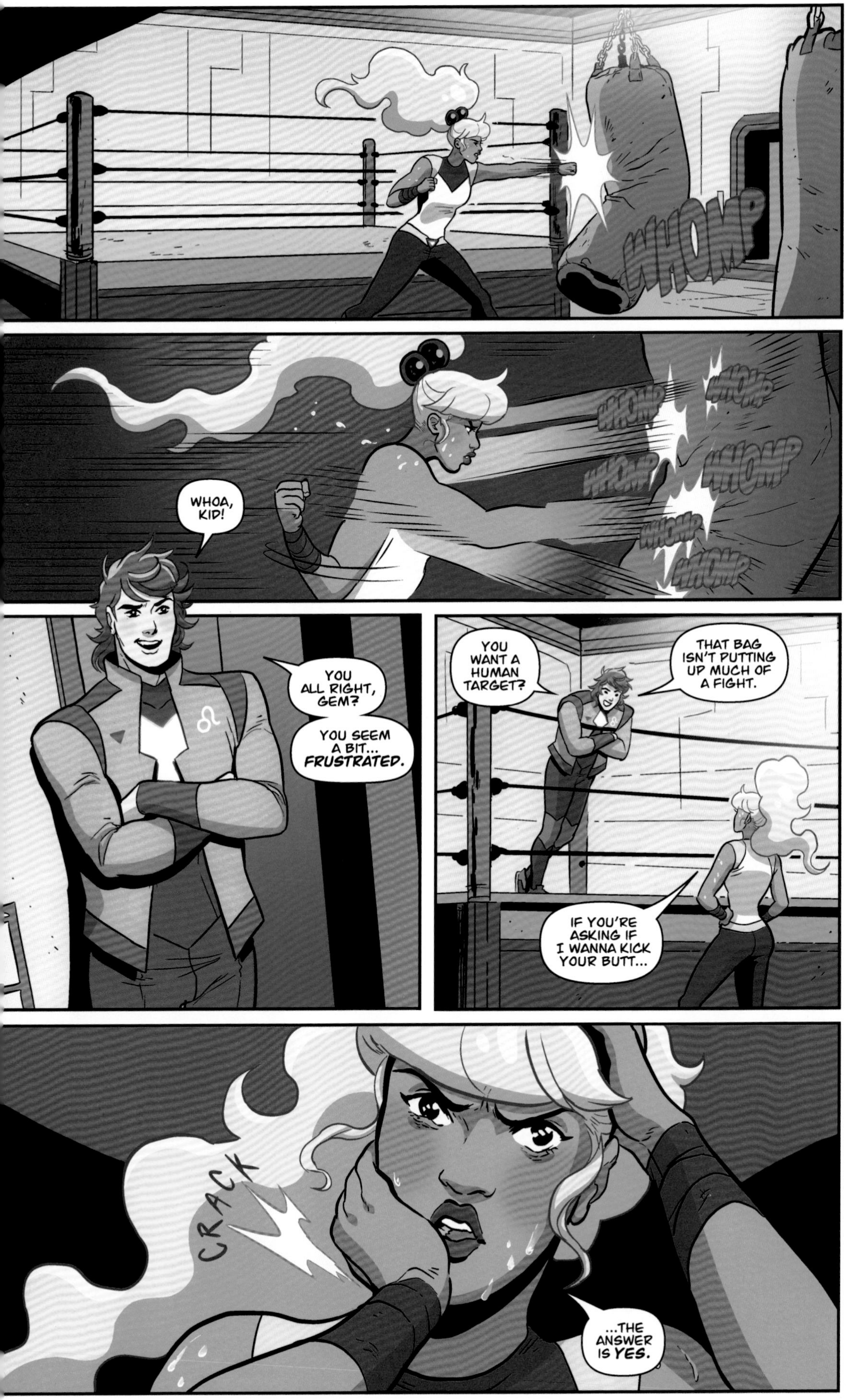
WHOMP
WHOA, KID!
WHOMP
WHOMP
WHOMP
WHOMP
WHOMP
WHOMP
YOU ALL RIGHT, GEM?
YOU SEEM A BIT... FRUSTRATED.
YOU WANT A HUMAN TARGET?
THAT BAG ISN'T PUTTING UP MUCH OF A FIGHT.
IF YOU'RE ASKING IF I WANNA KICK YOUR BUTT...
CRACK
...THE ANSWER IS YES.

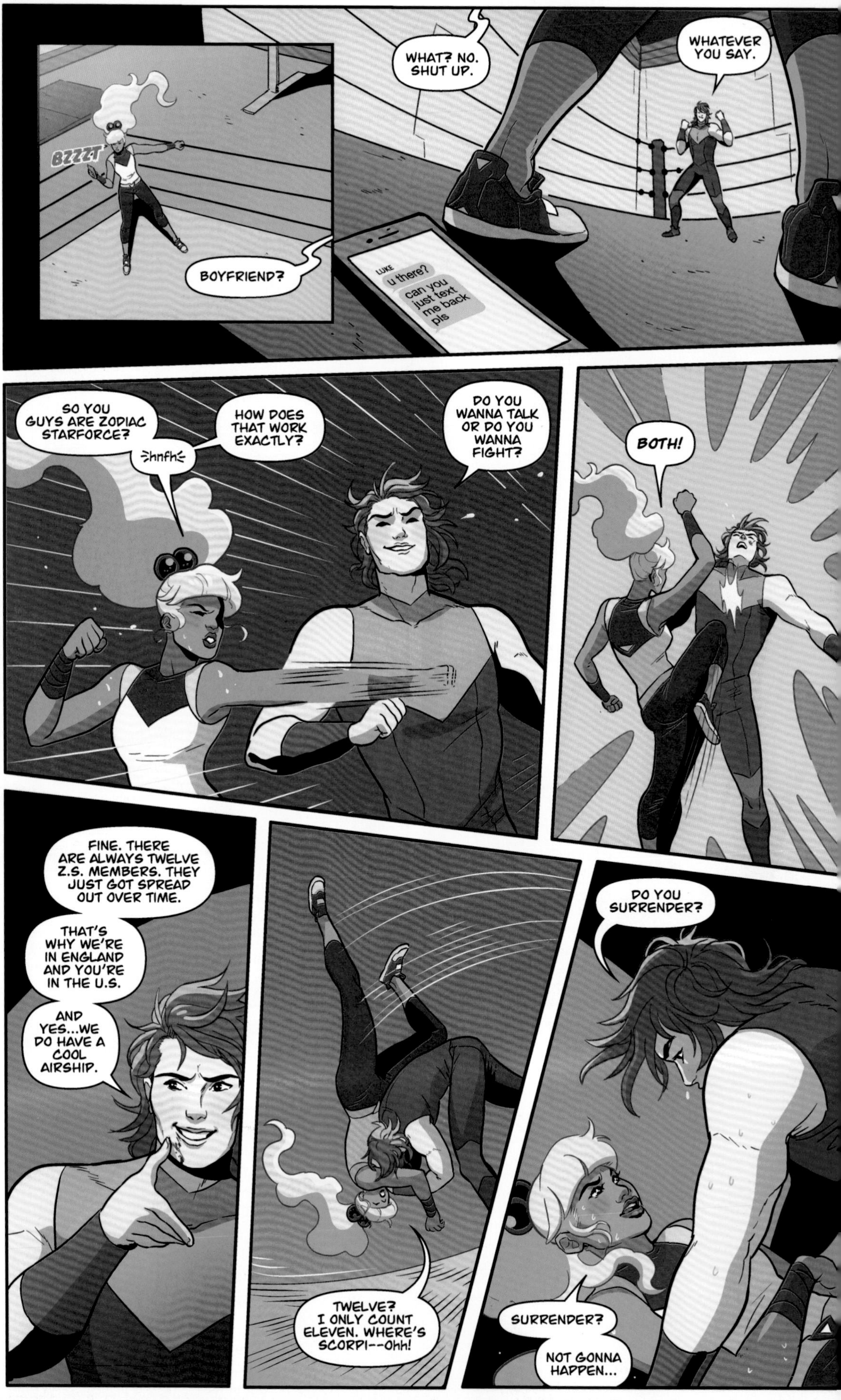
BZZZT
BOYFRIEND?
WHAT? NO. SHUT UP.
WHATEVER YOU SAY.
LUKE
u there?
can you just text me back pls
SO YOU GUYS ARE ZODIAC STARFORCE?
hnfh
HOW DOES THAT WORK EXACTLY?
DO YOU WANNA TALK OR DO YOU WANNA FIGHT?
BOTH!
FINE. THERE ARE ALWAYS TWELVE Z.S. MEMBERS. THEY JUST GOT SPREAD OUT OVER TIME.
THAT'S WHY WE'RE IN ENGLAND AND YOU'RE IN THE U.S.
AND YES...WE DO HAVE A COOL AIRSHIP.
TWELVE? I ONLY COUNT ELEVEN. WHERE'S SCORPI--OHH!
DO YOU SURRENDER?
SURRENDER?
NOT GONNA HAPPEN...

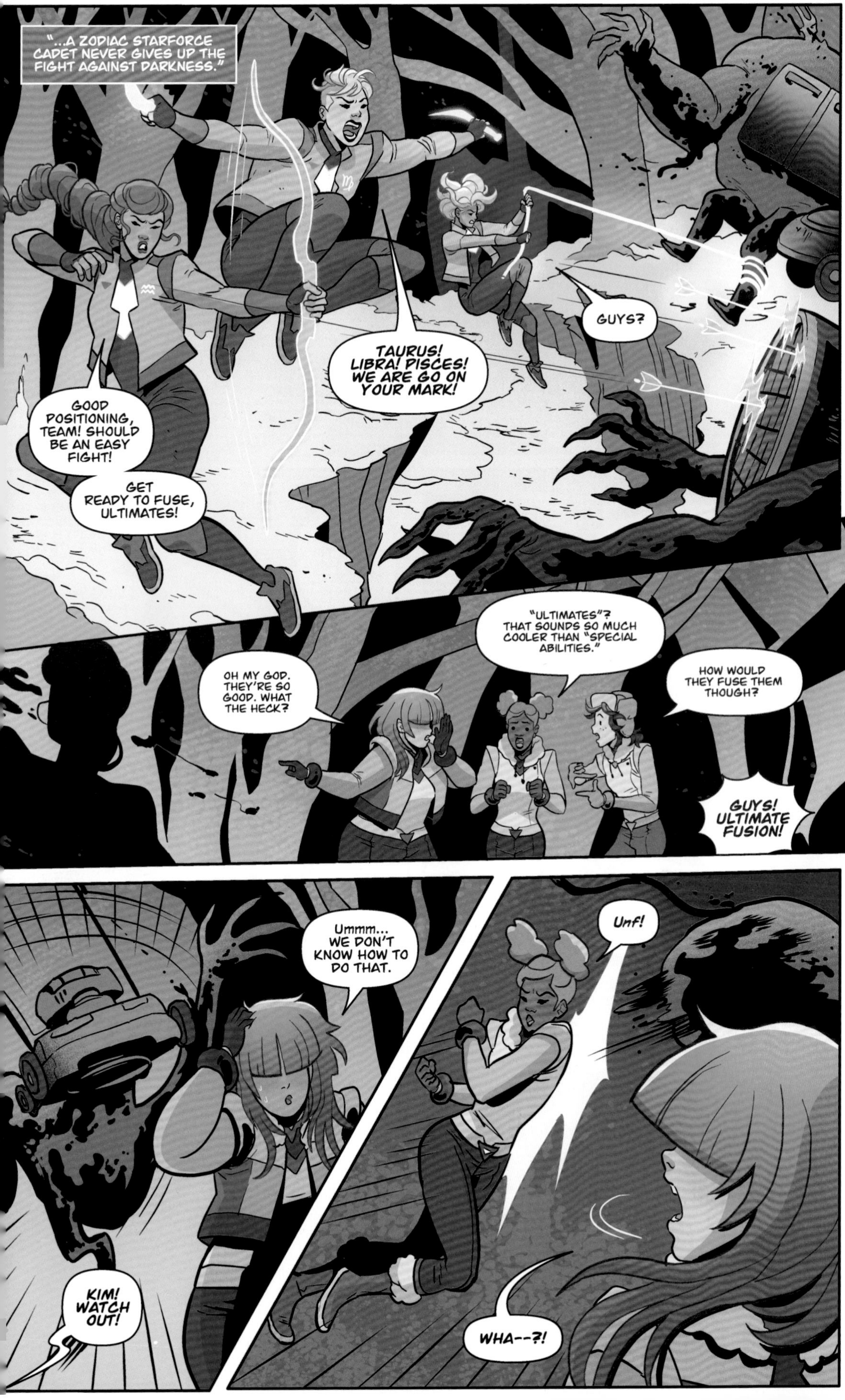
"...A ZODIAC STARFORCE CADET NEVER GIVES UP THE FIGHT AGAINST DARKNESS."
GOOD POSITIONING, TEAM! SHOULD BE AN EASY FIGHT!
GET READY TO FUSE, ULTIMATES!
TAURUS! LIBRA! PISCES! WE ARE GO ON YOUR MARK!
GUYS?
OH MY GOD. THEY'RE SO GOOD. WHAT THE HECK?
"ULTIMATES"? THAT SOUNDS SO MUCH COOLER THAN "SPECIAL ABILITIES."
HOW WOULD THEY FUSE THEM THOUGH?
GUYS! ULTIMATE FUSION!
Ummm... WE DON'T KNOW HOW TO DO THAT.
KIM! WATCH OUT!
Unf!
WHA--?!

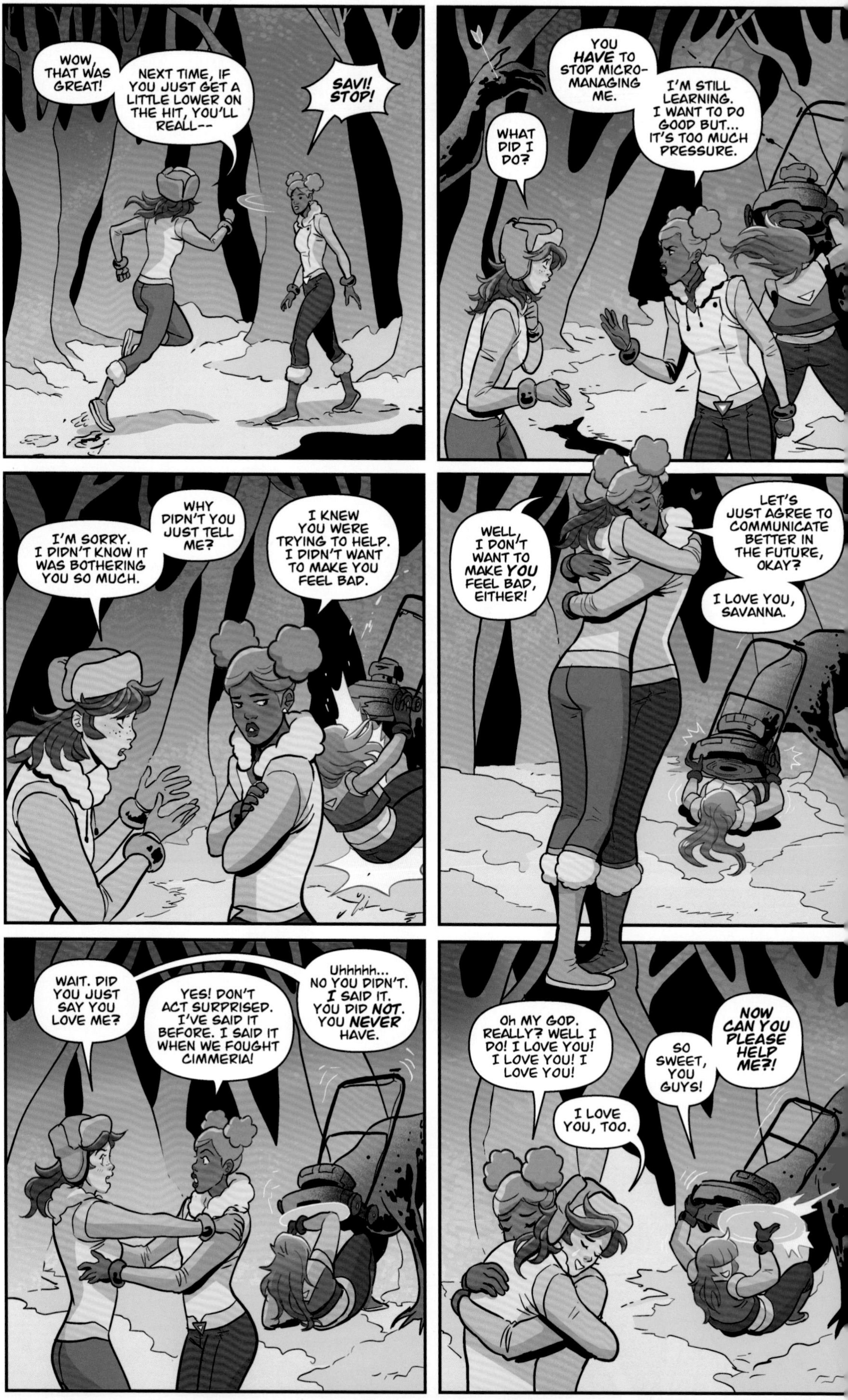
WOW, THAT WAS GREAT!
NEXT TIME, IF YOU JUST GET A LITTLE LOWER ON THE HIT, YOU'LL REALL--
SAVI! STOP!
WHAT DID I DO?
YOU HAVE TO STOP MICRO-MANAGING ME.
I'M STILL LEARNING. I WANT TO DO GOOD BUT... IT'S TOO MUCH PRESSURE.
I'M SORRY. I DIDN'T KNOW IT WAS BOTHERING YOU SO MUCH.
WHY DIDN'T YOU JUST TELL ME?
I KNEW YOU WERE TRYING TO HELP. I DIDN'T WANT TO MAKE YOU FEEL BAD.
WELL, I DON'T WANT TO MAKE YOU FEEL BAD, EITHER!
LET'S JUST AGREE TO COMMUNICATE BETTER IN THE FUTURE, OKAY?
I LOVE YOU, SAVANNA.
WAIT. DID YOU JUST SAY YOU LOVE ME?
YES! DON'T ACT SURPRISED. I'VE SAID IT BEFORE. I SAID IT WHEN WE FOUGHT CIMMERIA!
Uhhhhh... NO YOU DIDN'T. I SAID IT. YOU DID NOT. YOU NEVER HAVE.
Oh MY GOD. REALLY? WELL I DO! I LOVE YOU! I LOVE YOU! I LOVE YOU!
I LOVE YOU, TOO.
SO SWEET, YOU GUYS!
NOW CAN YOU PLEASE HELP ME?!

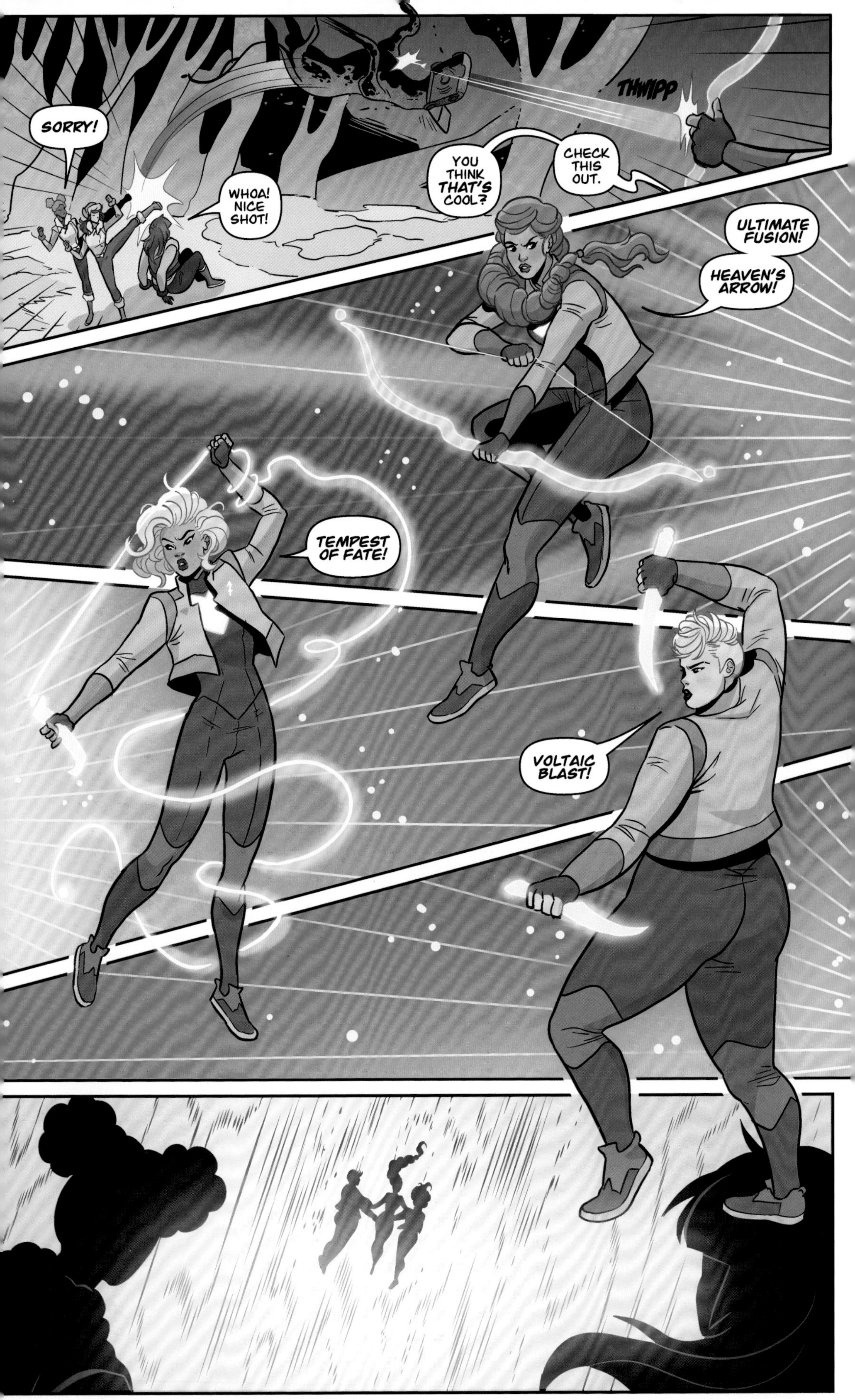
THWIPP
SORRY!
WHOA! NICE SHOT!
YOU THINK THAT'S COOL?
CHECK THIS OUT.
ULTIMATE FUSION!
HEAVEN'S ARROW!
TEMPEST OF FATE!
VOLTAIC BLAST!

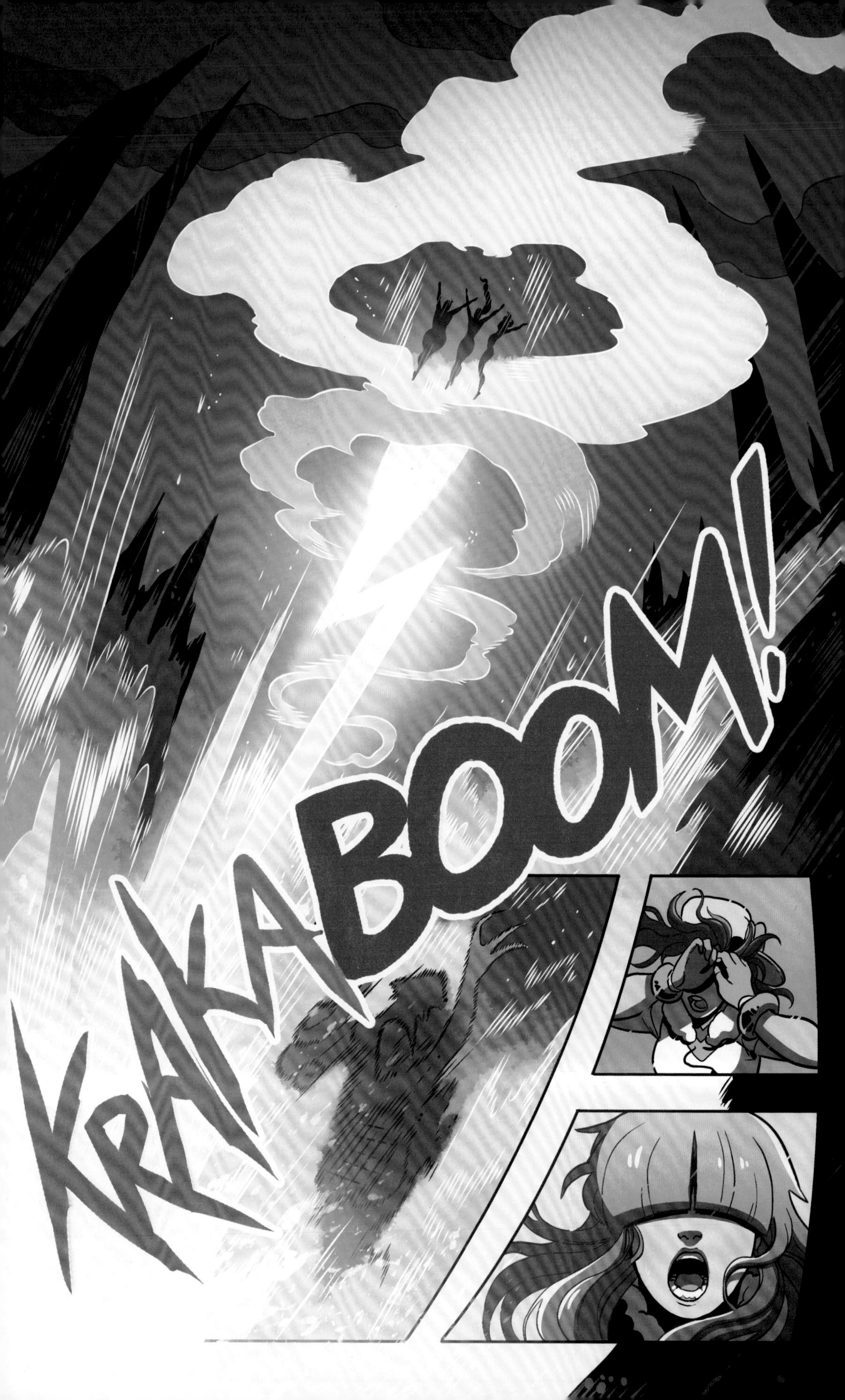
KRAKABOOM!

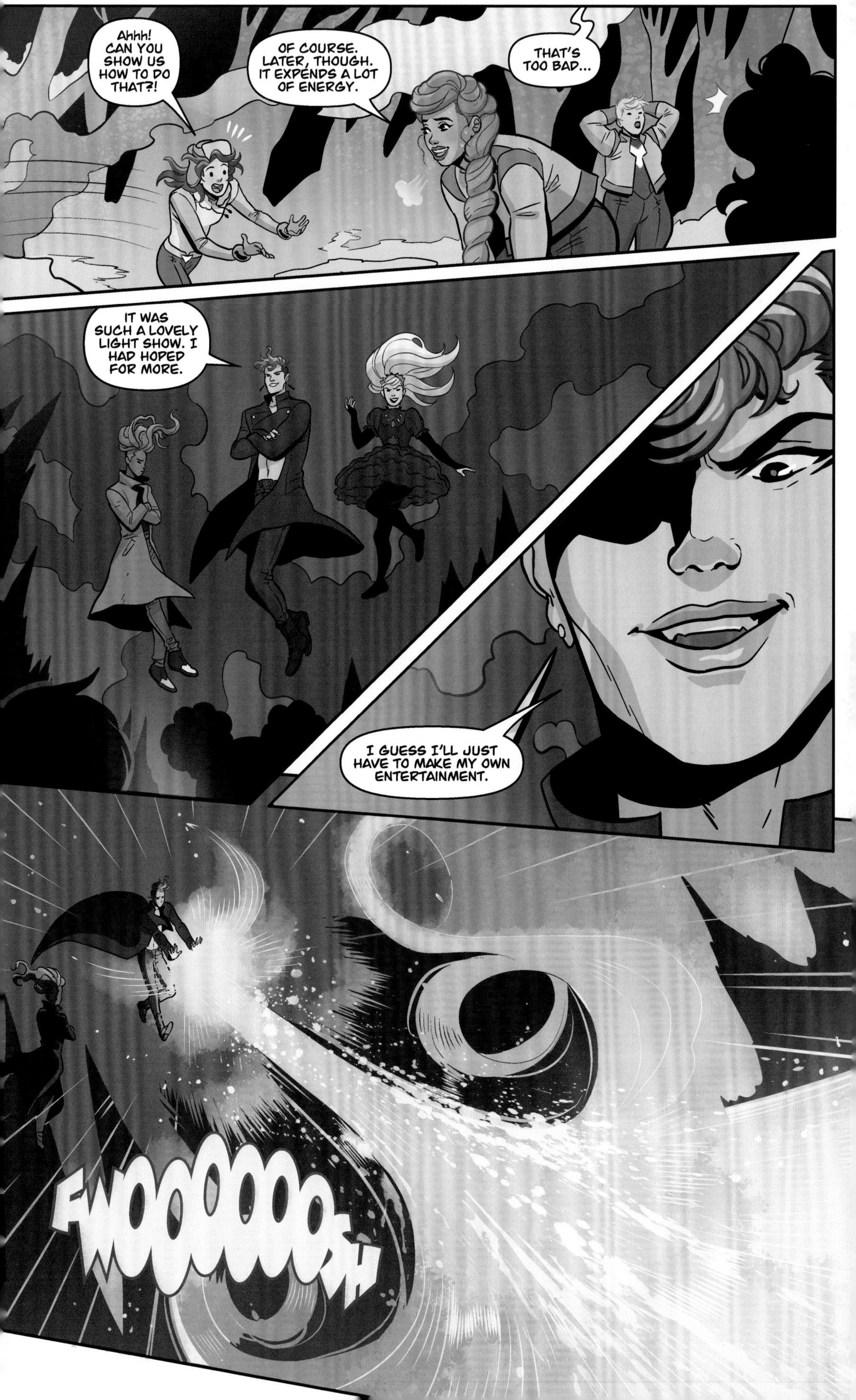
Ahhh! CAN YOU SHOW US HOW TO DO THAT?!
OF COURSE. LATER, THOUGH. IT EXPENDS A LOT OF ENERGY.
THAT'S TOO BAD...
IT WAS SUCH A LOVELY LIGHT SHOW. I HAD HOPED FOR MORE.
I GUESS I'LL JUST HAVE TO MAKE MY OWN ENTERTAINMENT.
FWOOOOOSH

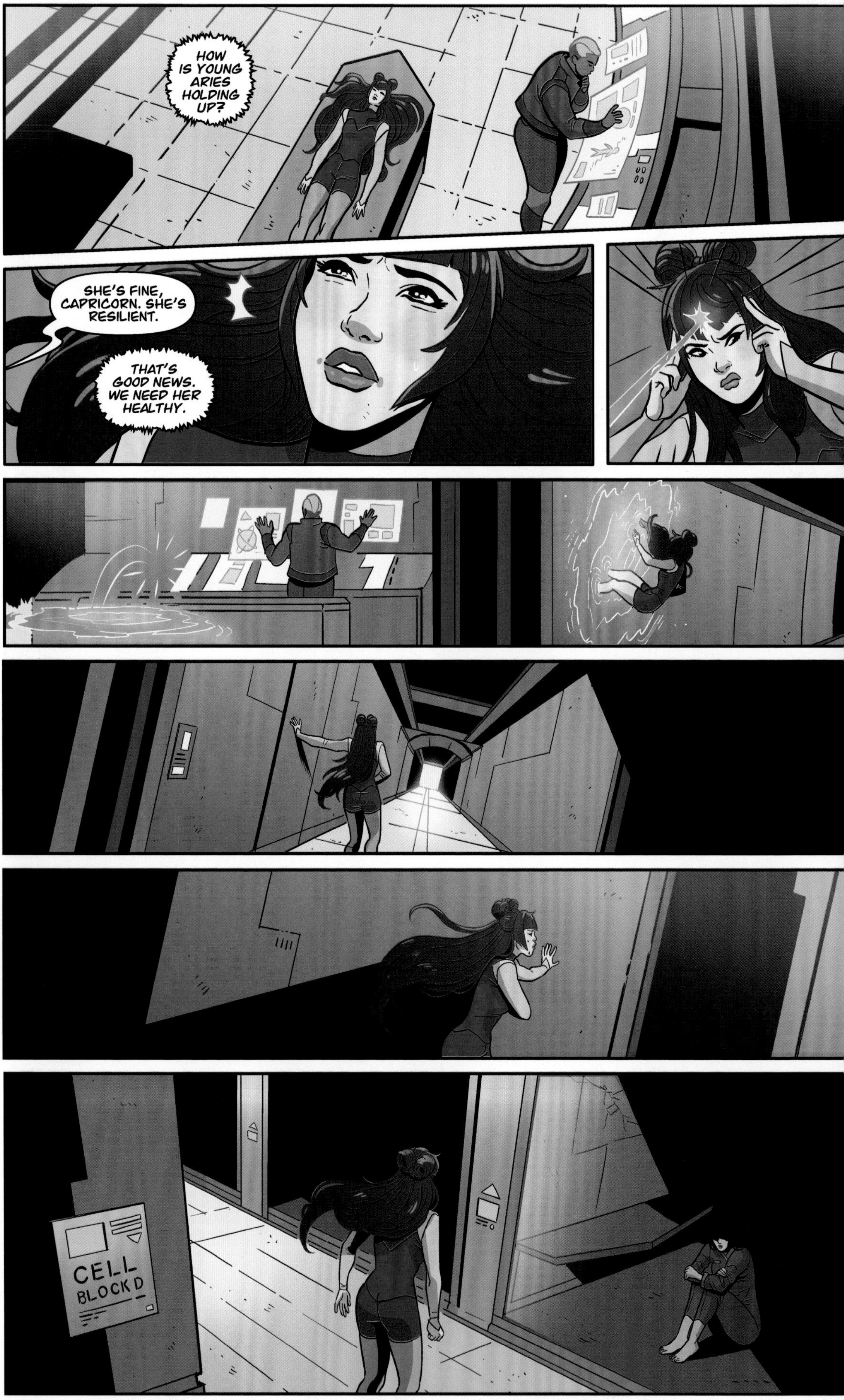
HOW IS YOUNG ARIES HOLDING UP?
SHE'S FINE, CAPRICORN. SHE'S RESILIENT.
THAT'S GOOD NEWS. WE NEED HER HEALTHY.
CELL BLOCK D

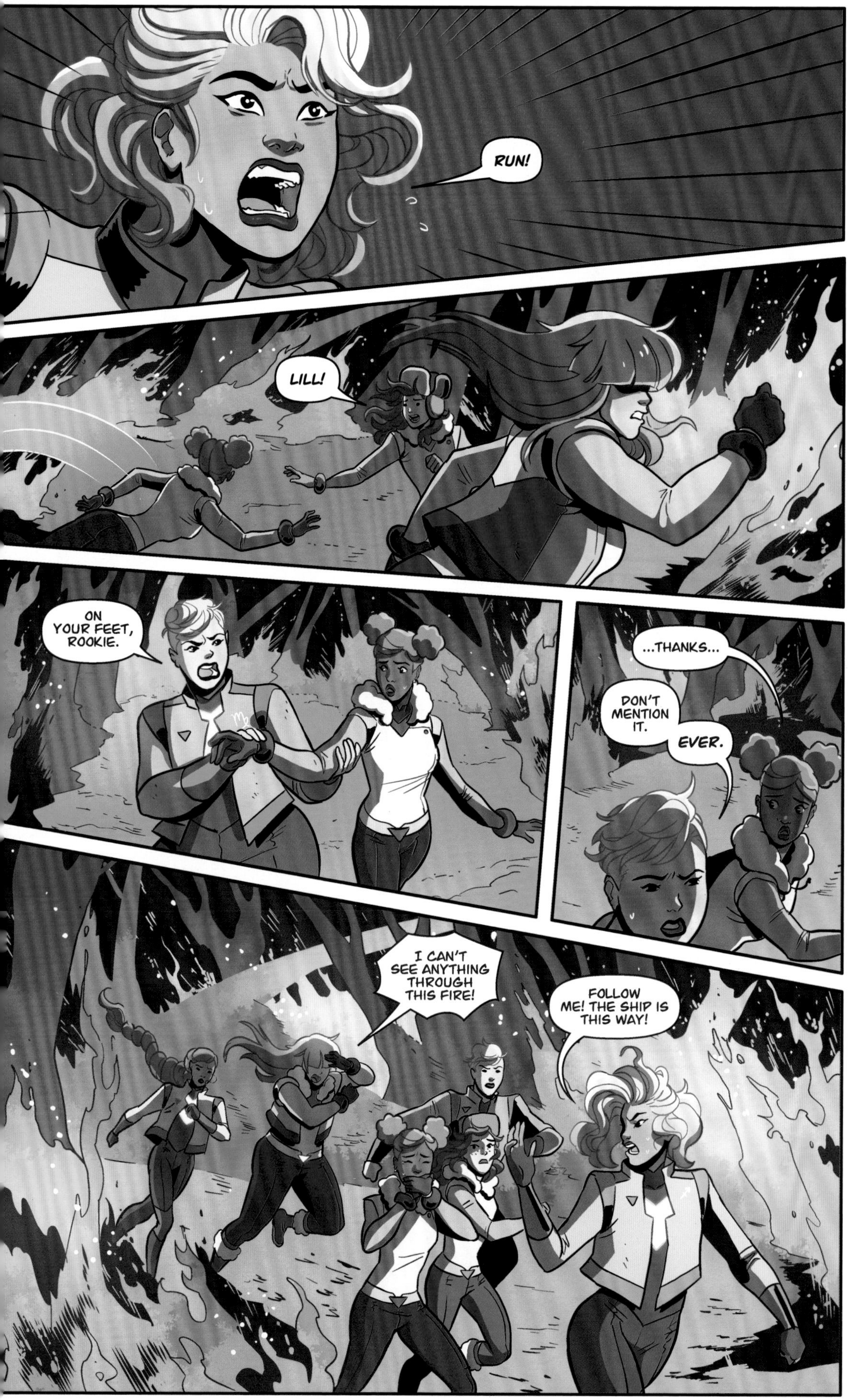
RUN!
LILL!
ON YOUR FEET, ROOKIE.
...THANKS...
DON'T MENTION IT.
EVER.
I CAN'T SEE ANYTHING THROUGH THIS FIRE!
FOLLOW ME! THE SHIP IS THIS WAY!

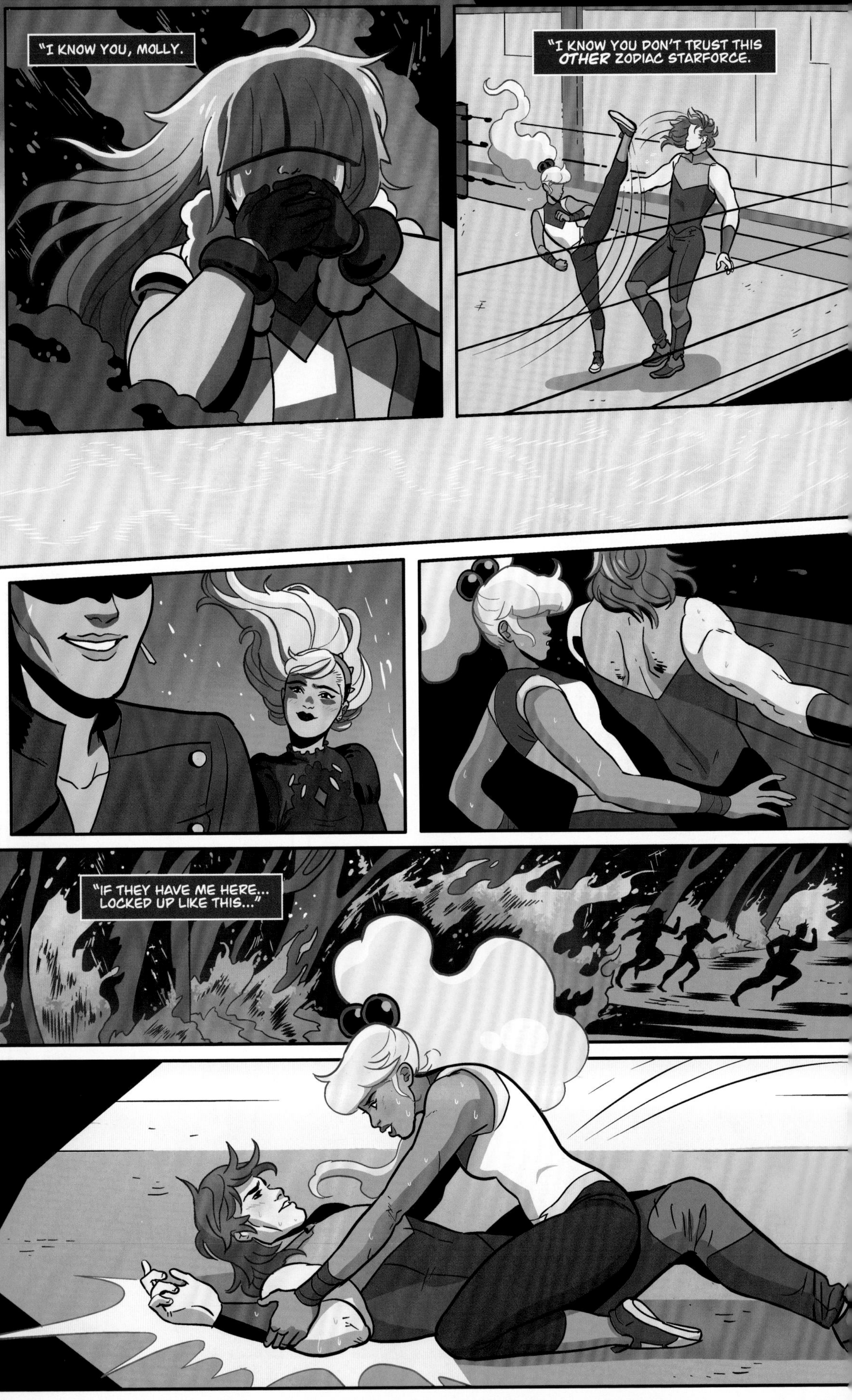
"I KNOW YOU, MOLLY.
"I KNOW YOU DON'T TRUST THIS OTHER ZODIAC STARFORCE.
"IF THEY HAVE ME HERE... LOCKED UP LIKE THIS..."

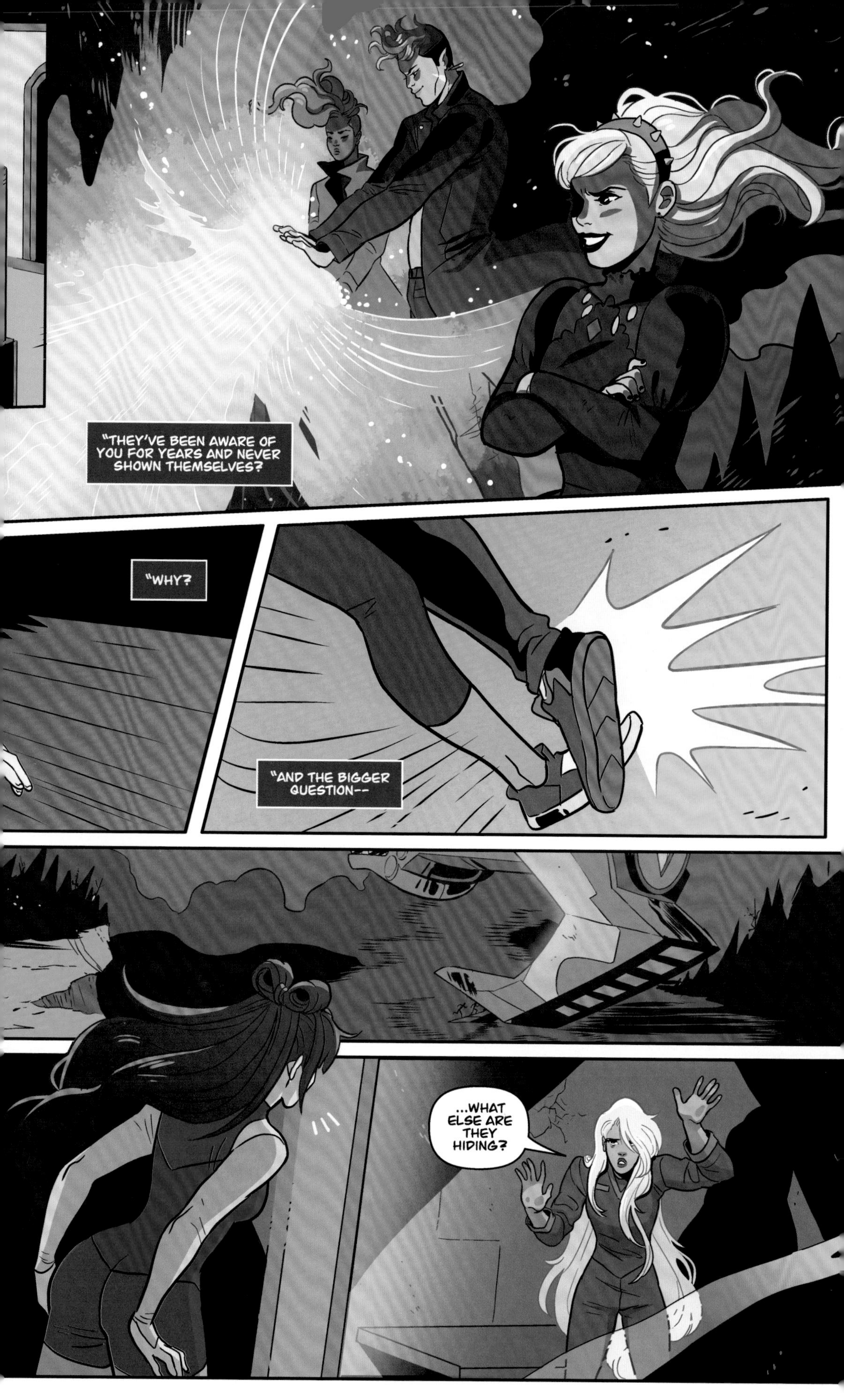
"THEY'VE BEEN AWARE OF YOU FOR YEARS AND NEVER SHOWN THEMSELVES?
"WHY?
"AND THE BIGGER QUESTION--
...WHAT ELSE ARE THEY HIDING?

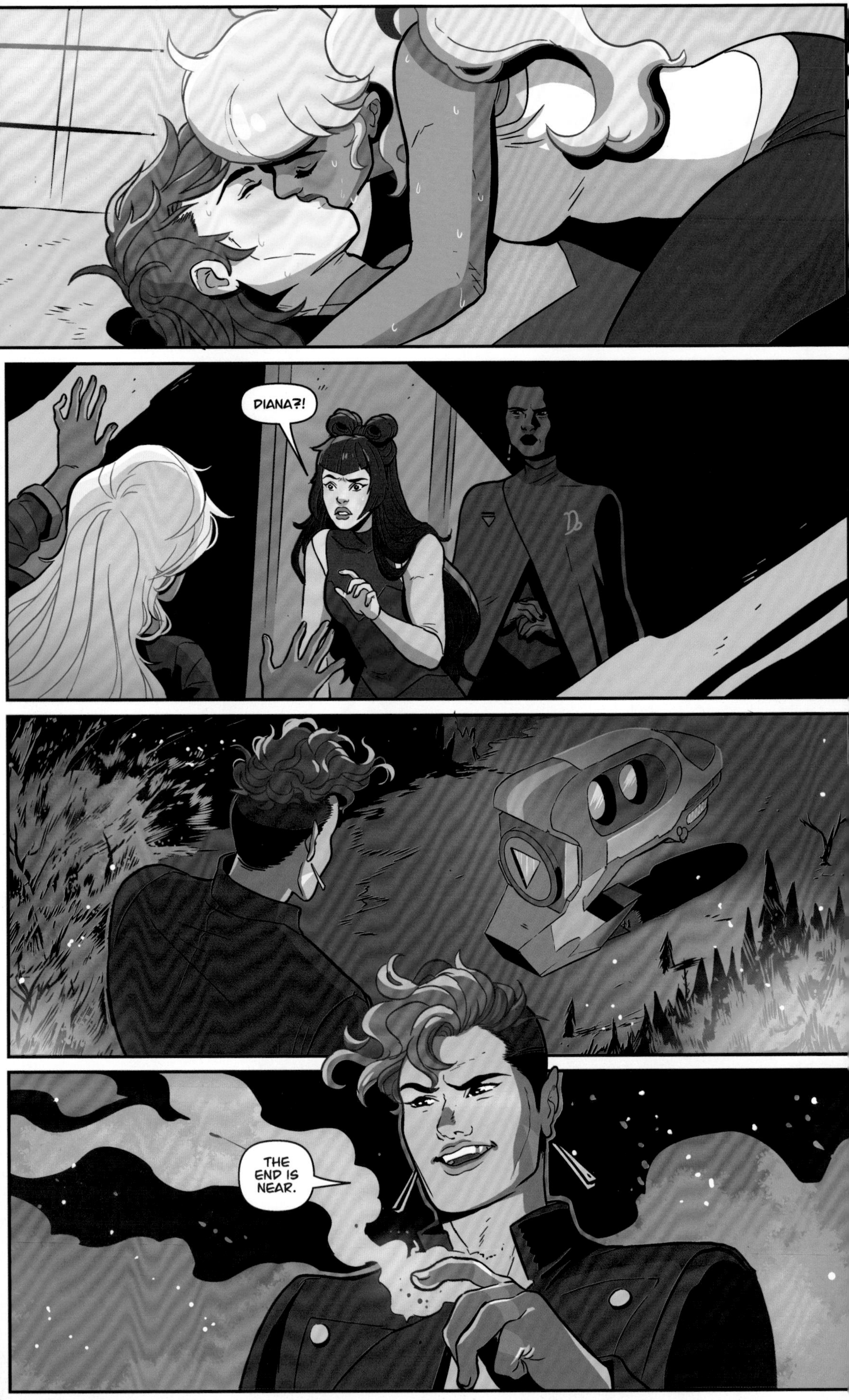
DIANA?!
THE END IS NEAR.

CHAPTER FOUR

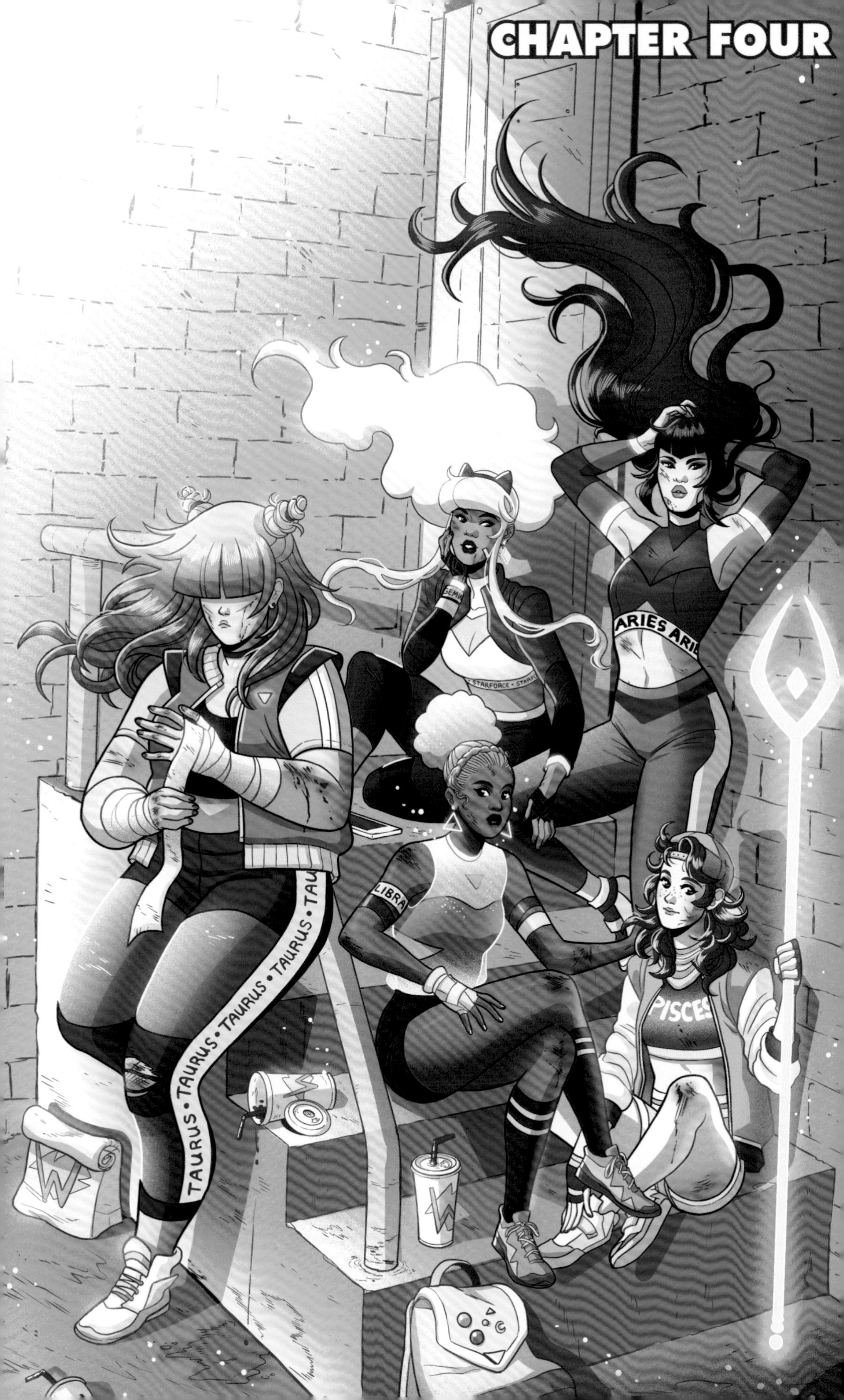

TAURUS • TAURUS • TAURUS • TAURUS • TAURUS
ARIES
STARFORCE
LIBRA
PISCES

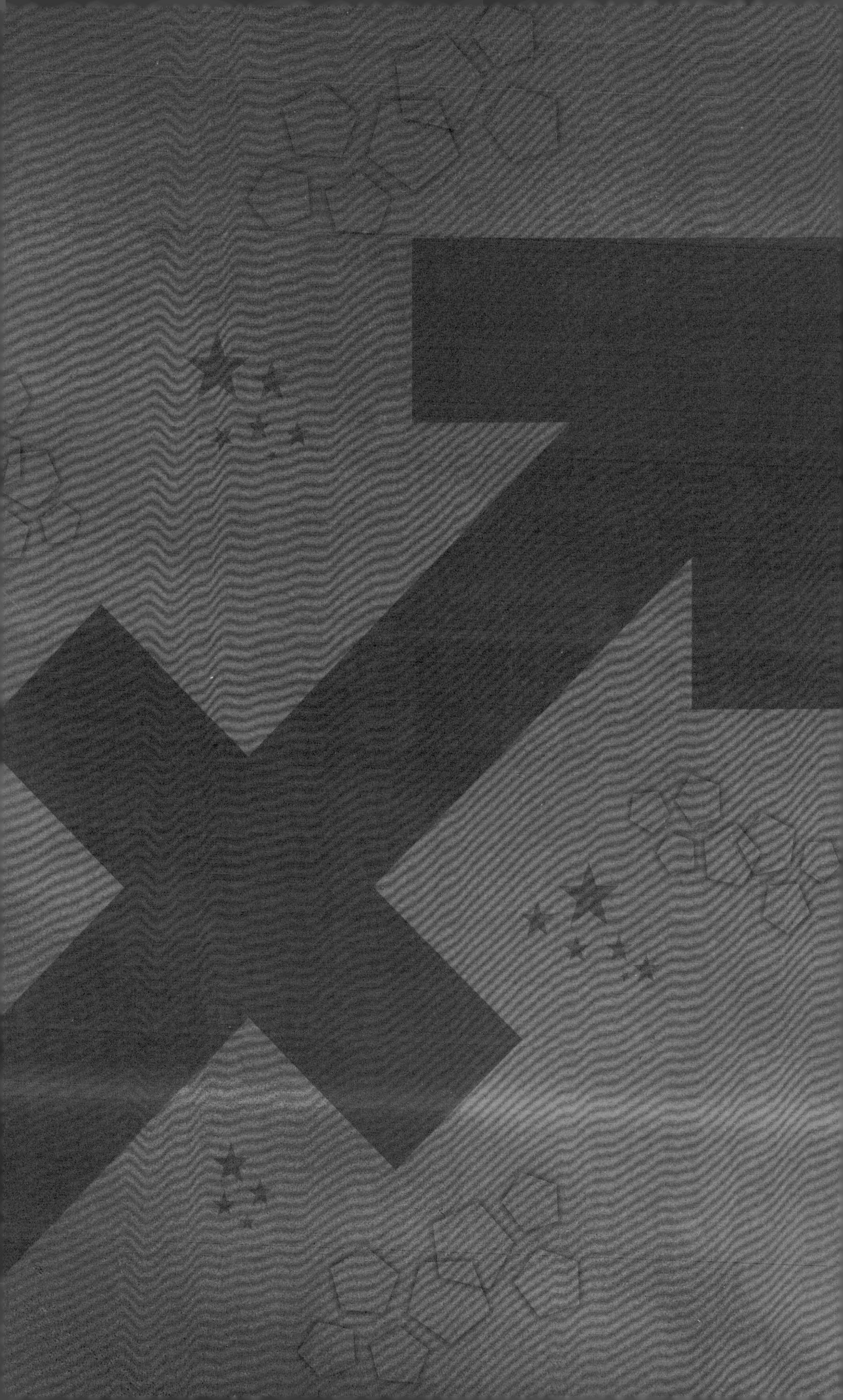

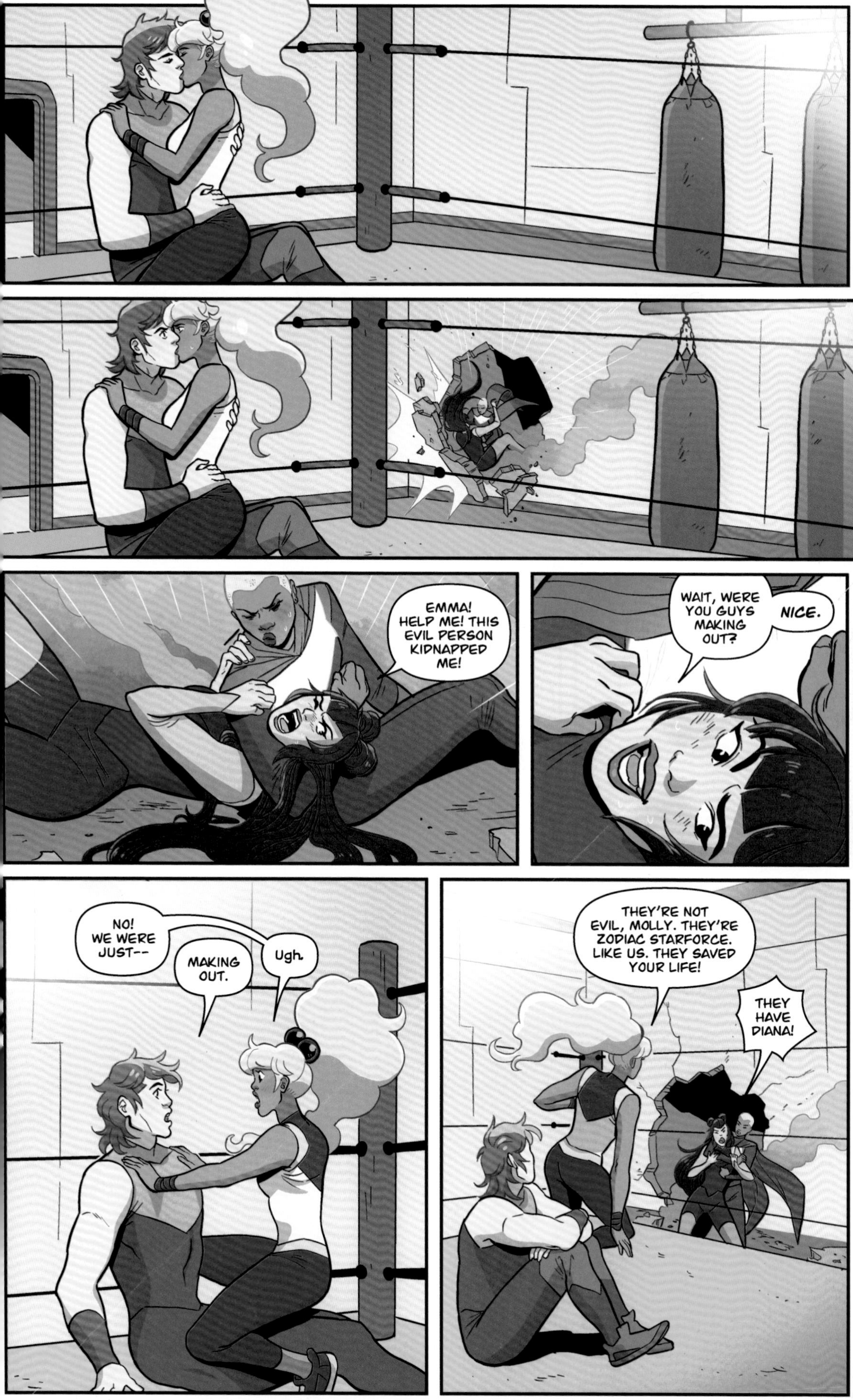
EMMA! HELP ME! THIS EVIL PERSON KIDNAPPED ME!
WAIT, WERE YOU GUYS MAKING OUT?
NICE.
NO! WE WERE JUST--
MAKING OUT.
Ugh.
THEY'RE NOT EVIL, MOLLY. THEY'RE ZODIAC STARFORCE. LIKE US. THEY SAVED YOUR LIFE!
THEY HAVE DIANA!

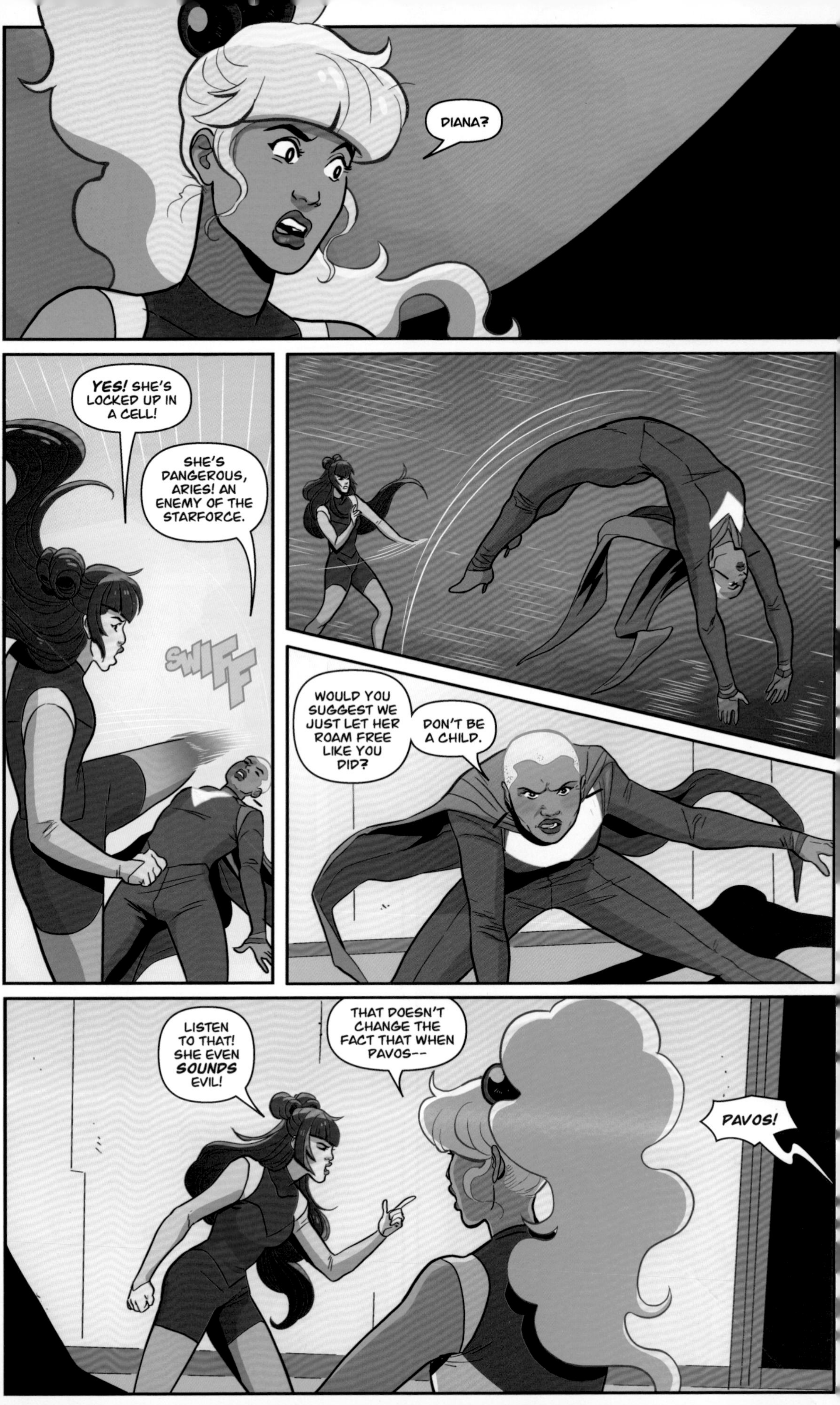
DIANA?
YES! SHE'S LOCKED UP IN A CELL!
SHE'S DANGEROUS, ARIES! AN ENEMY OF THE STARFORCE.
SWIFF
WOULD YOU SUGGEST WE JUST LET HER ROAM FREE LIKE YOU DID?
DON'T BE A CHILD.
LISTEN TO THAT! SHE EVEN SOUNDS EVIL!
THAT DOESN'T CHANGE THE FACT THAT WHEN PAVOS--
PAVOS!

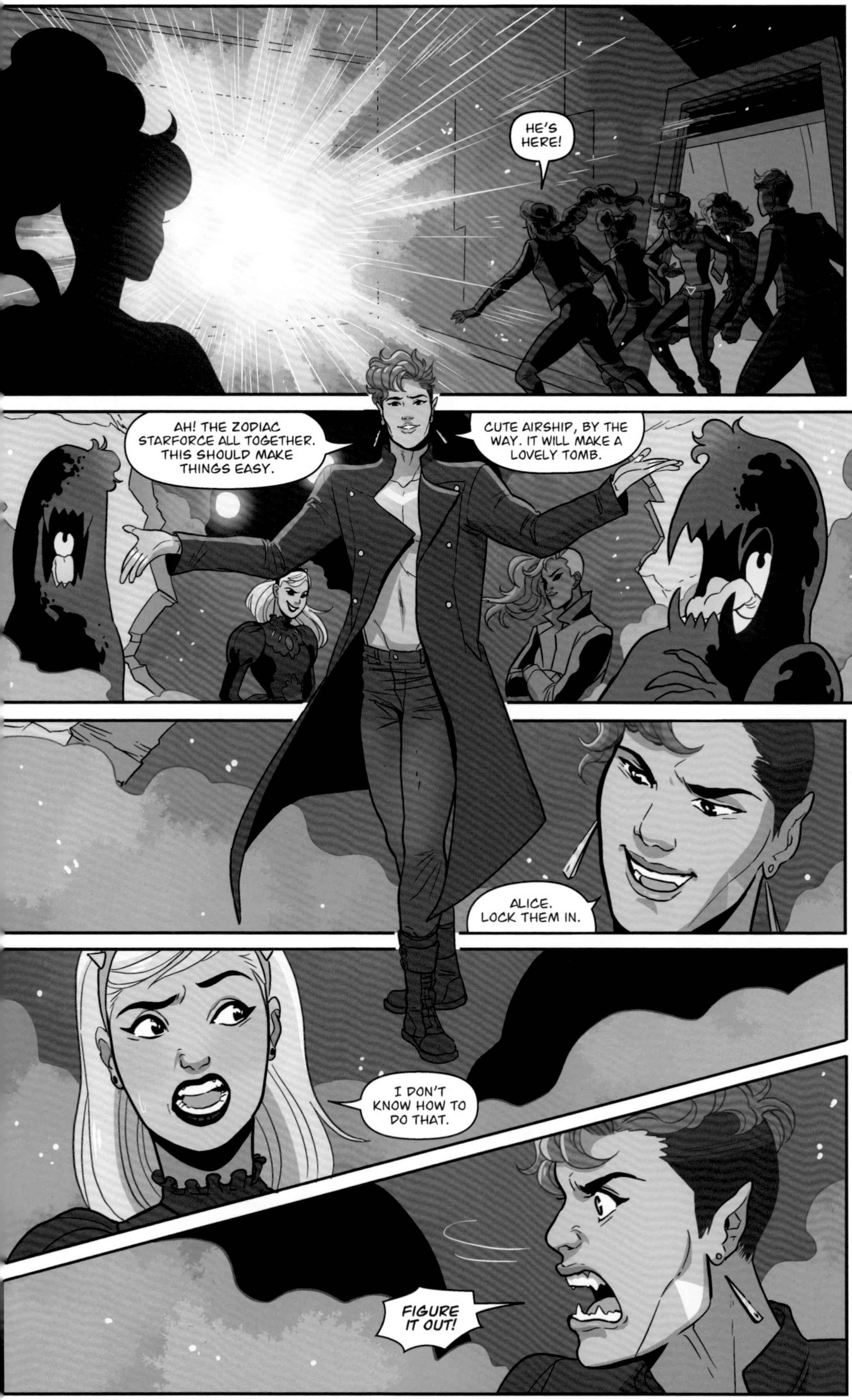
HE'S HERE!
AH! THE ZODIAC STARFORCE ALL TOGETHER. THIS SHOULD MAKE THINGS EASY.
CUTE AIRSHIP, BY THE WAY. IT WILL MAKE A LOVELY TOMB.
ALICE. LOCK THEM IN.
I DON'T KNOW HOW TO DO THAT.
FIGURE IT OUT!

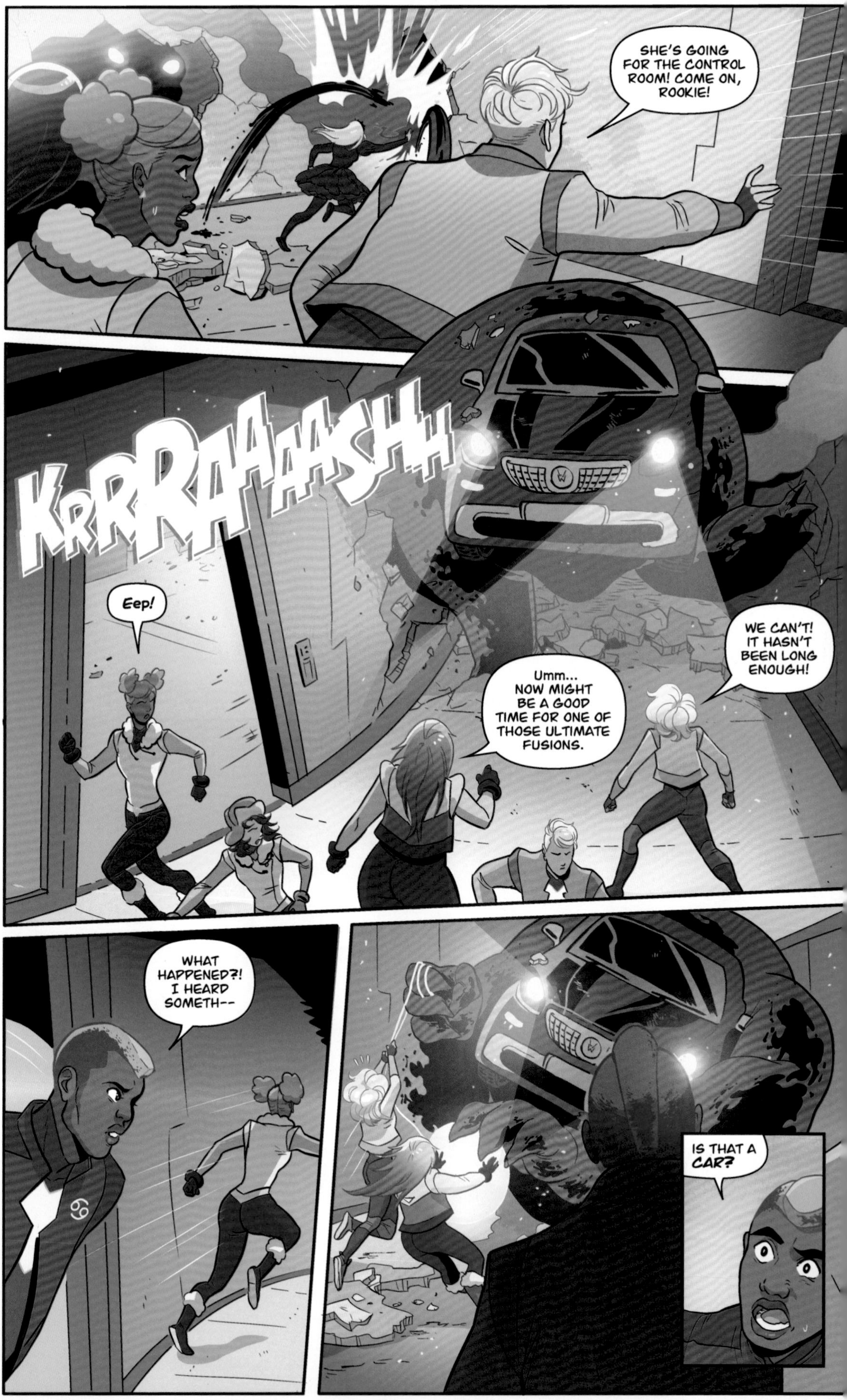
SHE'S GOING FOR THE CONTROL ROOM! COME ON, ROOKIE!
KRRRAAAASHH
Eep!
Umm... NOW MIGHT BE A GOOD TIME FOR ONE OF THOSE ULTIMATE FUSIONS.
WE CAN'T! IT HASN'T BEEN LONG ENOUGH!
WHAT HAPPENED?! I HEARD SOMETH--
IS THAT A CAR?

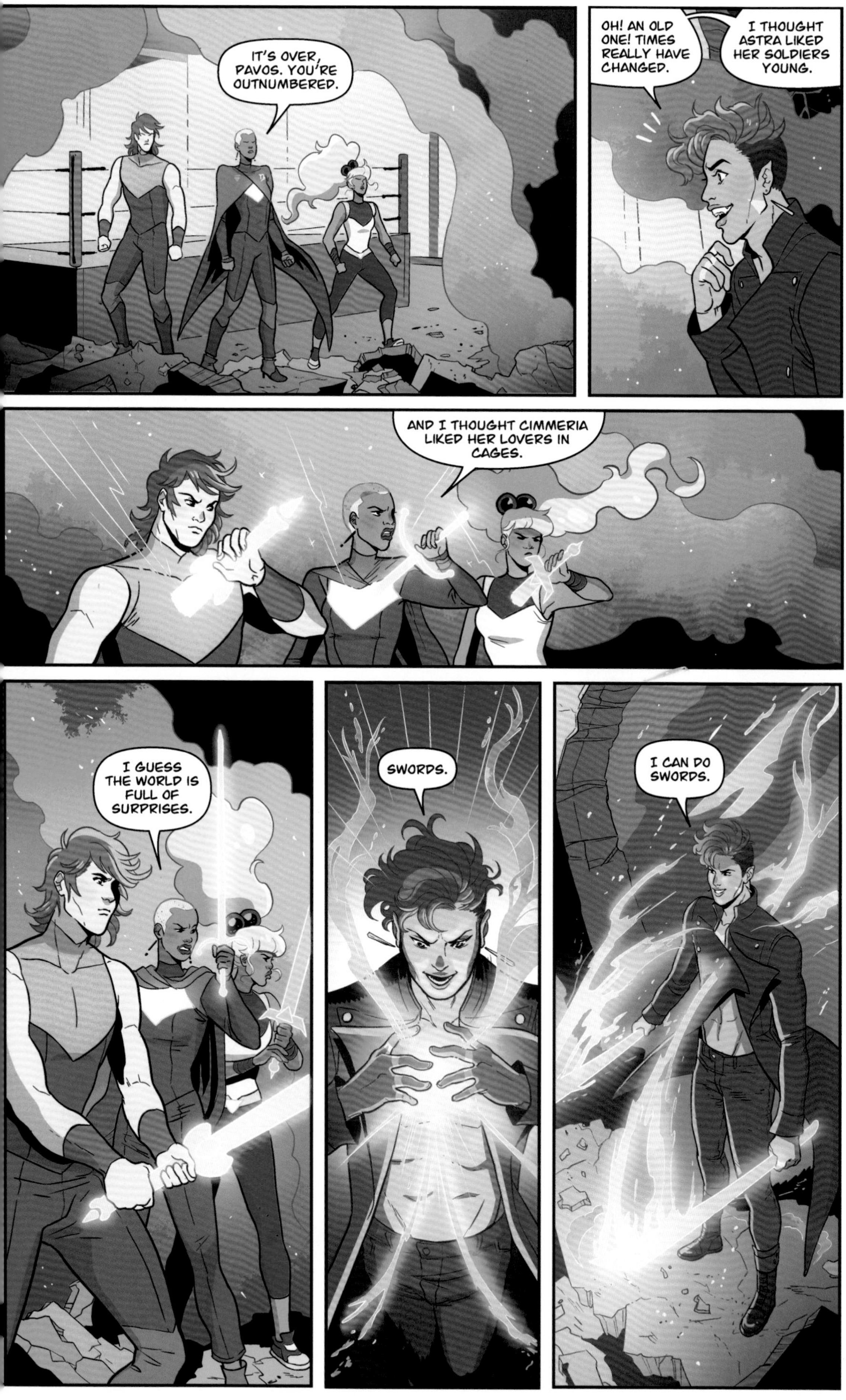
IT'S OVER, PAVOS. YOU'RE OUTNUMBERED.
OH! AN OLD ONE! TIMES REALLY HAVE CHANGED.
I THOUGHT ASTRA LIKED HER SOLDIERS YOUNG.
AND I THOUGHT CIMMERIA LIKED HER LOVERS IN CAGES.
I GUESS THE WORLD IS FULL OF SURPRISES.
SWORDS.
I CAN DO SWORDS.

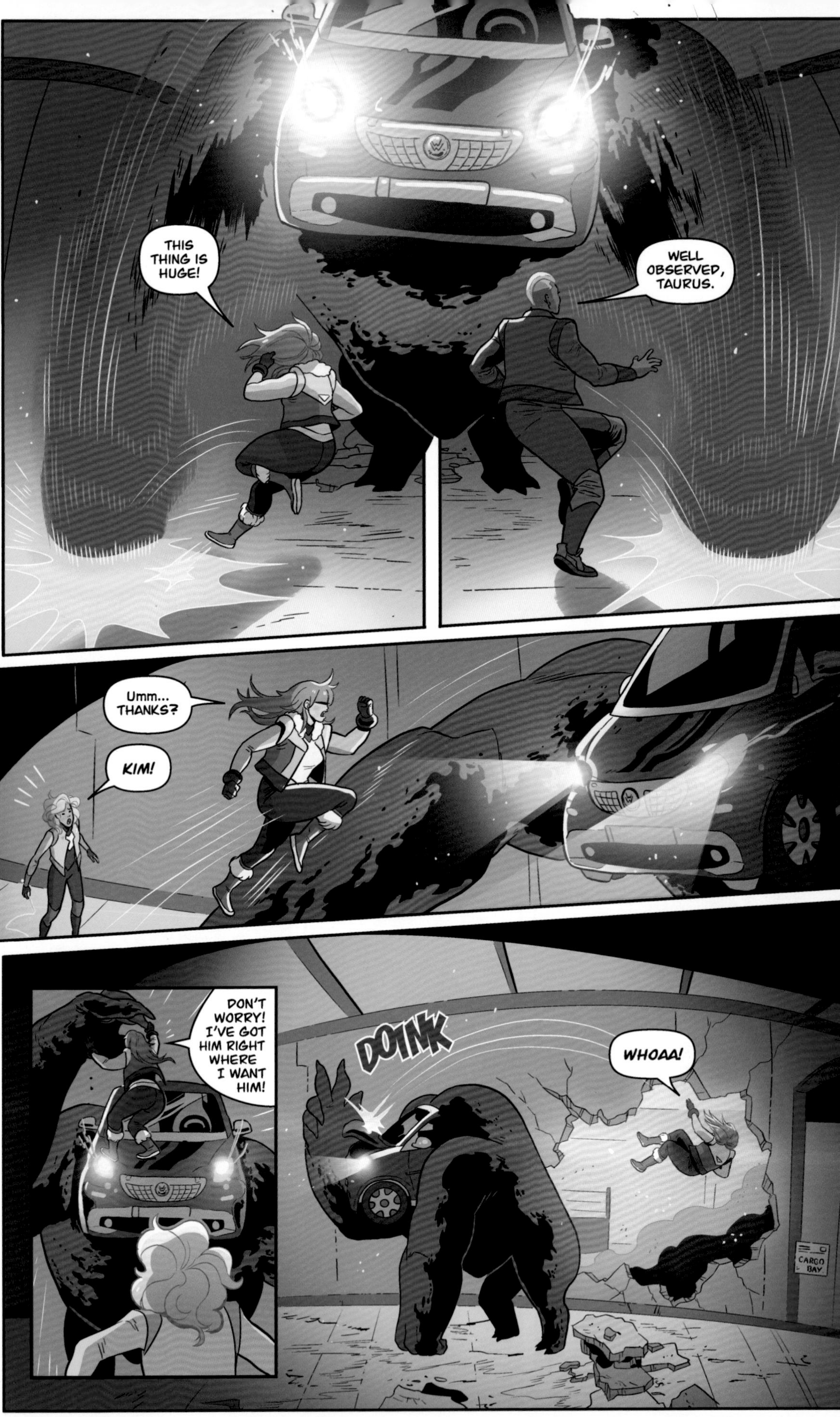
THIS THING IS HUGE!
WELL OBSERVED, TAURUS.
Umm... THANKS?
KIM!
DON'T WORRY! I'VE GOT HIM RIGHT WHERE I WANT HIM!
DOINK
WHOAA!
CARGO BAY

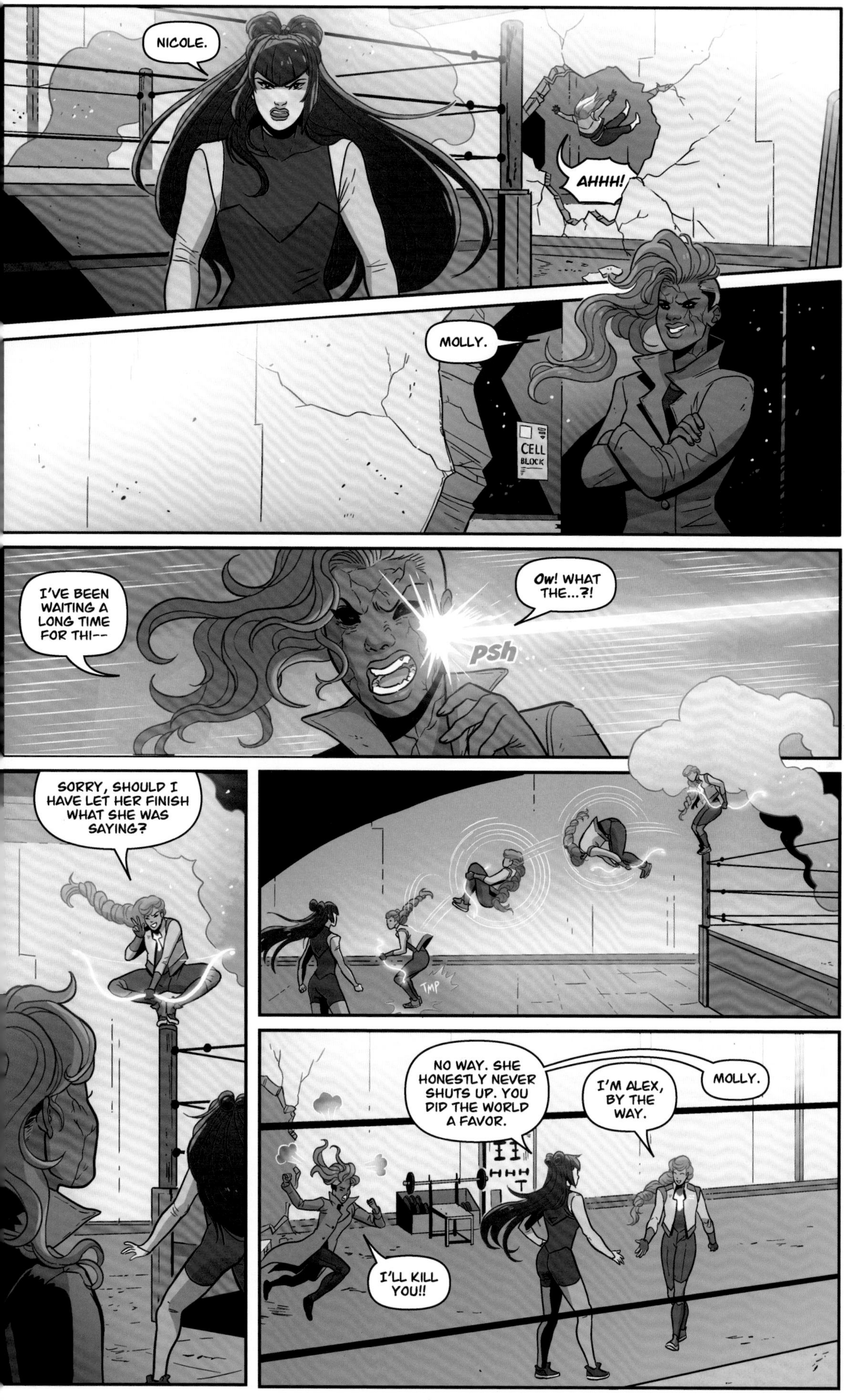
NICOLE.
AHHH!
MOLLY.
CELL BLOCK
I'VE BEEN WAITING A LONG TIME FOR THI--
OW! WHAT THE...?!
PSH
SORRY, SHOULD I HAVE LET HER FINISH WHAT SHE WAS SAYING?
TMP
NO WAY. SHE HONESTLY NEVER SHUTS UP. YOU DID THE WORLD A FAVOR.
MOLLY.
I'M ALEX, BY THE WAY.
I'LL KILL YOU!!

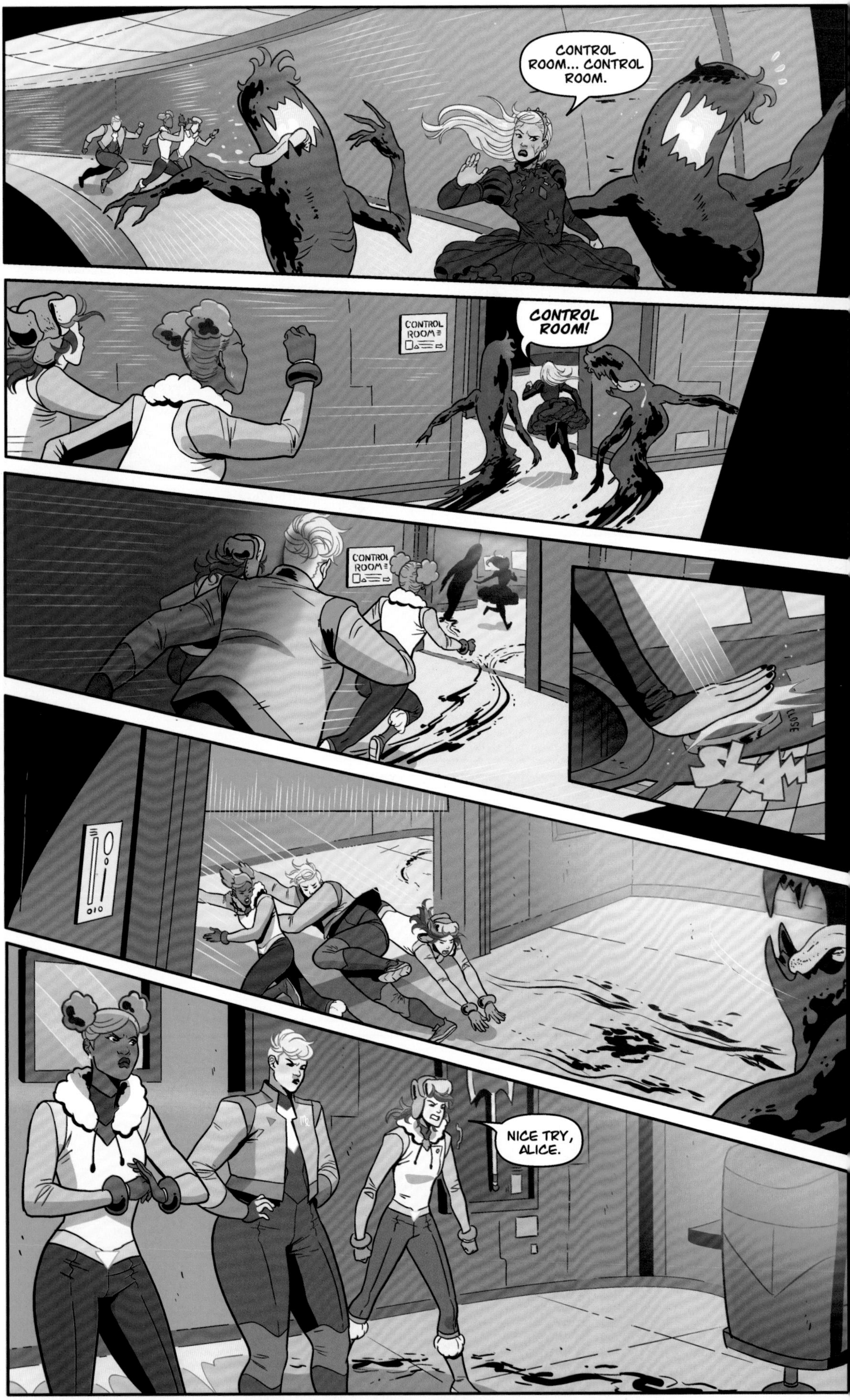

CONTROL ROOM... CONTROL ROOM.
CONTROL ROOM
CONTROL ROOM!
CONTROL ROOM
CLOSE
SLAM
NICE TRY, ALICE.

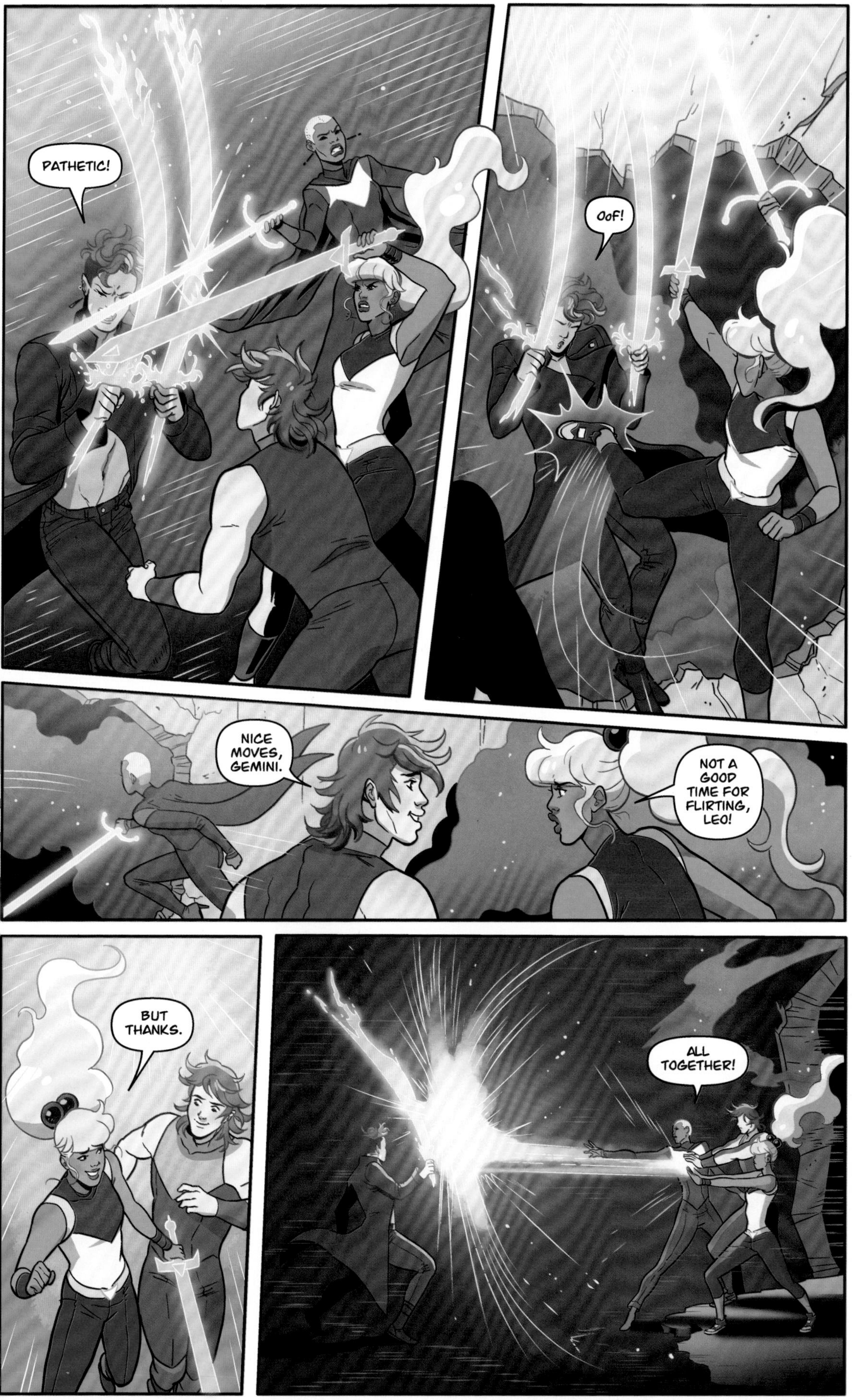
PATHETIC!
OOF!
NICE MOVES, GEMINI.
NOT A GOOD TIME FOR FLIRTING, LEO!
BUT THANKS.
ALL TOGETHER!

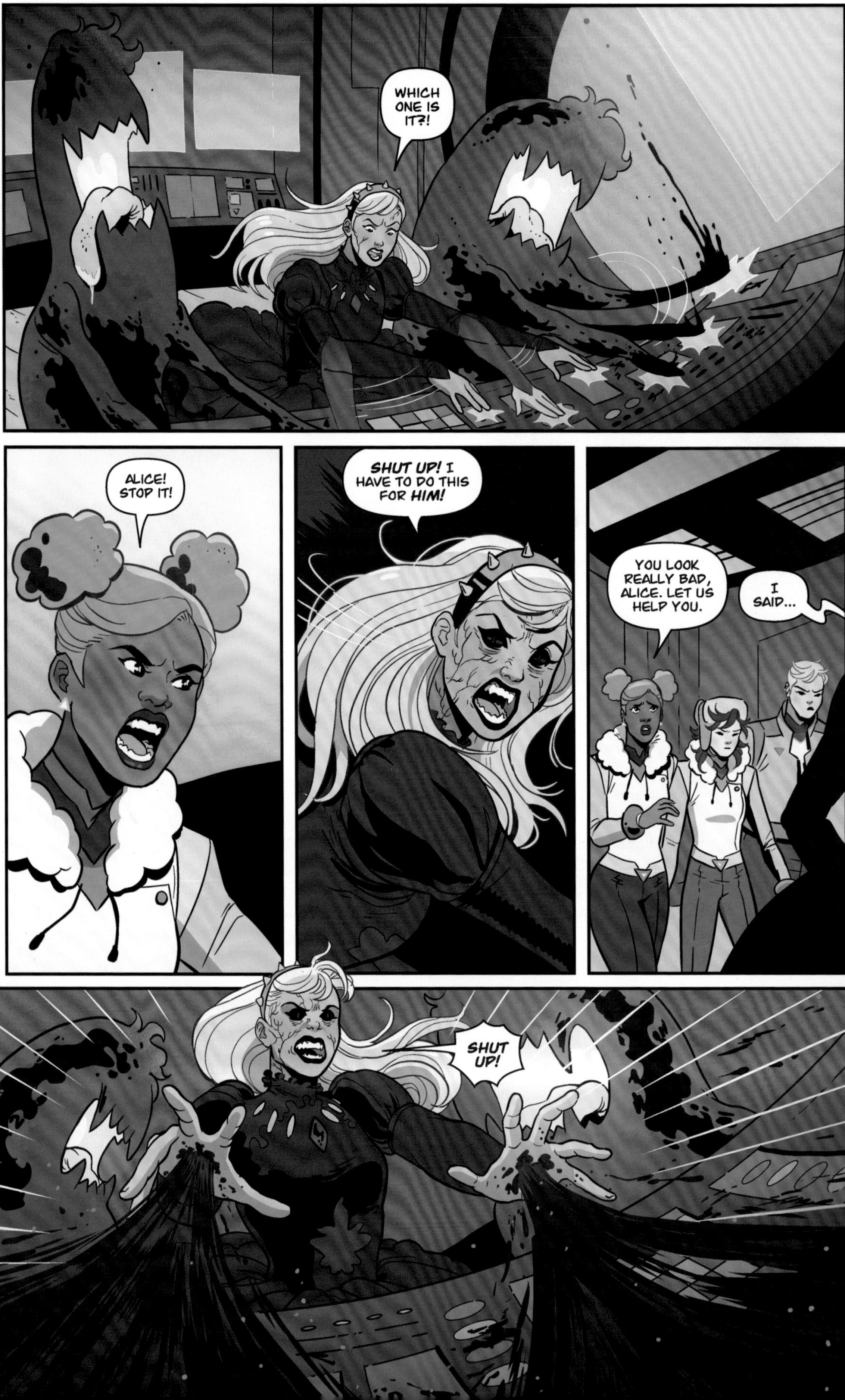
WHICH ONE IS IT?!
ALICE! STOP IT!
SHUT UP! I HAVE TO DO THIS FOR HIM!
YOU LOOK REALLY BAD, ALICE. LET US HELP YOU.
I SAID...
SHUT UP!

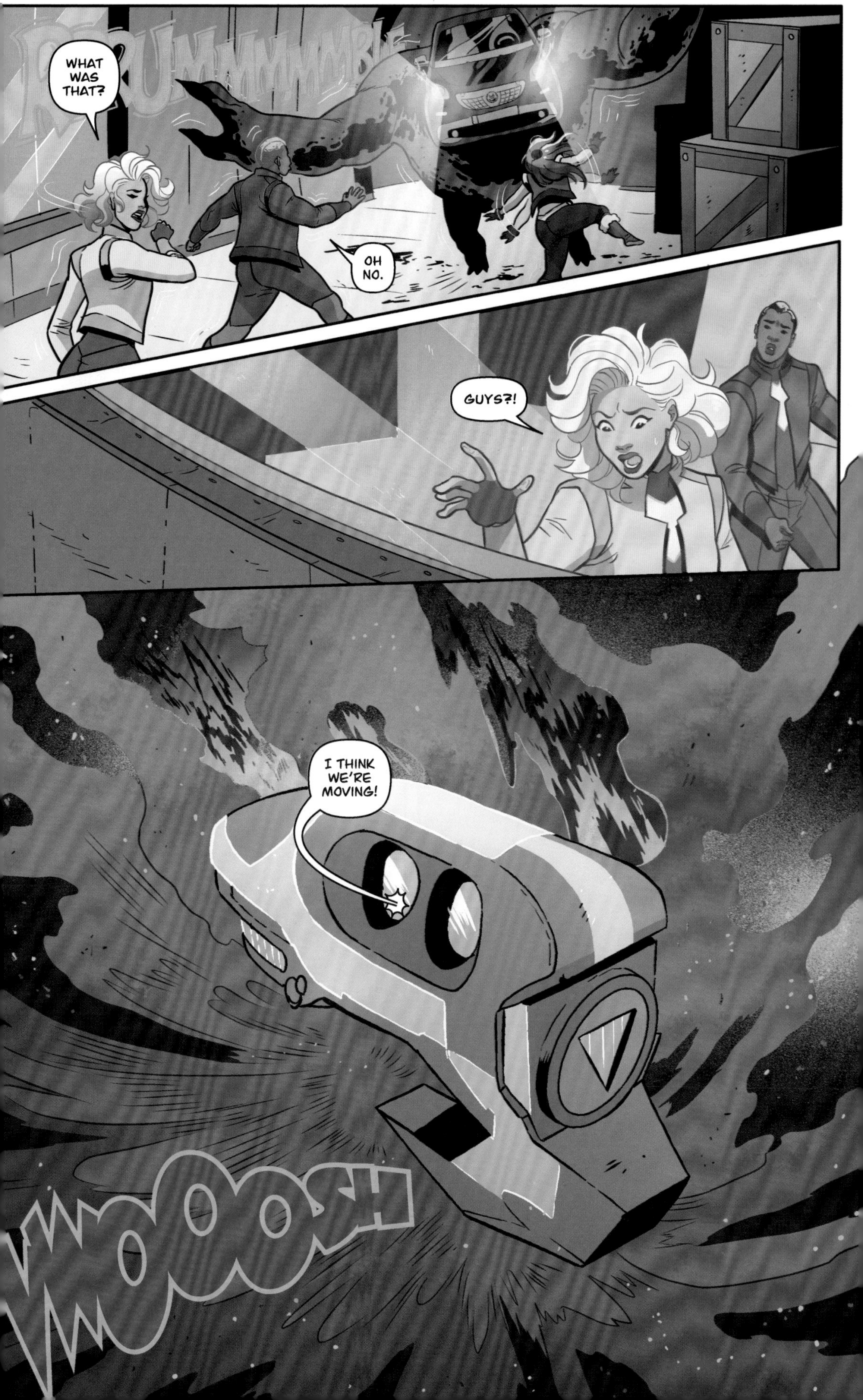
RRUMMMMMMBLE
WHAT WAS THAT?
OH NO.
GUYS?!
I THINK WE'RE MOVING!
WOOOSH

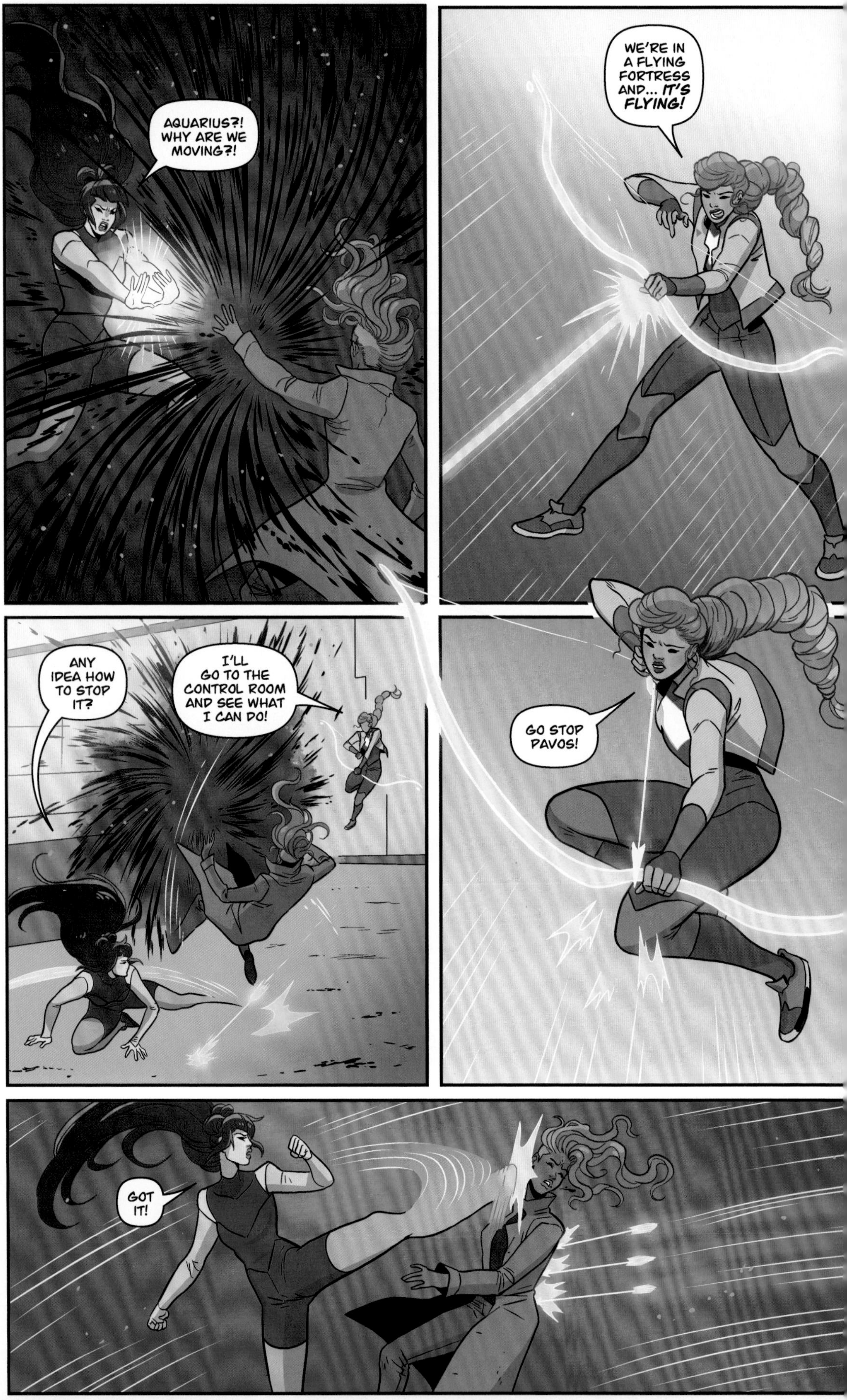
AQUARIUS?! WHY ARE WE MOVING?!
WE'RE IN A FLYING FORTRESS AND... *IT'S FLYING!*
ANY IDEA HOW TO STOP IT?
I'LL GO TO THE CONTROL ROOM AND SEE WHAT I CAN DO!
GO STOP PAVOS!
GOT IT!

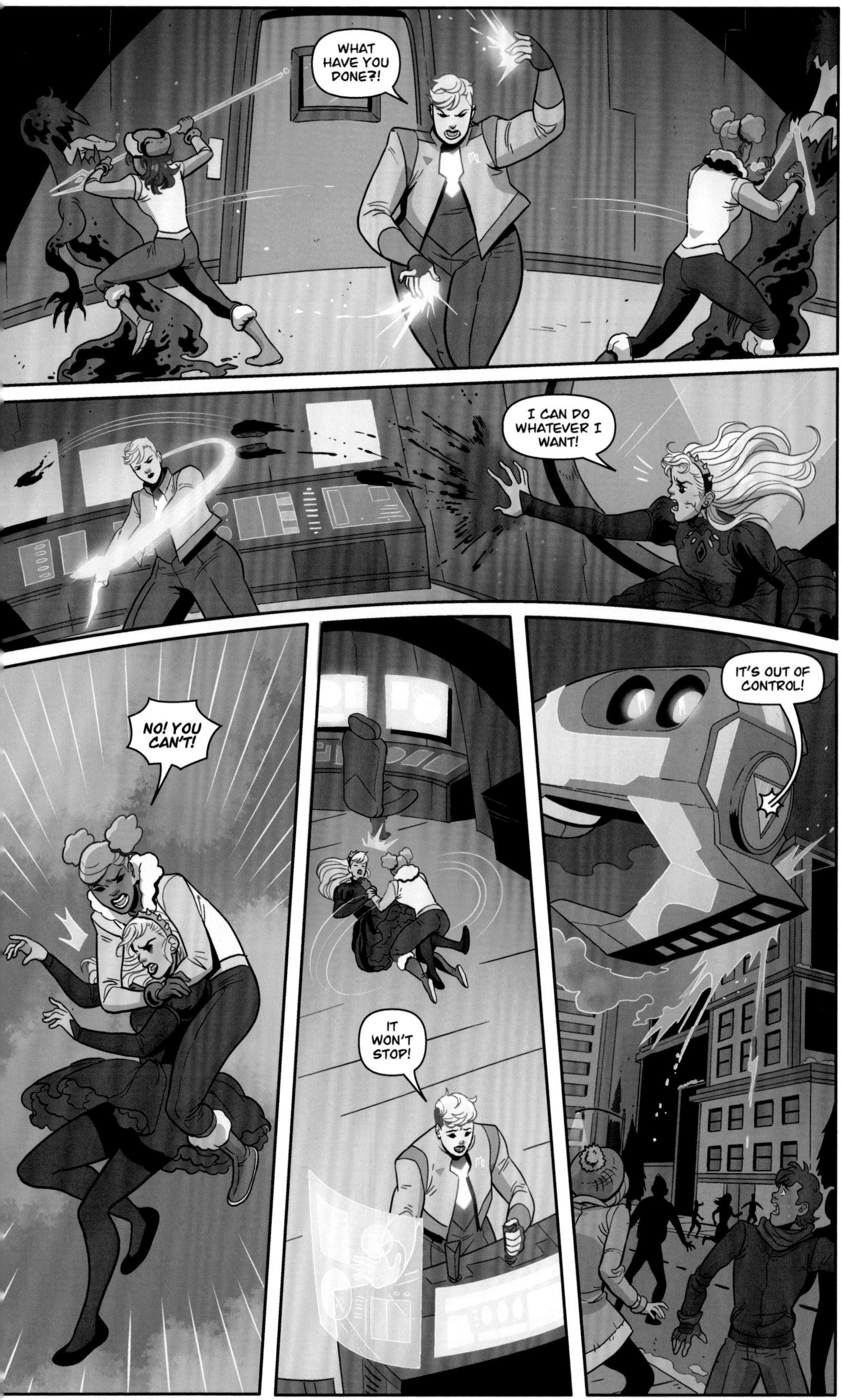
WHAT HAVE YOU DONE?!
I CAN DO WHATEVER I WANT!
NO! YOU CAN'T!
IT WON'T STOP!
IT'S OUT OF CONTROL!

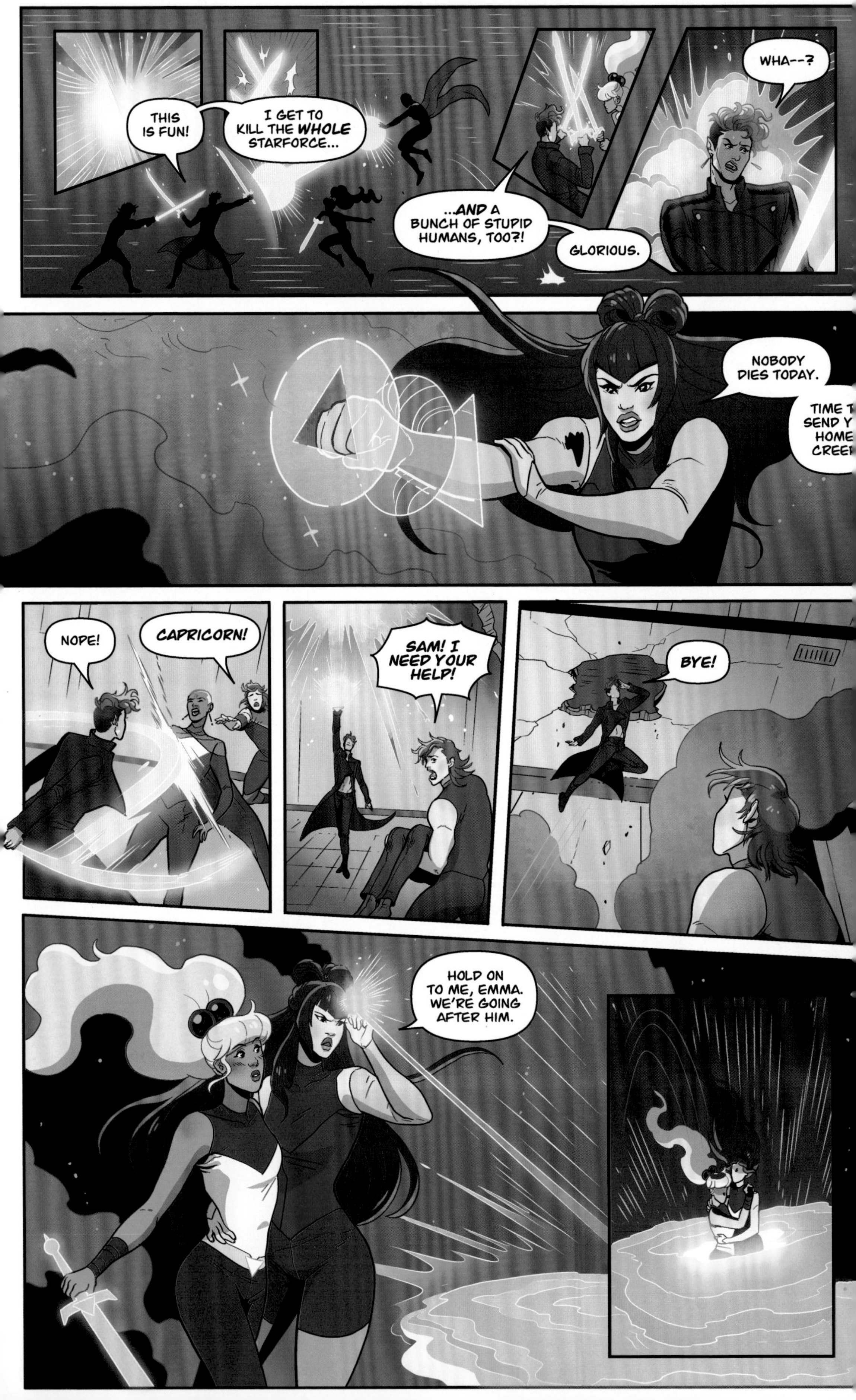
THIS IS FUN!
I GET TO KILL THE WHOLE STARFORCE...
...AND A BUNCH OF STUPID HUMANS, TOO?!
GLORIOUS.
WHA--?
NOBODY DIES TODAY.
TIME T SEND Y HOME CREE
NOPE!
CAPRICORN!
SAM! I NEED YOUR HELP!
BYE!
HOLD ON TO ME, EMMA. WE'RE GOING AFTER HIM.

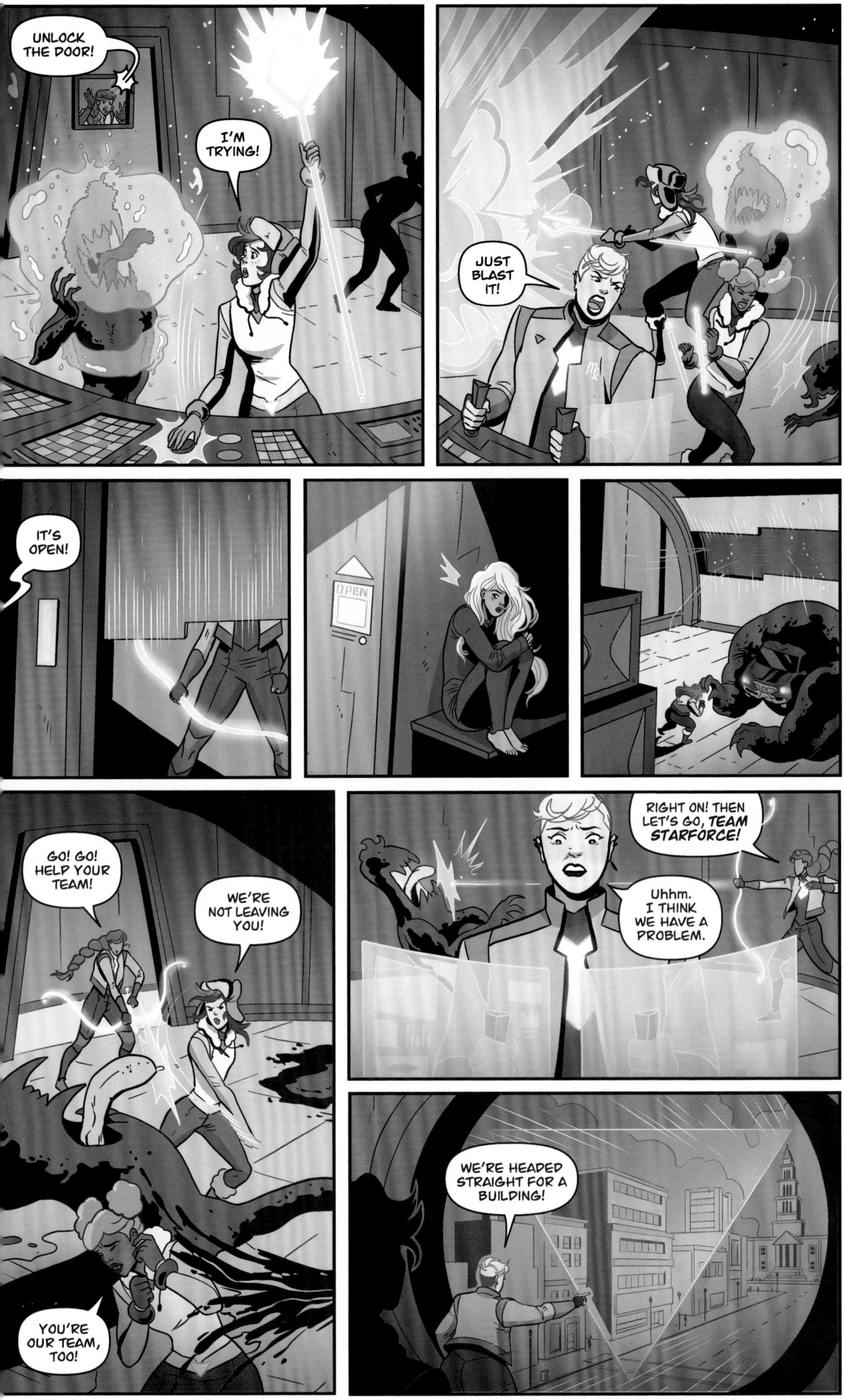
UNLOCK THE DOOR!
I'M TRYING!
JUST BLAST IT!
IT'S OPEN!
OPEN
GO! GO! HELP YOUR TEAM!
WE'RE NOT LEAVING YOU!
YOU'RE OUR TEAM, TOO!
RIGHT ON! THEN LET'S GO, TEAM STARFORCE!
Uhhm. I THINK WE HAVE A PROBLEM.
WE'RE HEADED STRAIGHT FOR A BUILDING!

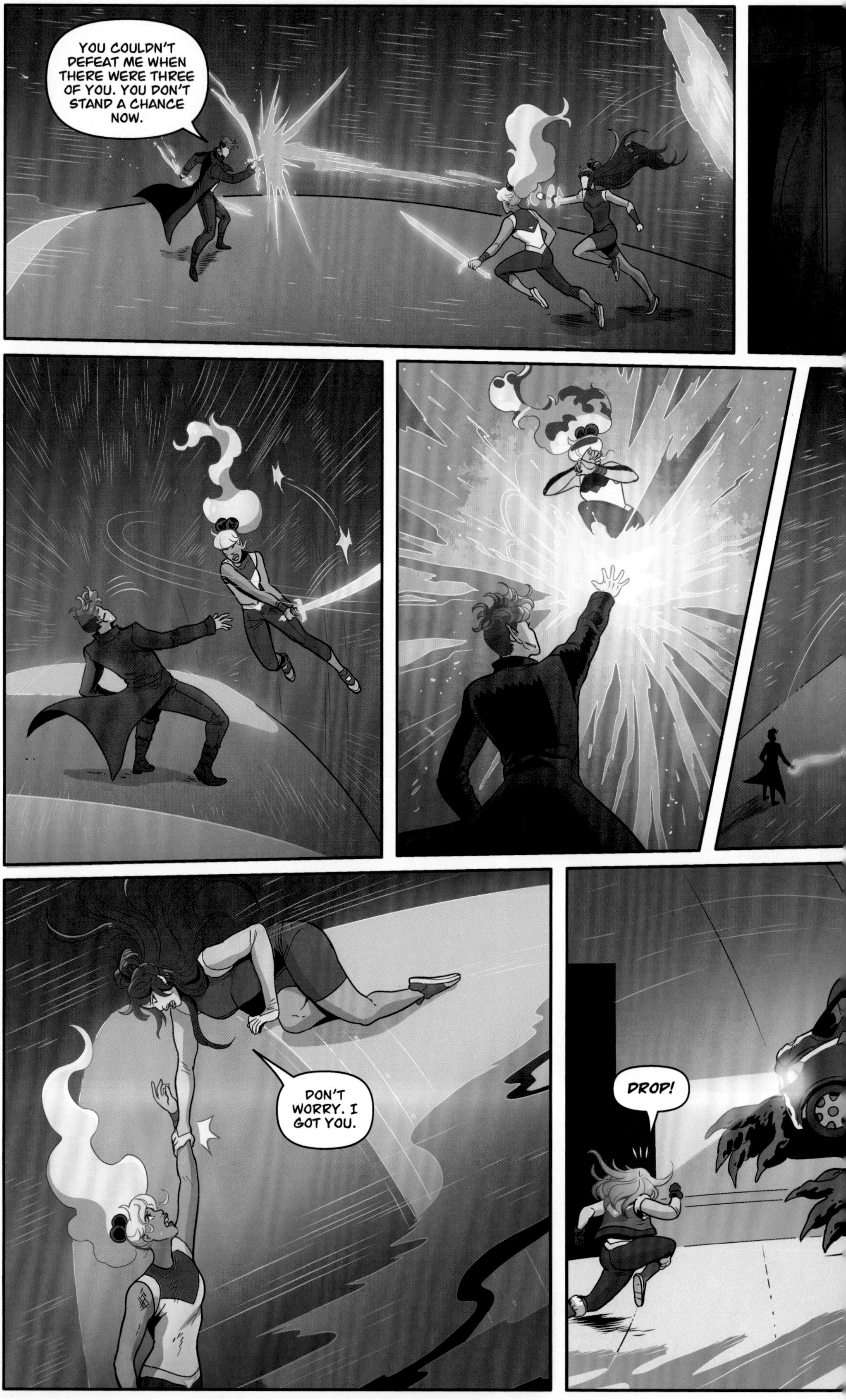
YOU COULDN'T DEFEAT ME WHEN THERE WERE THREE OF YOU. YOU DON'T STAND A CHANCE NOW.
DON'T WORRY. I GOT YOU.
DROP!

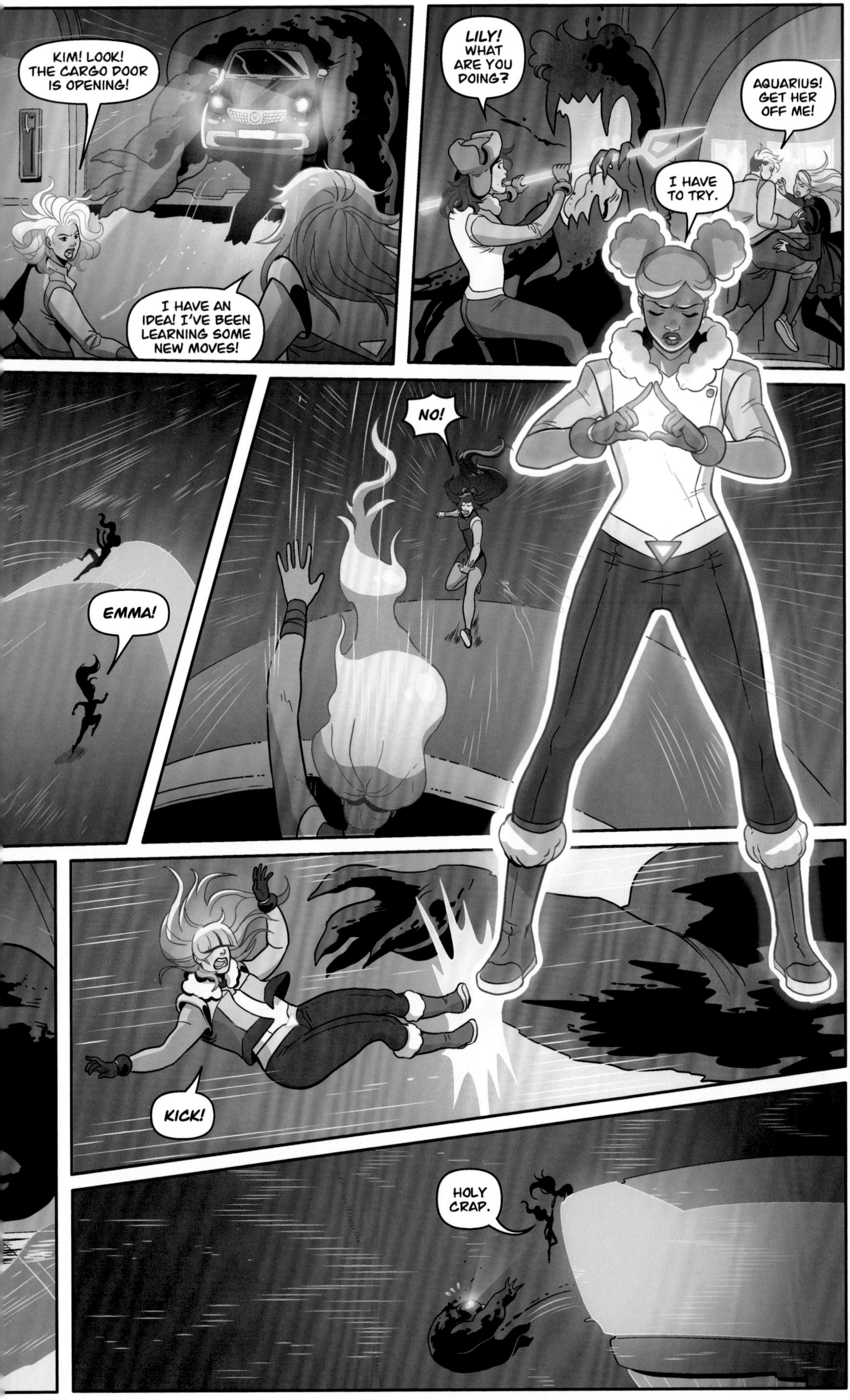
KIM! LOOK! THE CARGO DOOR IS OPENING!
I HAVE AN IDEA! I'VE BEEN LEARNING SOME NEW MOVES!
LILY! WHAT ARE YOU DOING?
AQUARIUS! GET HER OFF ME!
I HAVE TO TRY.
EMMA!
NO!
KICK!
HOLY CRAP.

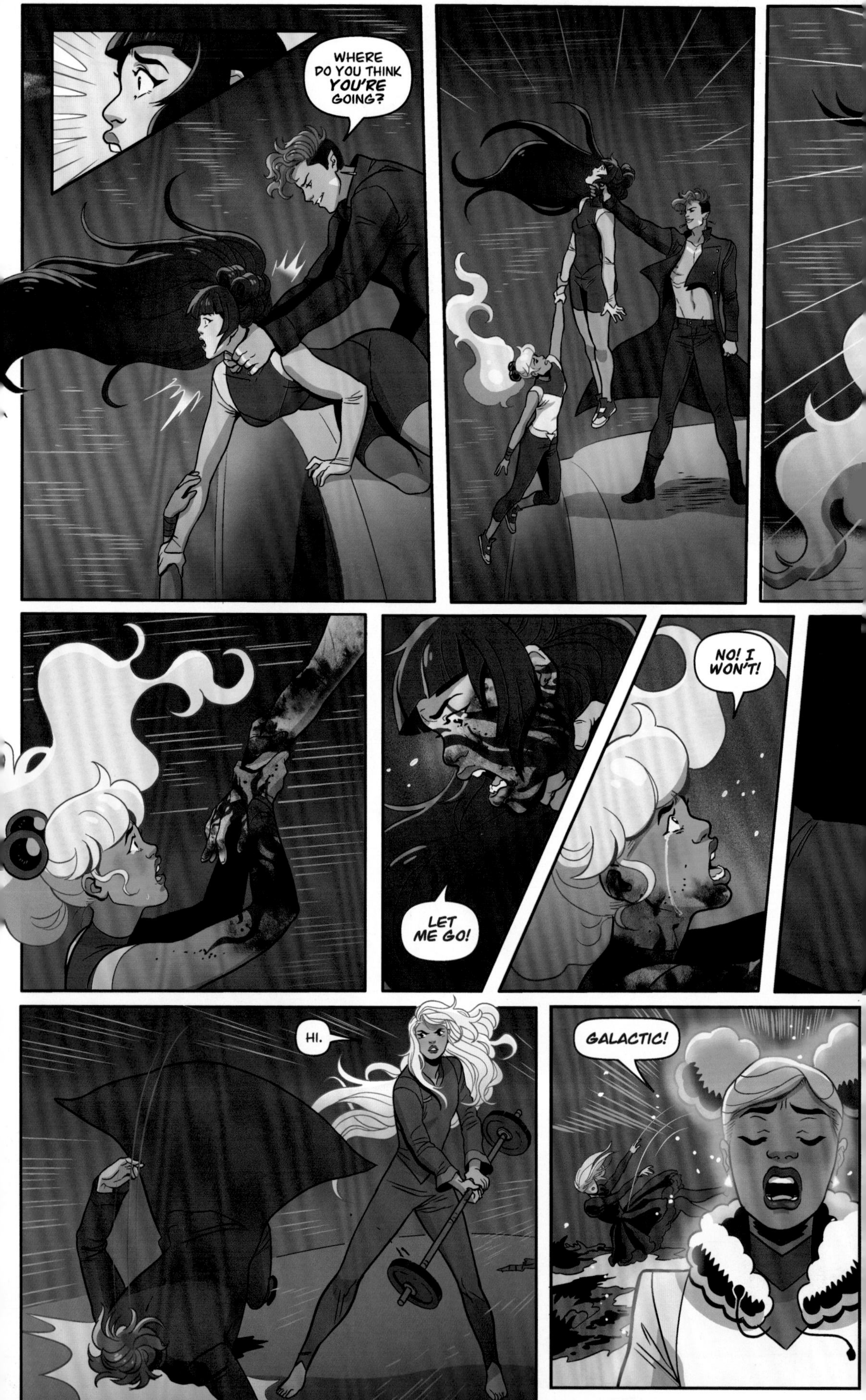
WHERE DO YOU THINK YOU'RE GOING?
LET ME GO!
NO! I WON'T!
HI.
GALACTIC!

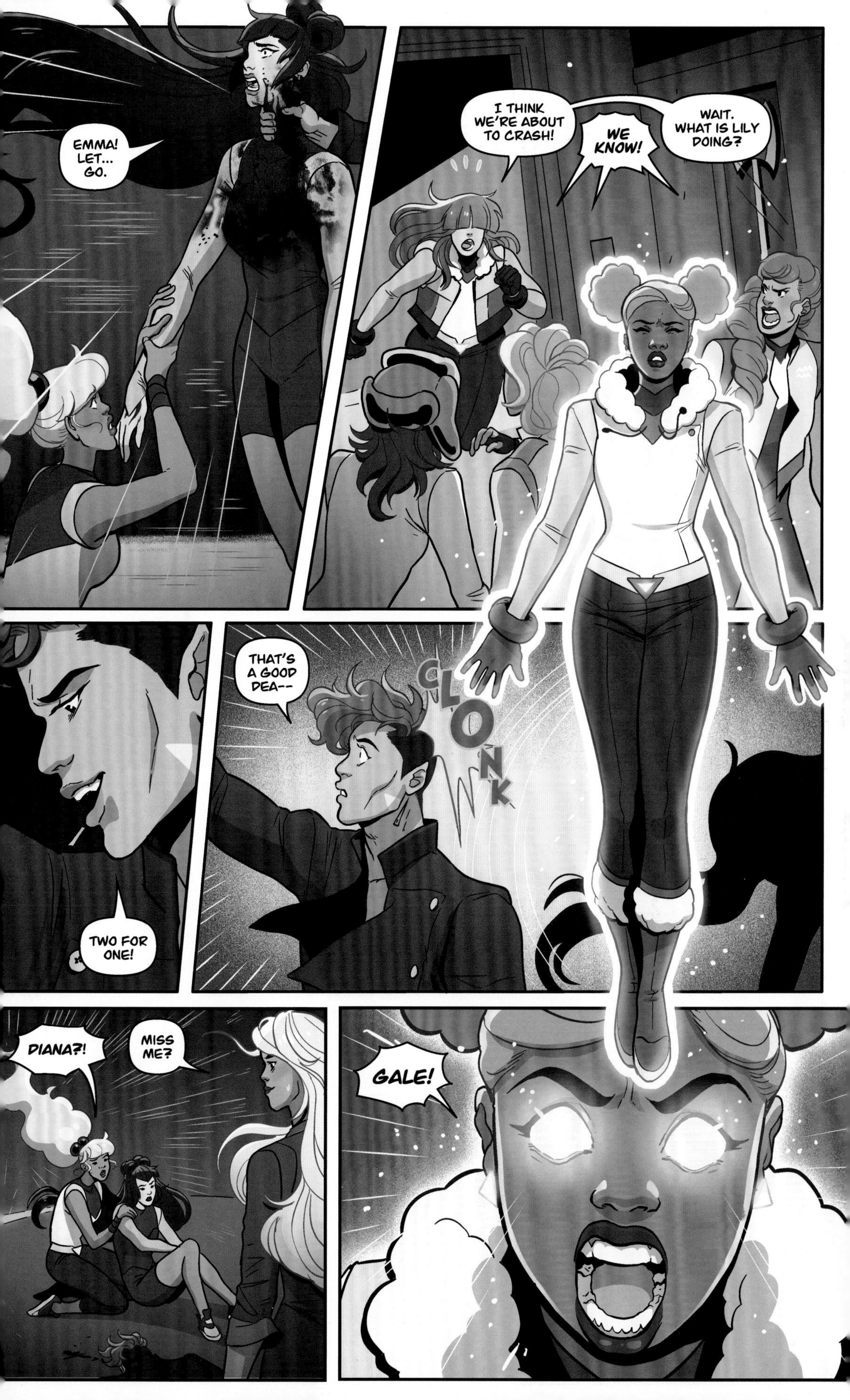
EMMA! LET... GO.
I THINK WE'RE ABOUT TO CRASH!
WE KNOW!
WAIT. WHAT IS LILY DOING?
TWO FOR ONE!
THAT'S A GOOD DEA--
CLONK
DIANA?!
MISS ME?
GALE!

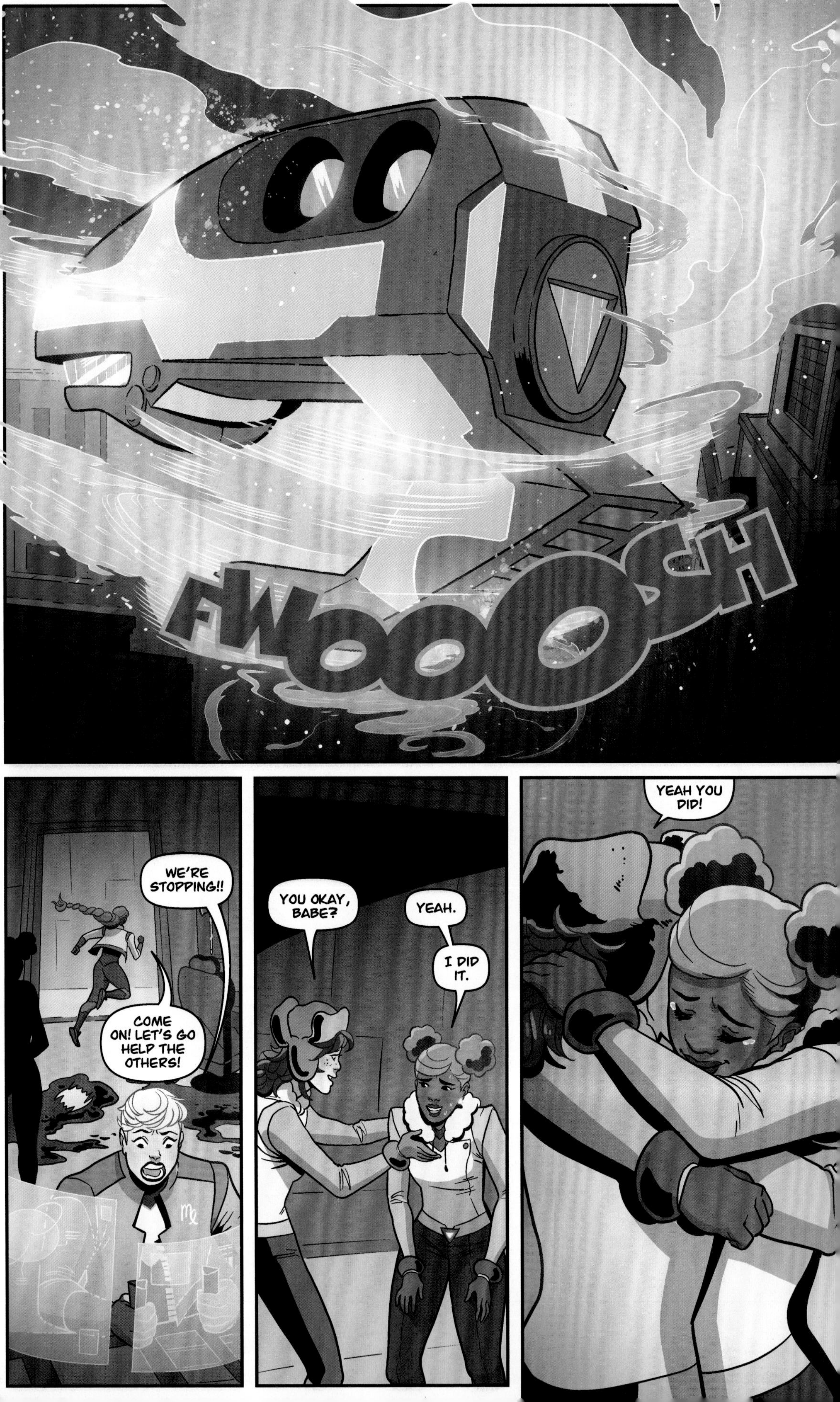
FWOOOSH
WE'RE STOPPING!!
COME ON! LET'S GO HELP THE OTHERS!
YOU OKAY, BABE?
YEAH.
I DID IT.
YEAH YOU DID!

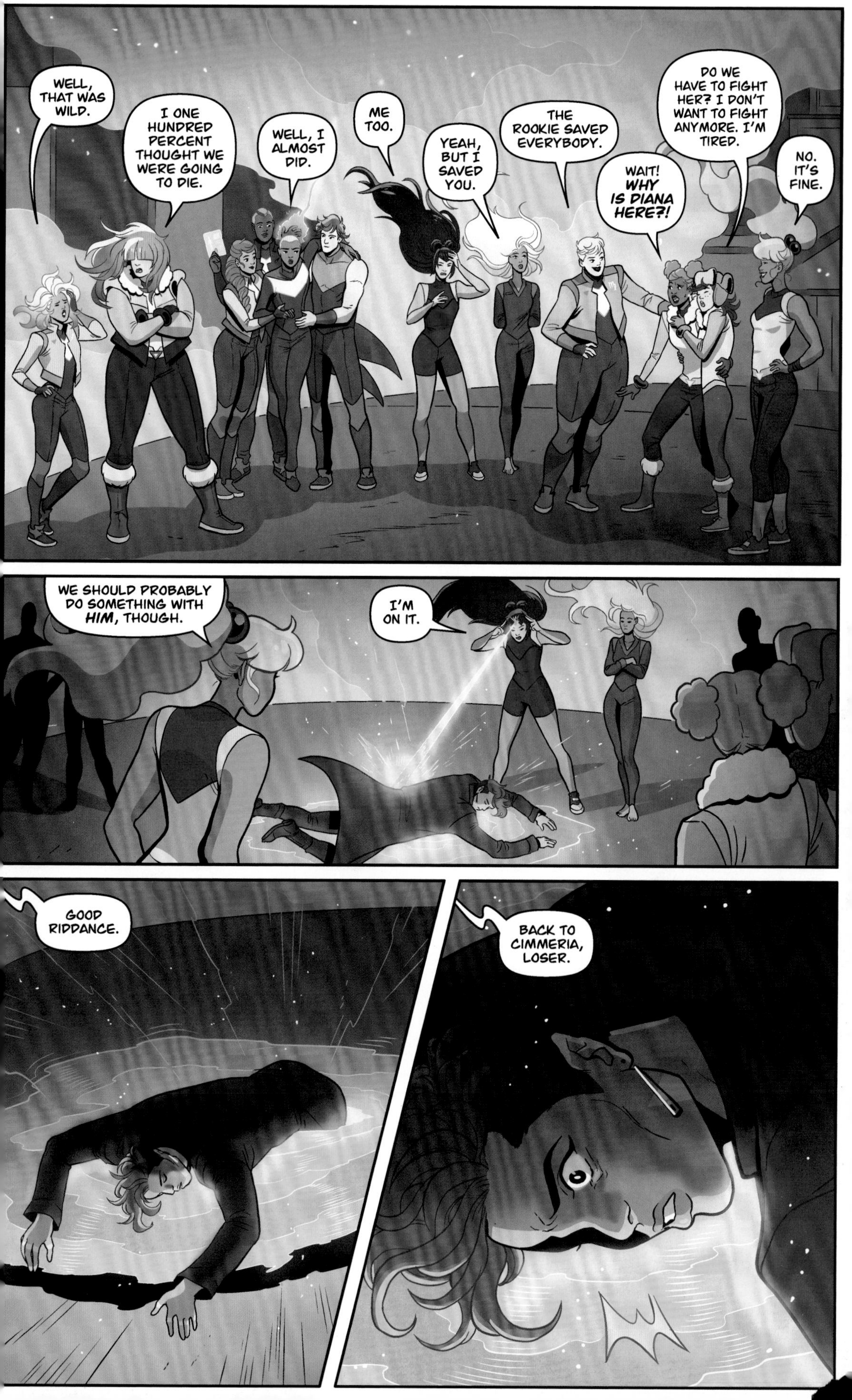
WELL, THAT WAS WILD.
I ONE HUNDRED PERCENT THOUGHT WE WERE GOING TO DIE.
WELL, I ALMOST DID.
ME TOO.
YEAH, BUT I SAVED YOU.
THE ROOKIE SAVED EVERYBODY.
WAIT! WHY IS DIANA HERE?!
DO WE HAVE TO FIGHT HER? I DON'T WANT TO FIGHT ANYMORE. I'M TIRED.
NO. IT'S FINE.
WE SHOULD PROBABLY DO SOMETHING WITH HIM, THOUGH.
I'M ON IT.
GOOD RIDDANCE.
BACK TO CIMMERIA, LOSER.

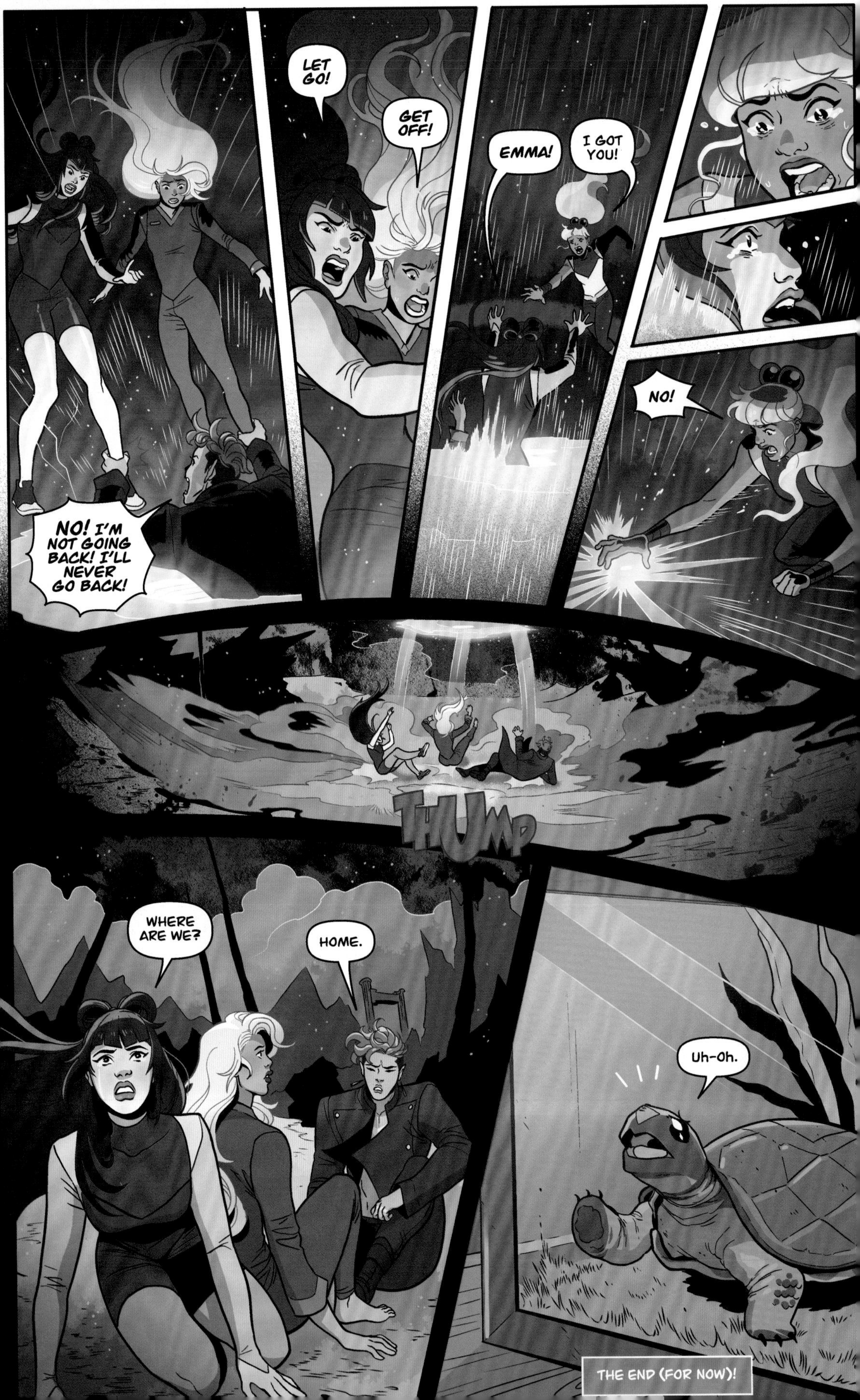
NO! I'M NOT GOING BACK! I'LL NEVER GO BACK!
LET GO!
GET OFF!
EMMA!
I GOT YOU!
NO!
THUMP
WHERE ARE WE?
HOME.
Uh-Oh.
THE END (FOR NOW)!

SKETCHBOOK

NOTES BY KEVIN AND PAULINA

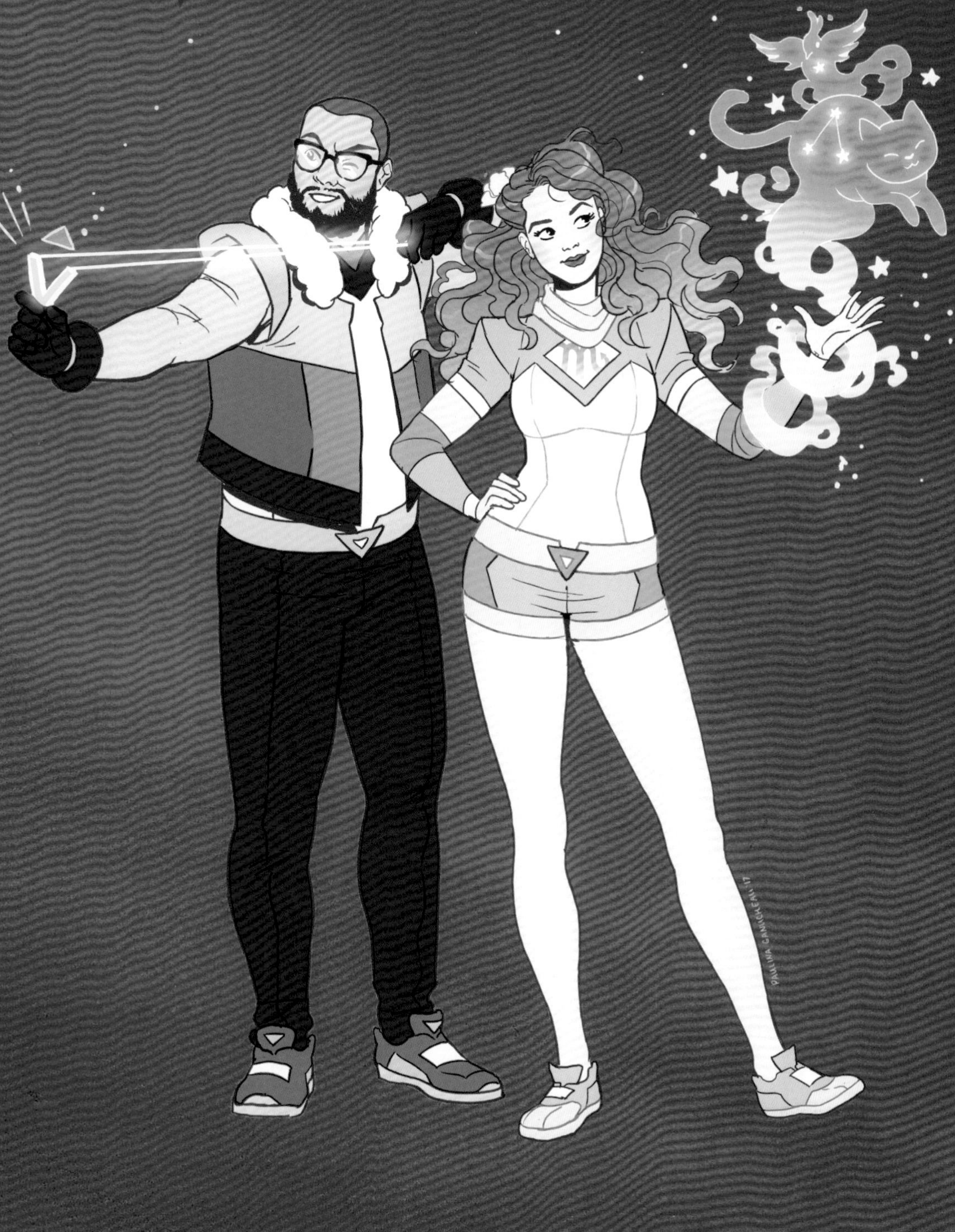

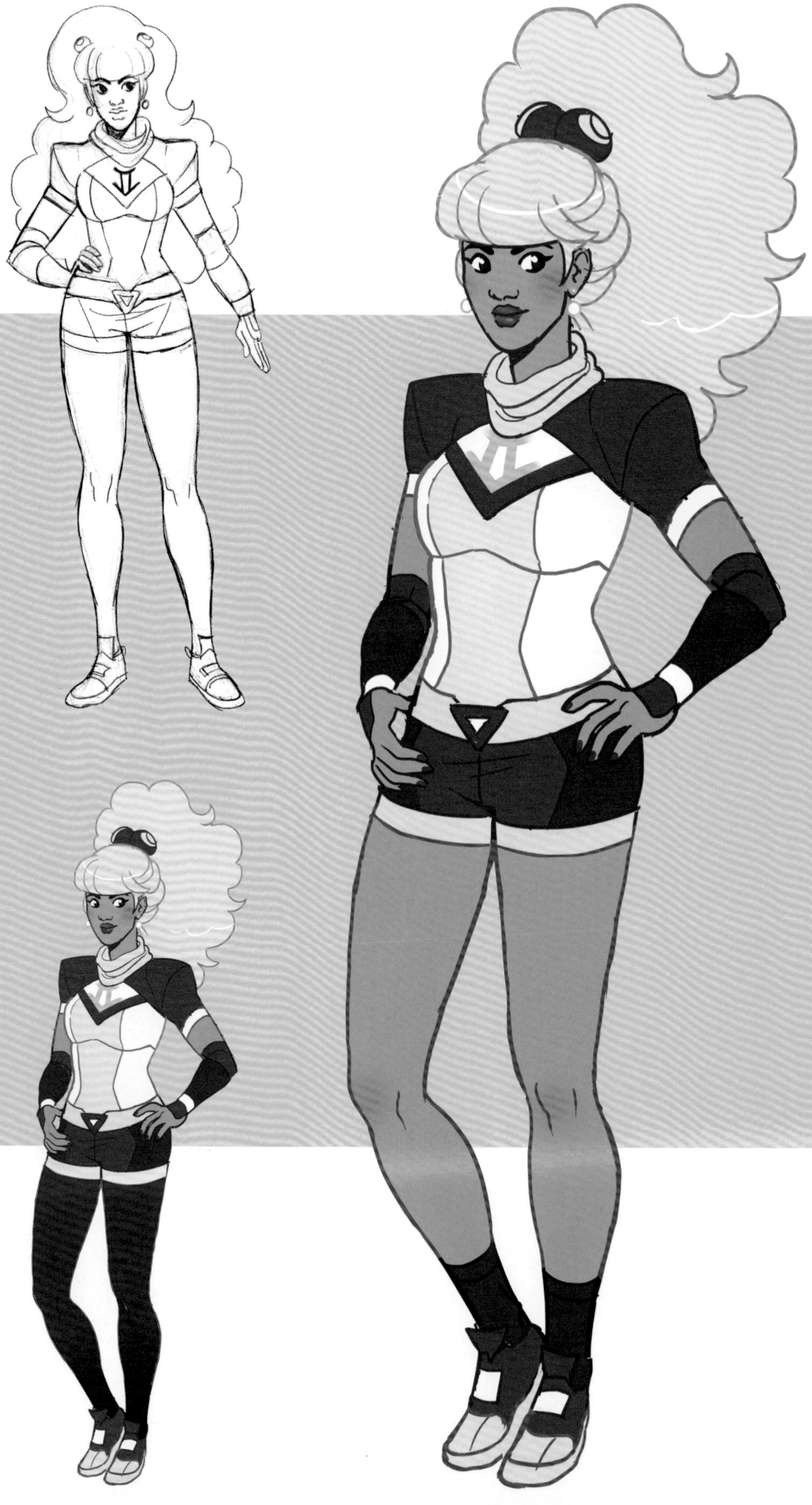

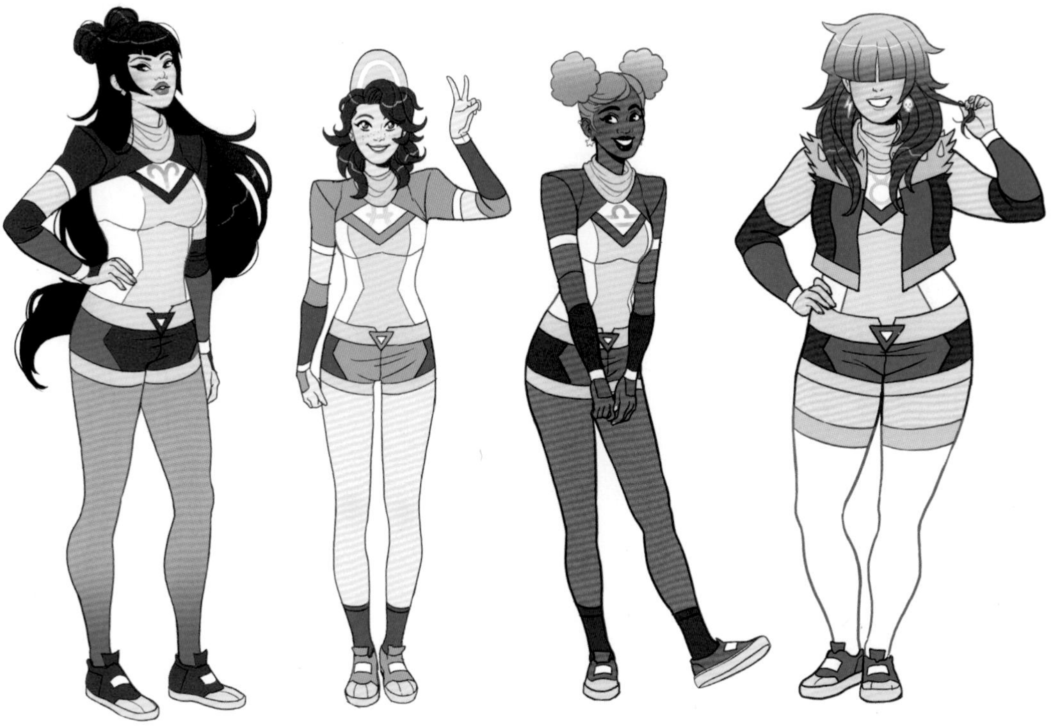

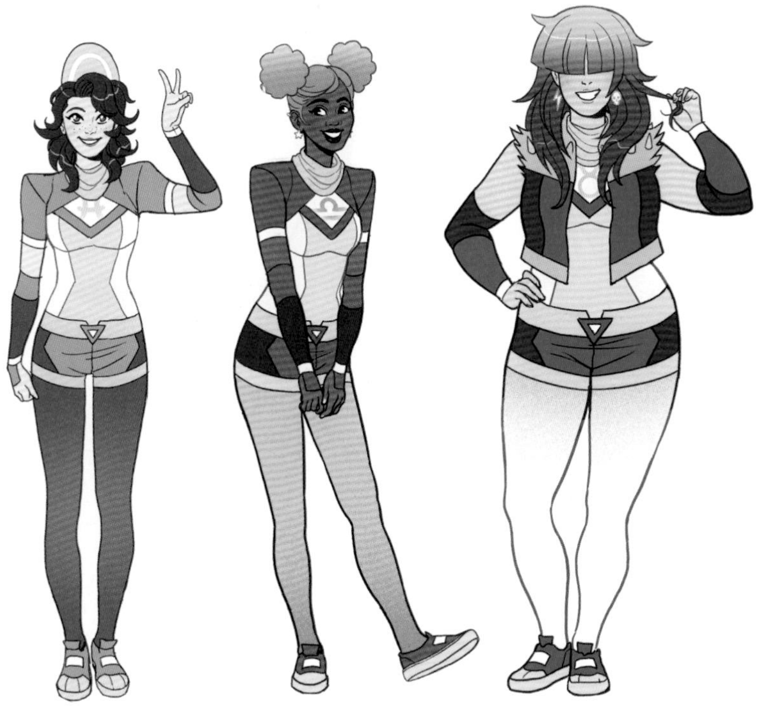

NEW UNIFORM

PAULINA: The first thing I thought when we were approved for series two was, "I GOTTA update the uniforms." I love the uniforms in the first series, but they were too complicated! So I went with a more streamlined look. Also, their uniforms should be ever evolving alongside the characters.

KEVIN: I love the shoulder-pads on the new uniforms. They make everybody look cool! I think these new uniforms make things much easier for cosplayers, too.

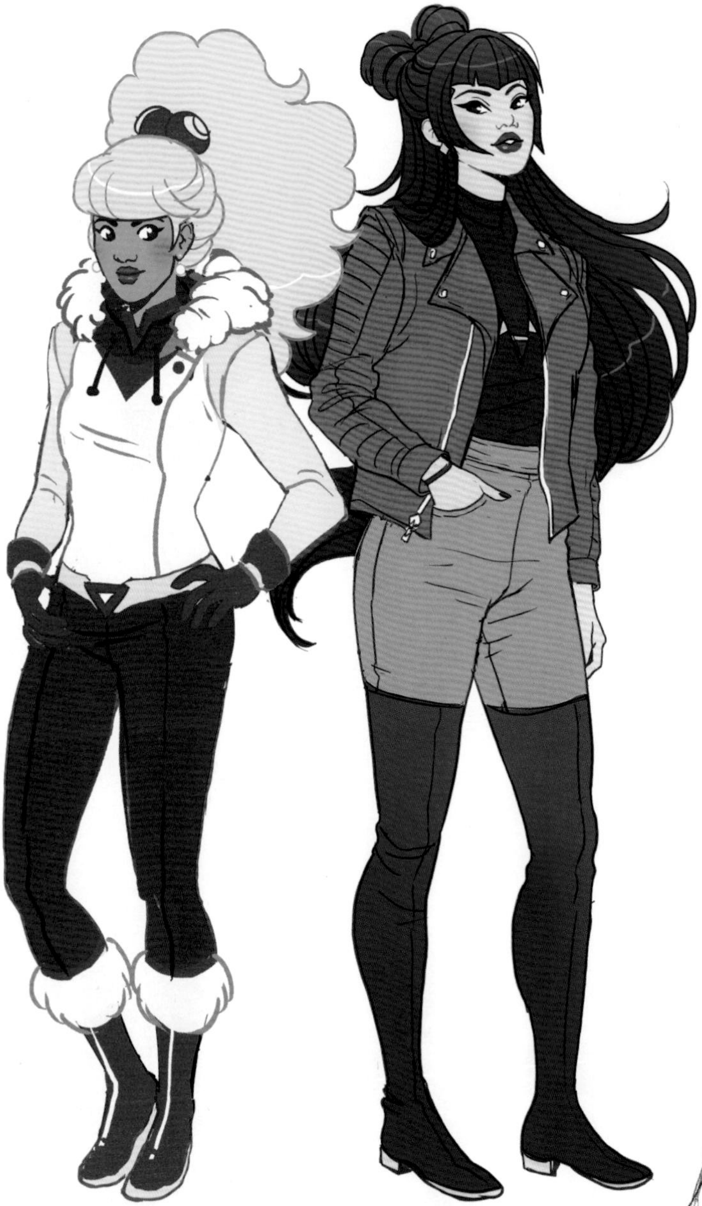

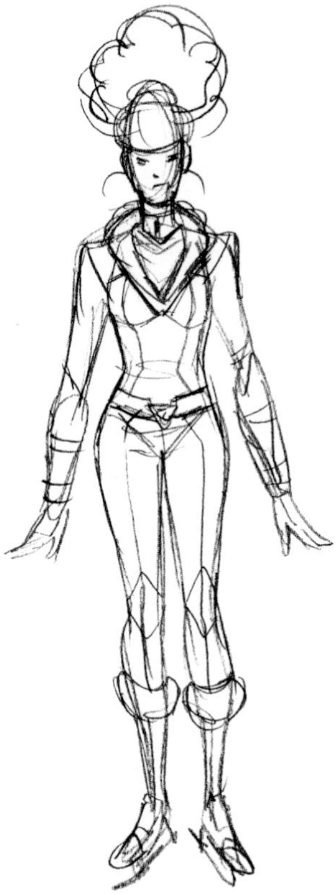

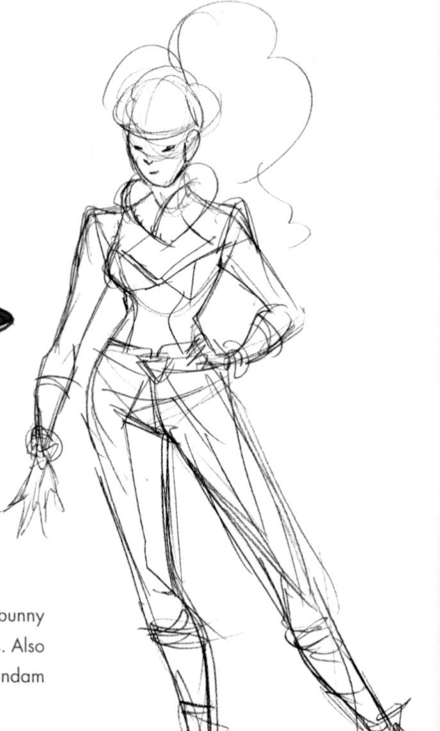

WINTER AND CASUAL CLOTHES

P: Bless this series for being set in winter 'cause I was finally able to design snow bunny ZS versions. If you couldn't already tell, I live for designing and costuming characters. Also the outfits aren't so much snow bunny as they are directly and truly inspired by Gundam pilot suits, haha.

K: I had to set this series during winter break so we could have an ICE SKATING BATTLE. It's my favorite fight scene in *ZS* so far and I'm glad the girls got to look fashionable while they were punching people.

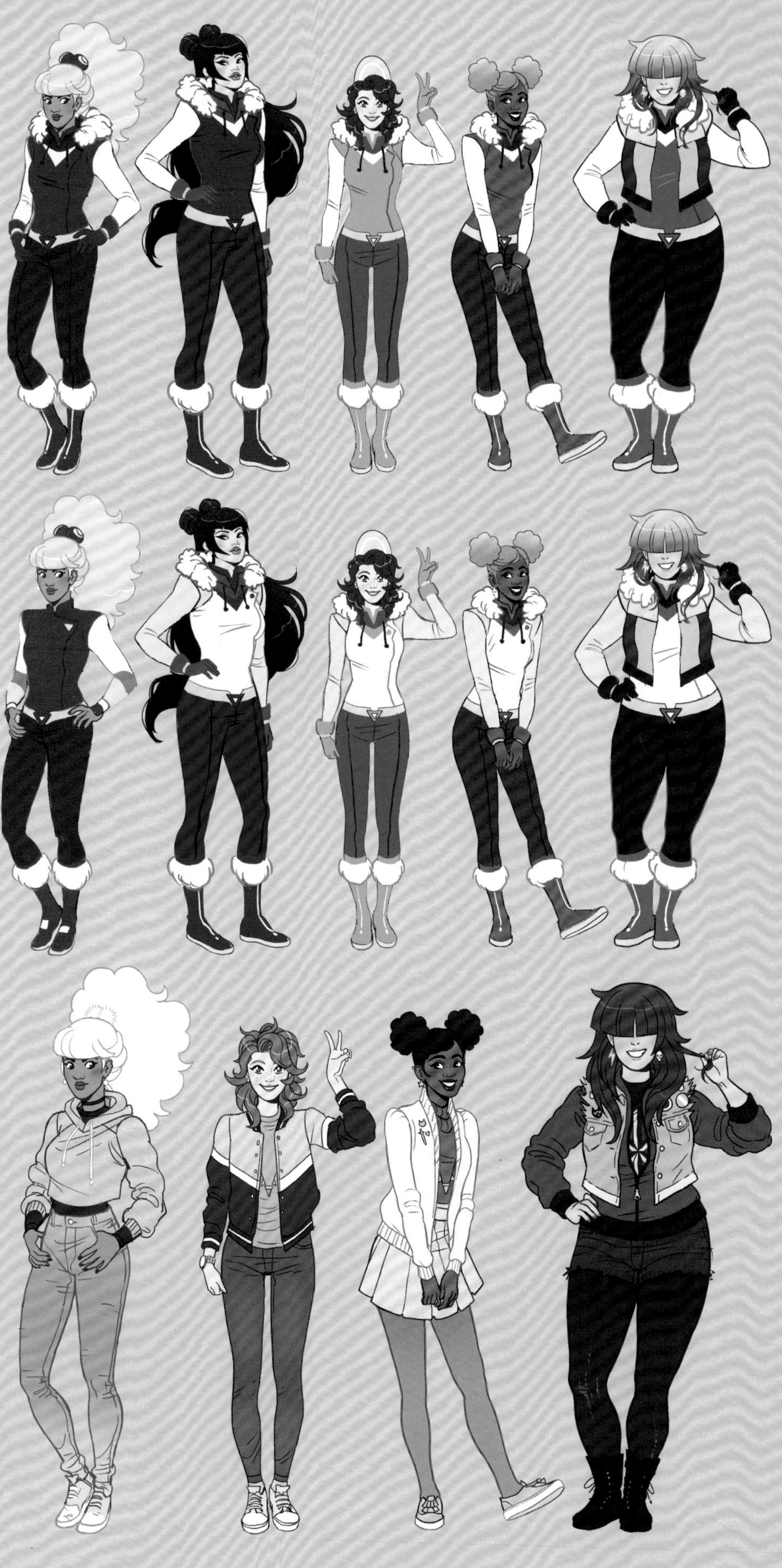

PAVOS

K: When I started writing Pavos, my goal was to make him the most hated creep in the history of *Zodiac Starforce*. I failed miserably and now everyone has a crush on him!

P: YOU'RE WELCOME! I live for this gorgeous creep. He is a direct descendent of all the beautiful and evil *Sailor Moon* villains that ever were. I'm so happy everyone fell in love with this weirdo the same way I did.

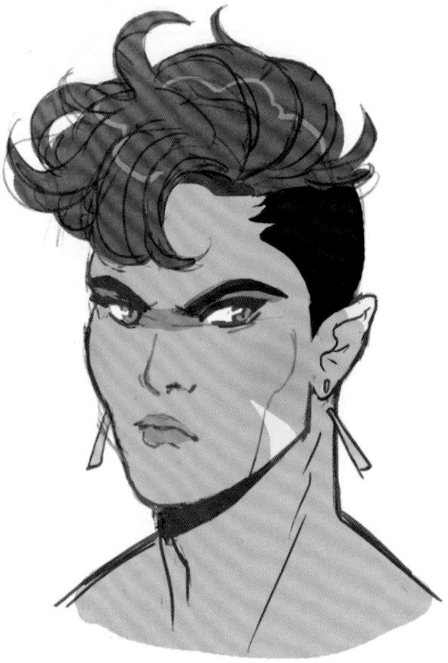

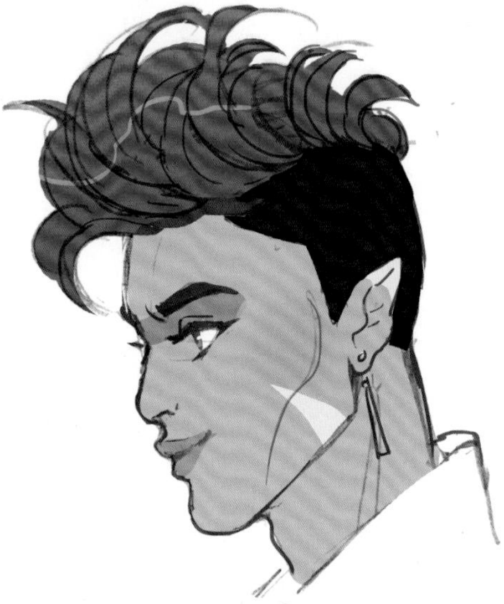

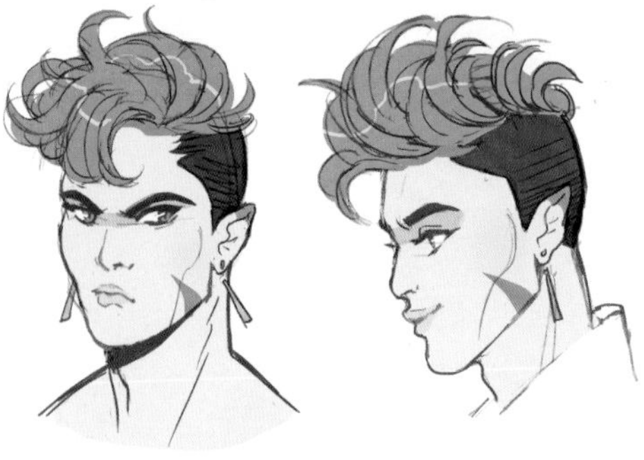

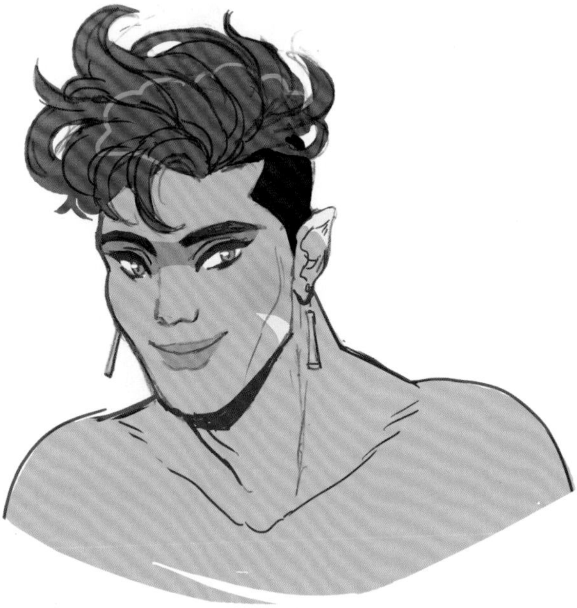

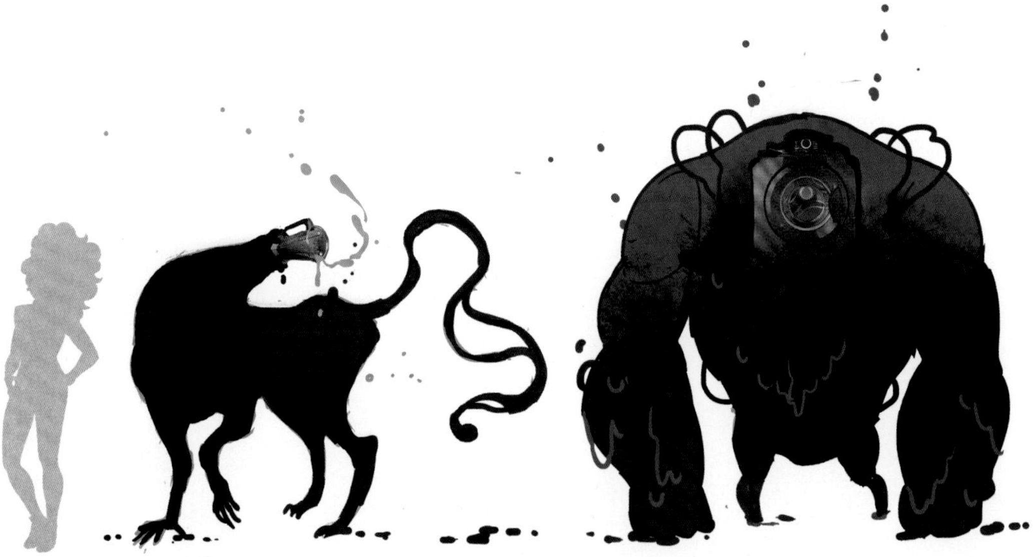

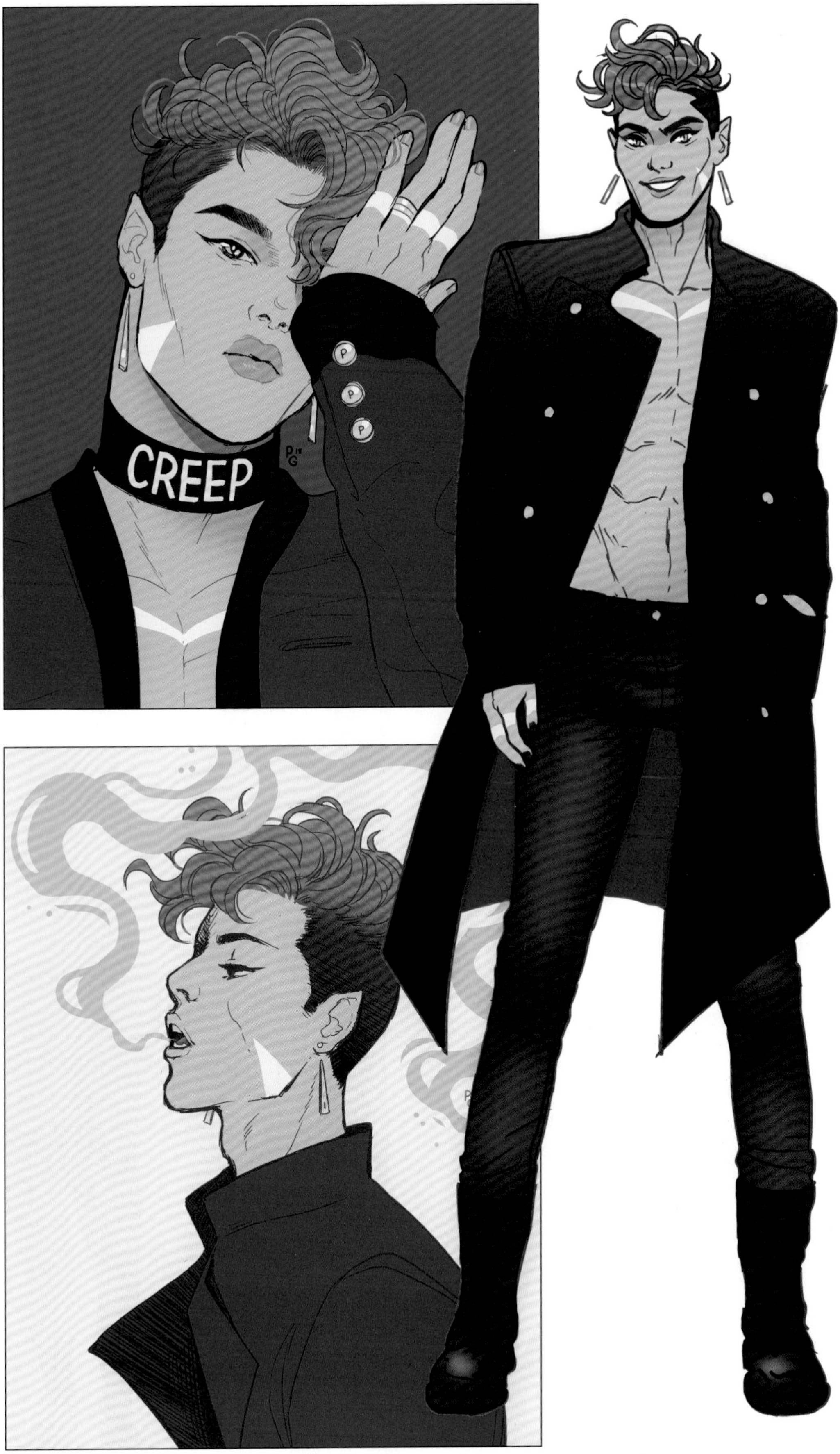
CREEP

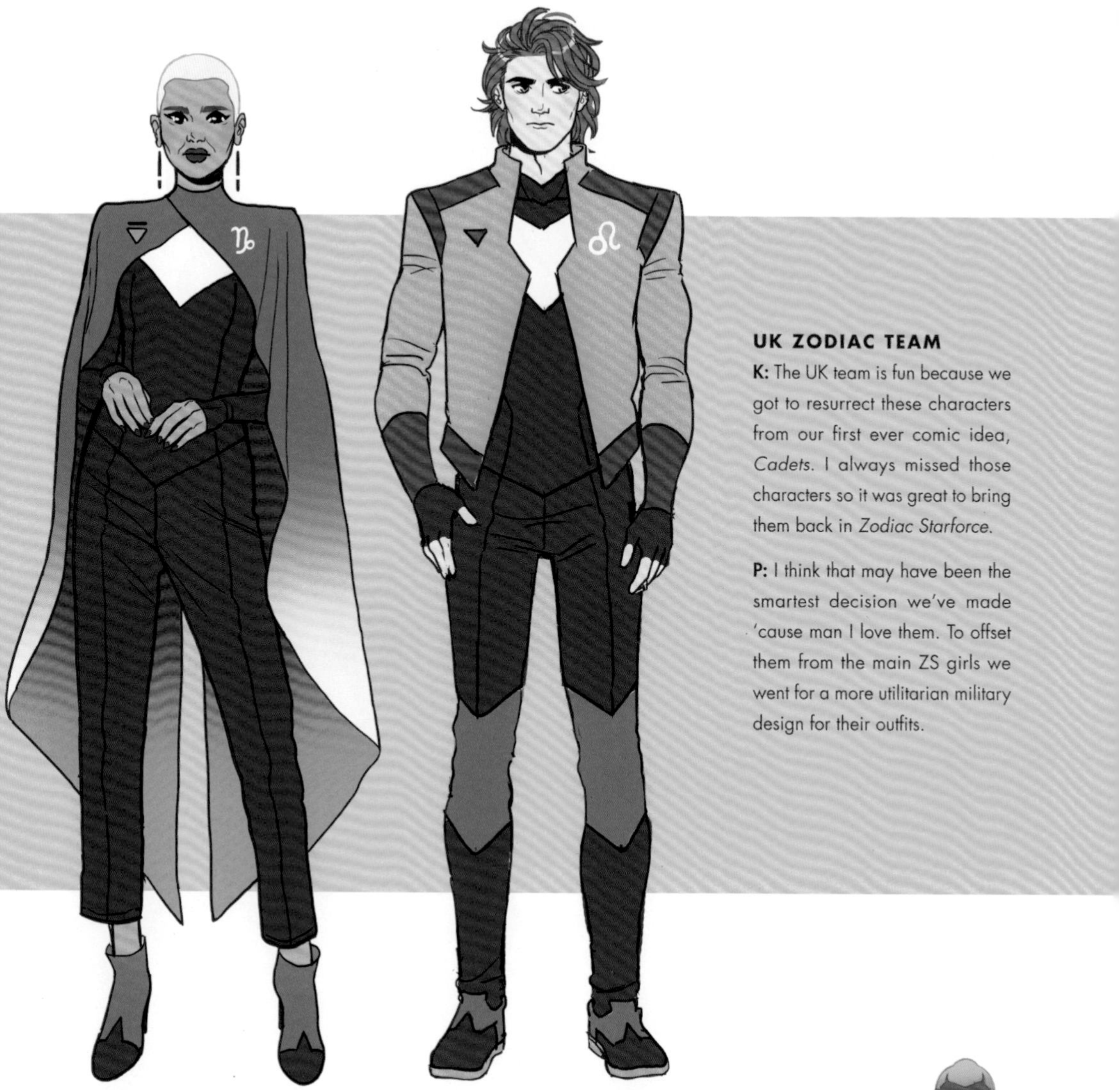

UK ZODIAC TEAM

K: The UK team is fun because we got to resurrect these characters from our first ever comic idea, *Cadets*. I always missed those characters so it was great to bring them back in *Zodiac Starforce*.

P: I think that may have been the smartest decision we've made 'cause man I love them. To offset them from the main ZS girls we went for a more utilitarian military design for their outfits.

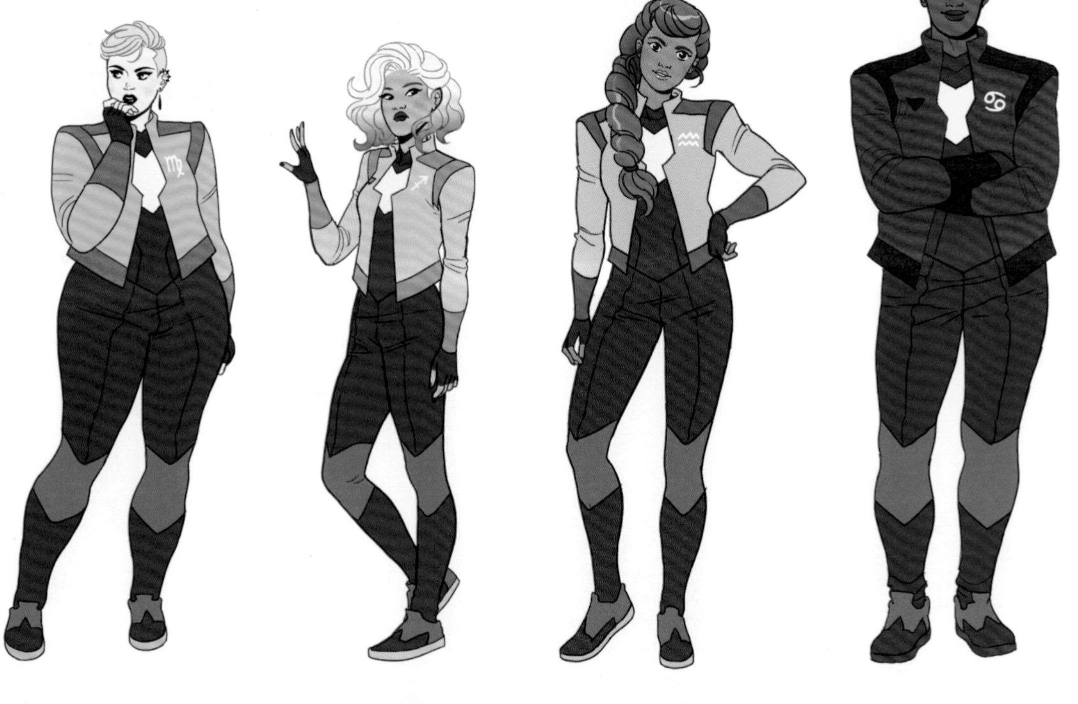

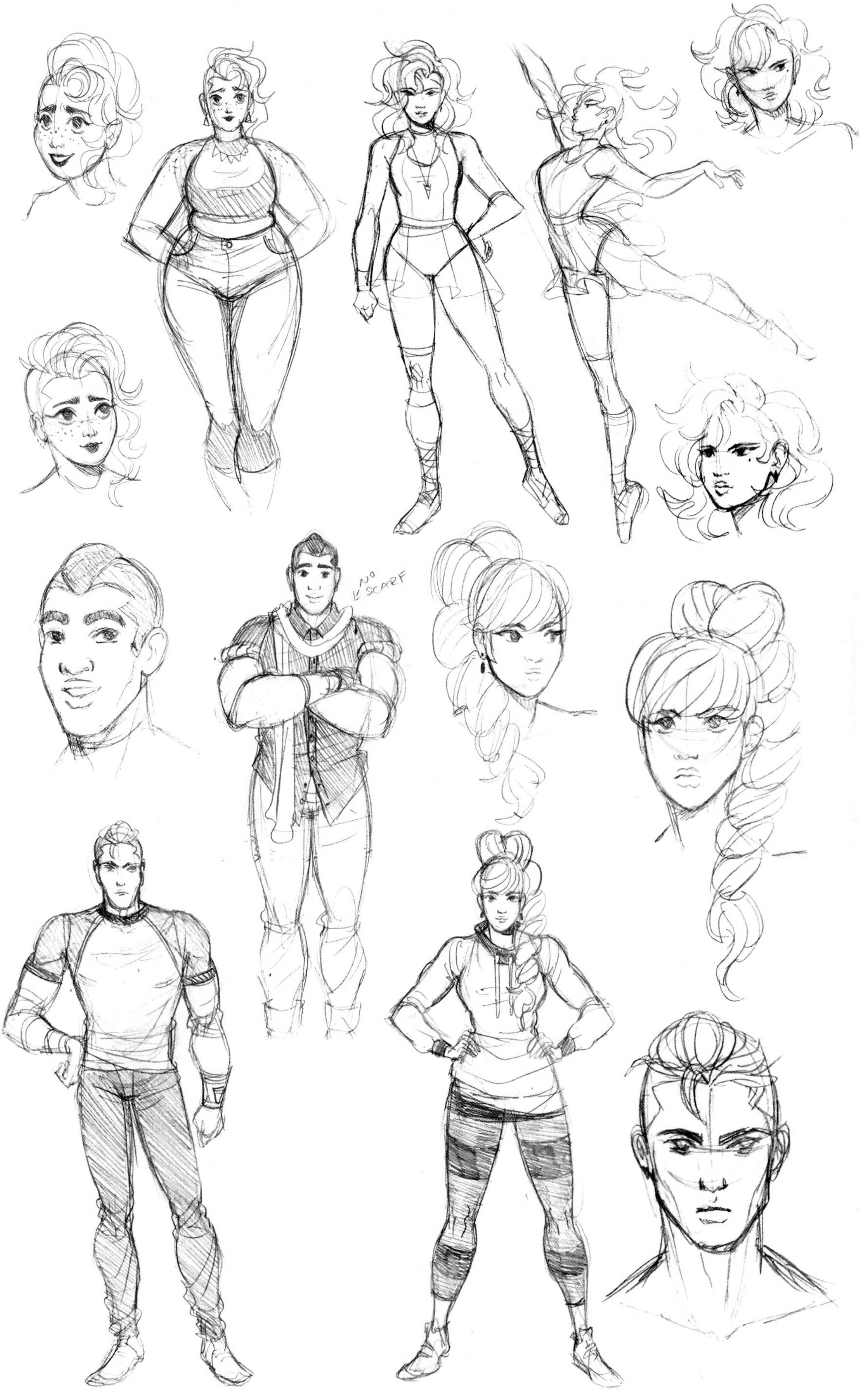
NO SCARF

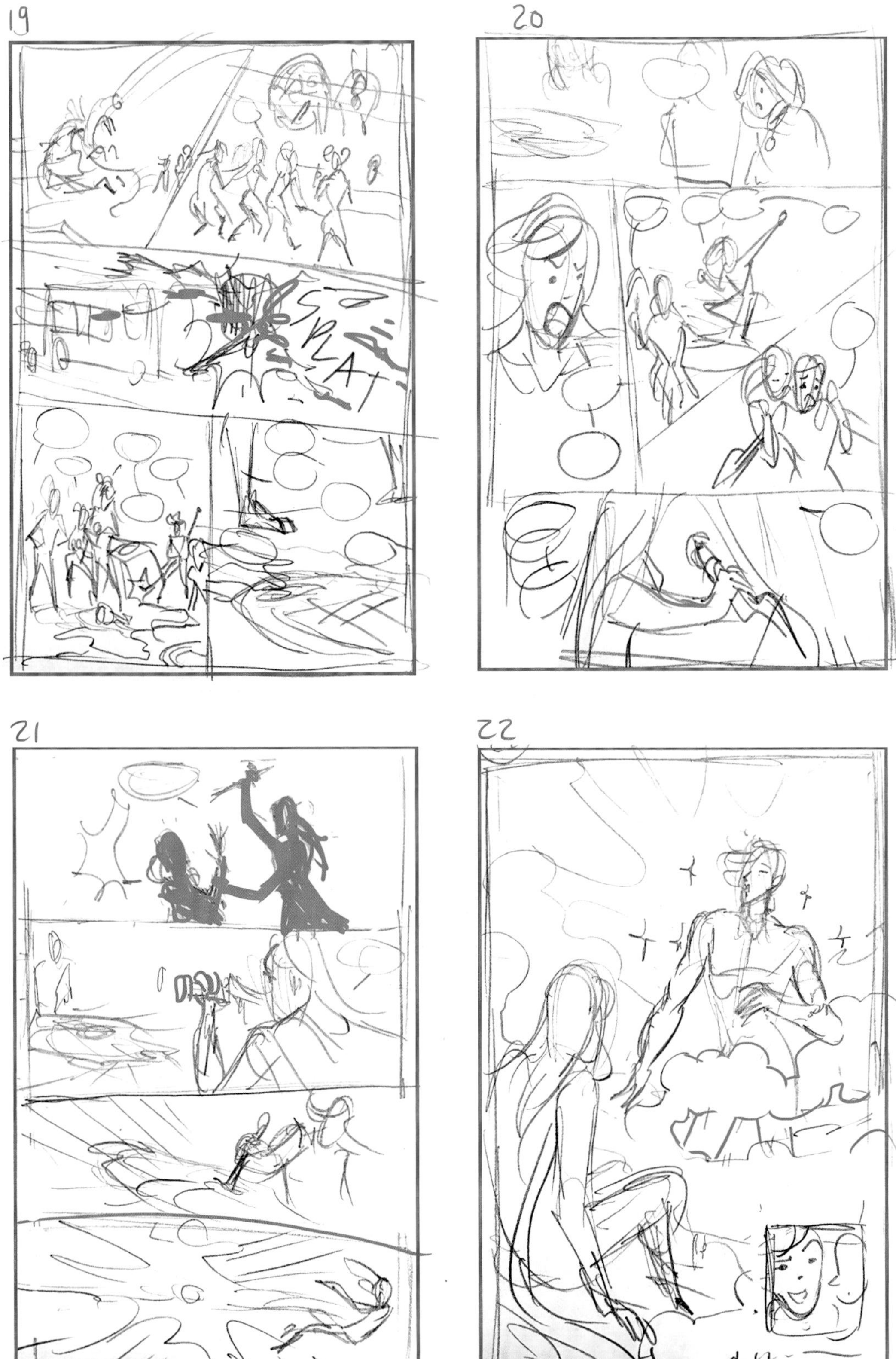
19
SPLAT
20
21
22

ISSUE #1, PAGES 19-22 LAYOUTS

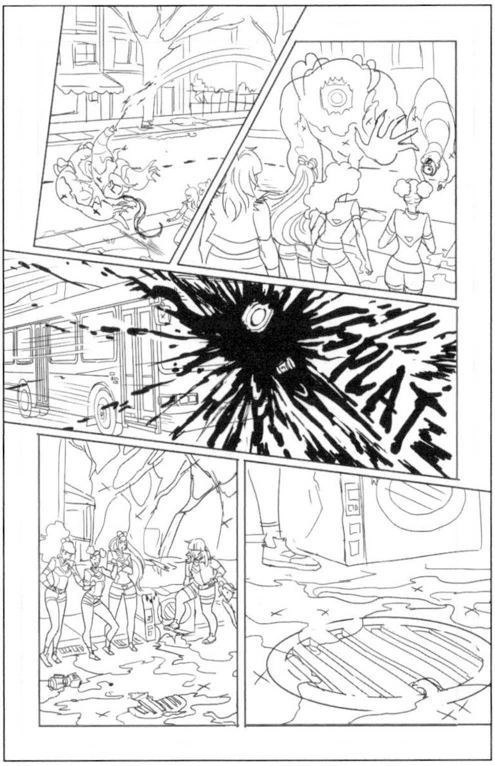
SPLAT

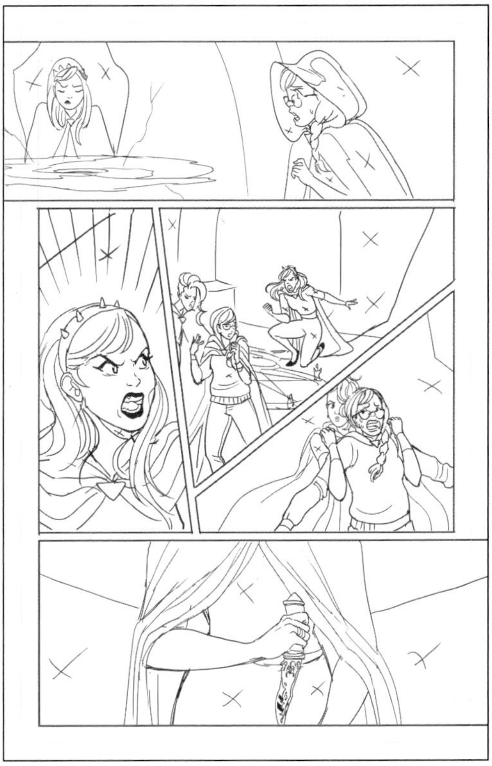

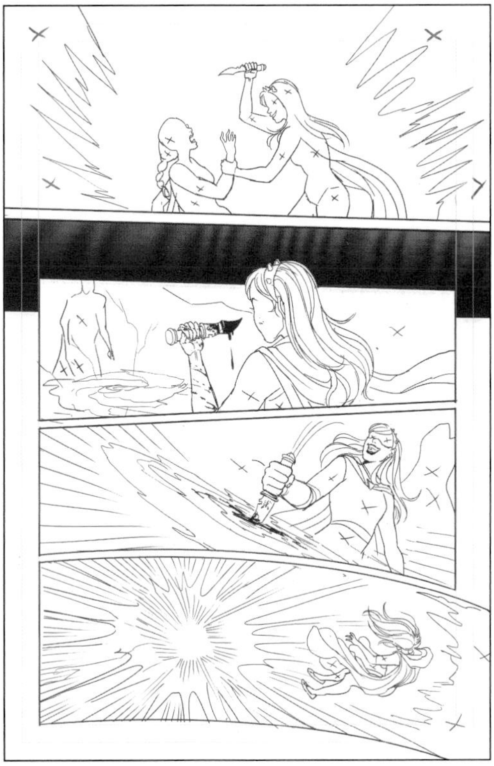

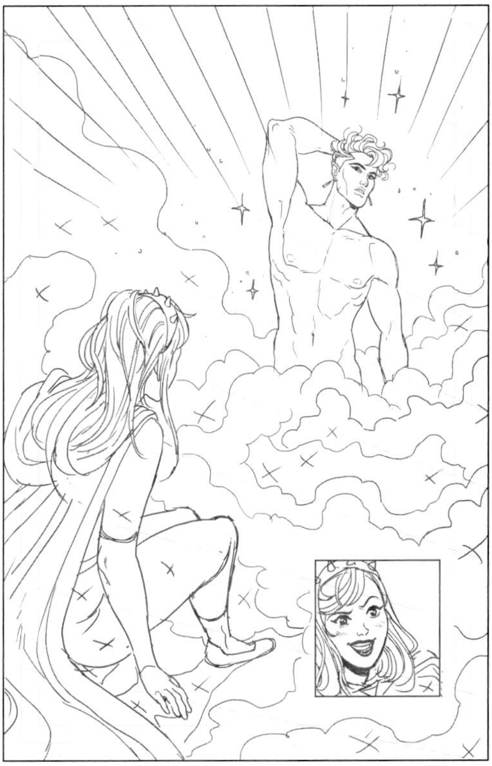

ISSUE #1, PAGES 19-22 PENCILS

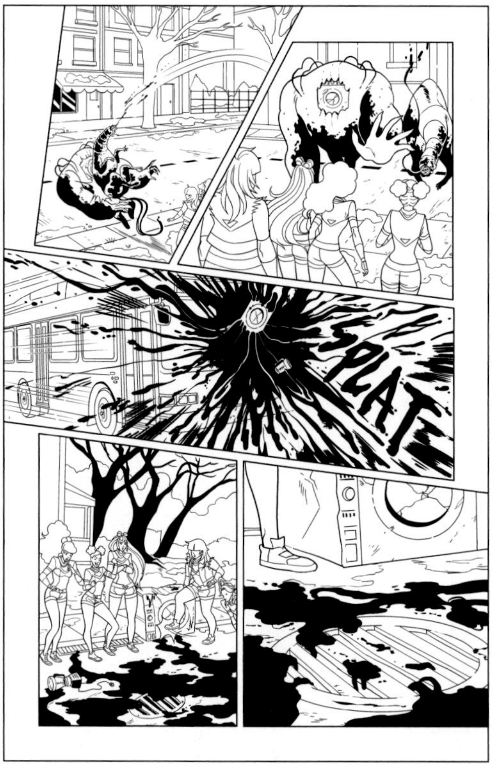
SPLAT

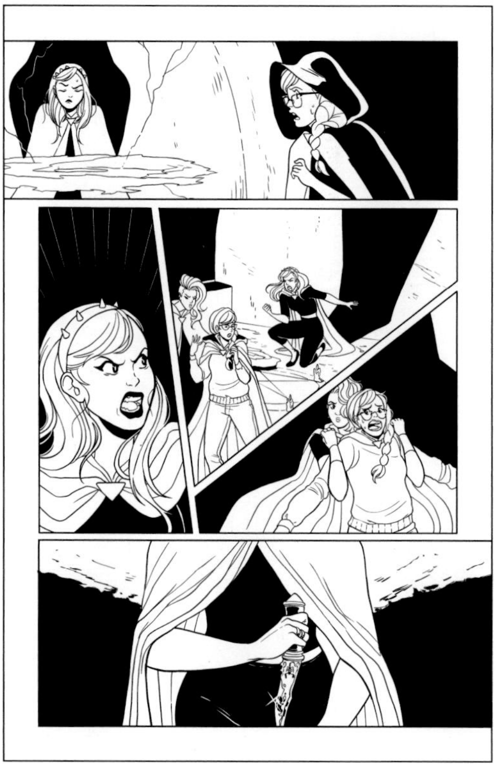

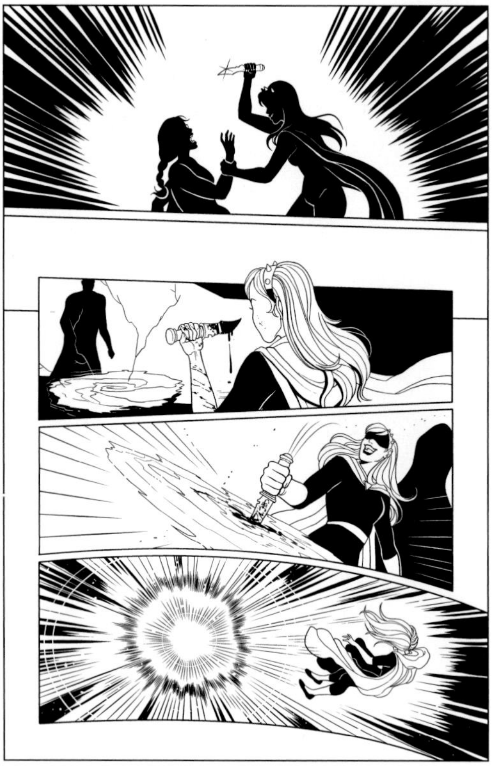

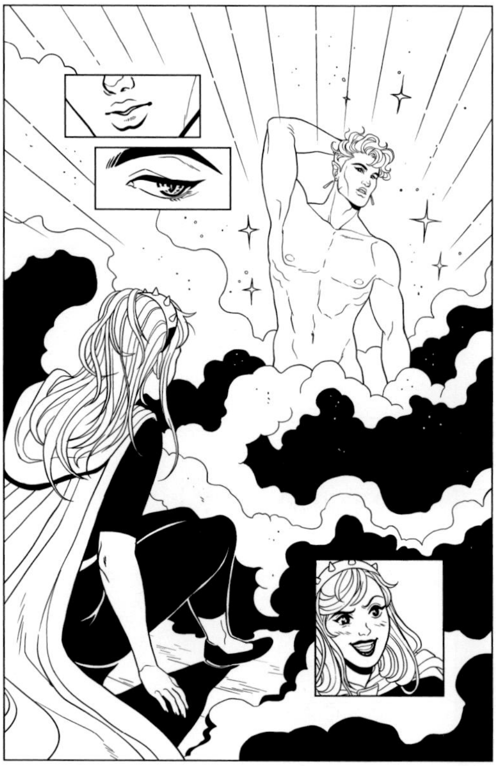

ISSUE #1, PAGES 19-22 INKS

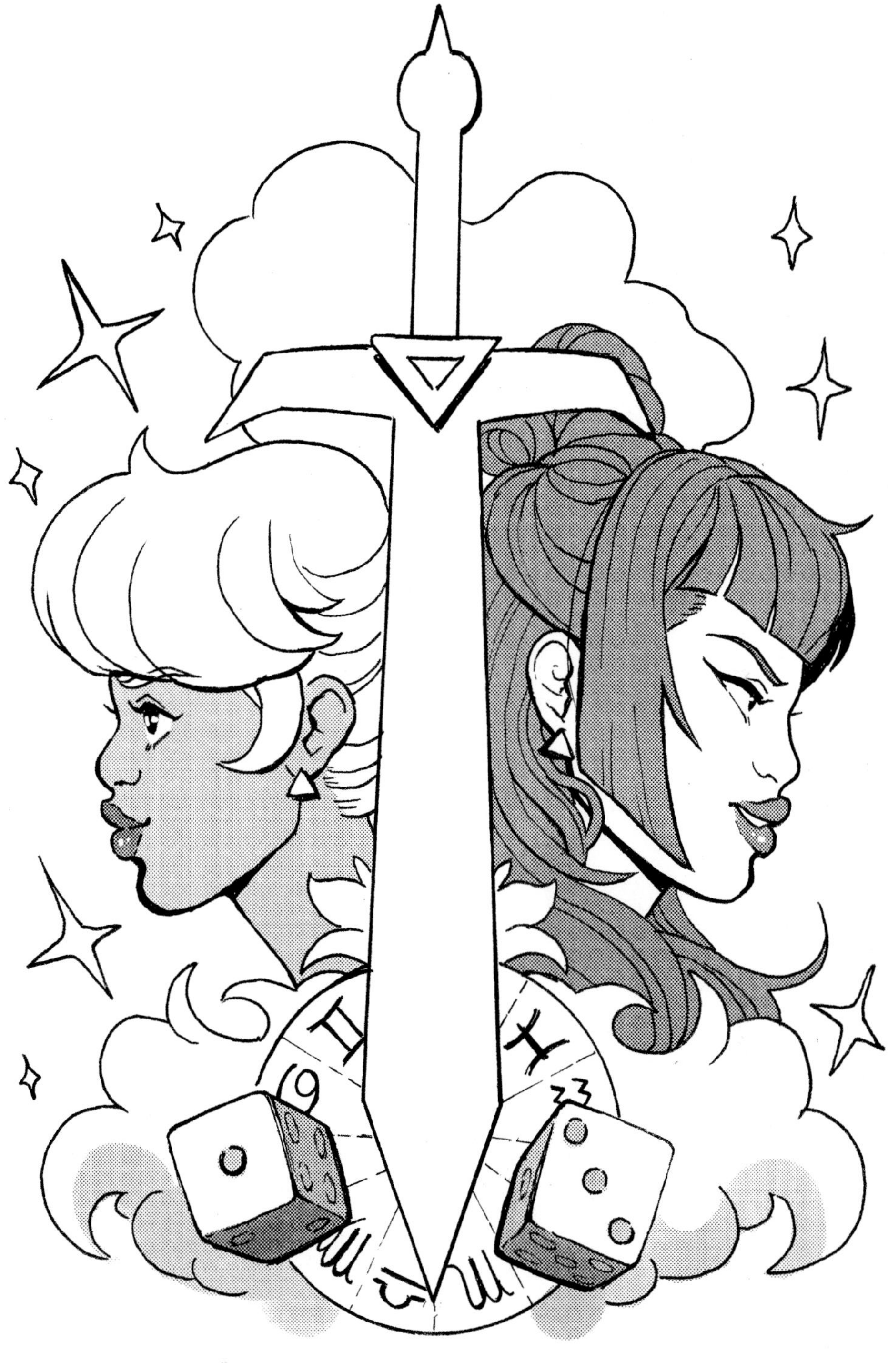

ZODIAC STARFORCE RPG

K: I had a lot of fun designing a D&D-style role-playing game for *Zodiac Starforce*. It was just a little mini-comic for the Small Press Expo convention, but it was a blast developing a whole rules system and adventure! Plus, Paulina drew this great cover!

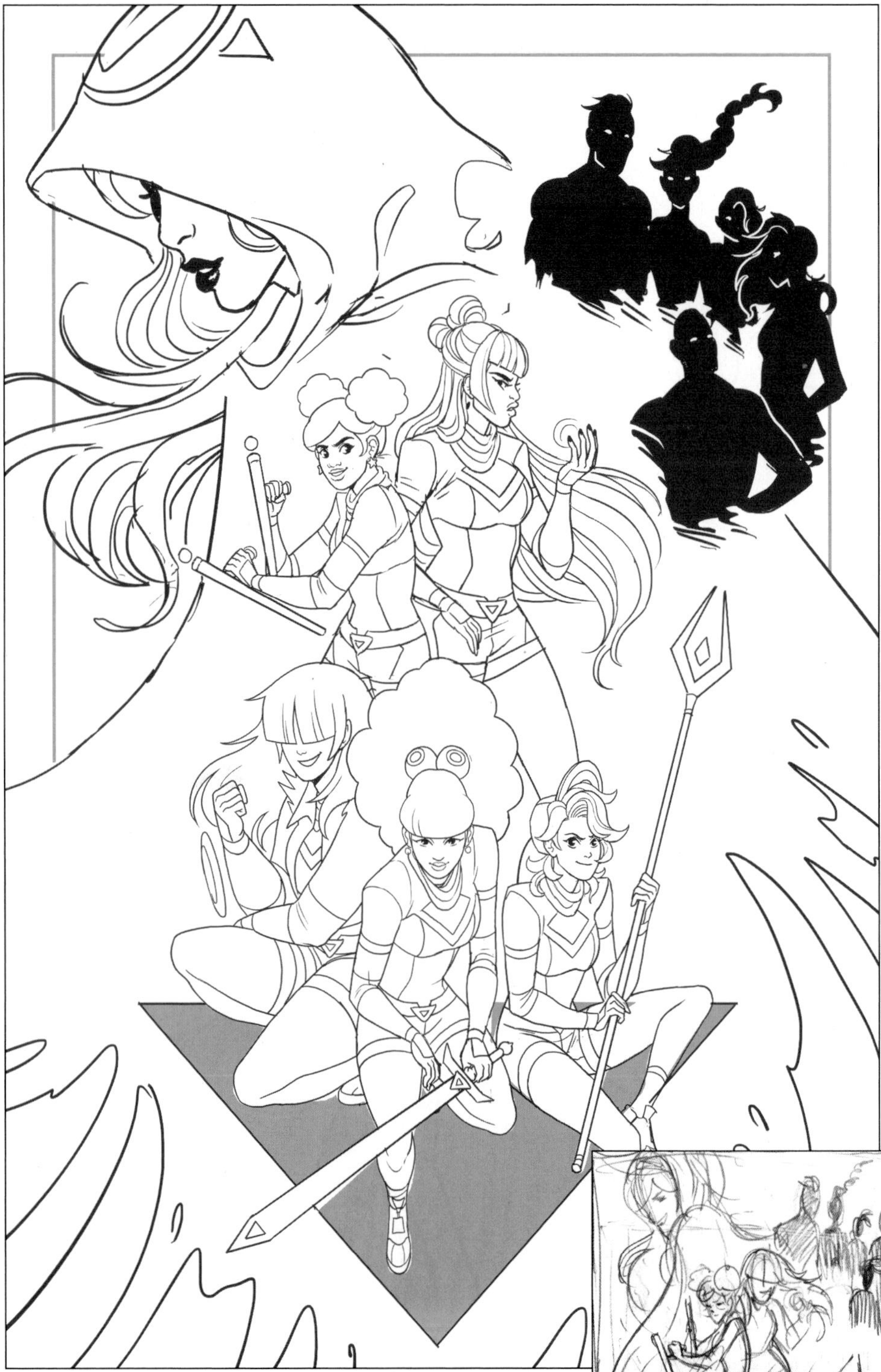

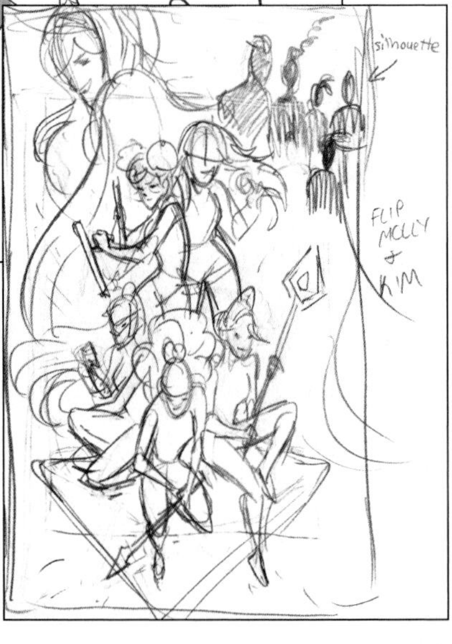
silhouette
FLIP
MOLLY
+
KIM

ZODIAC STARFORCE SERIES 2 ANNOUNCEMENT

K: Announcing this second series was one of the best moments I've had since I started writing comics. We always hoped we would get to do more than one series but you never know!

P: It was crazy exciting. I did this pin-up right away after we heard the news for our announcement. I think the girls have evolved so much even from this drawing in series two so it's cool to look back and see that. I love that this image has a bunch of secret stuff in it, too. UK ZS! Sneaky coven Alice!

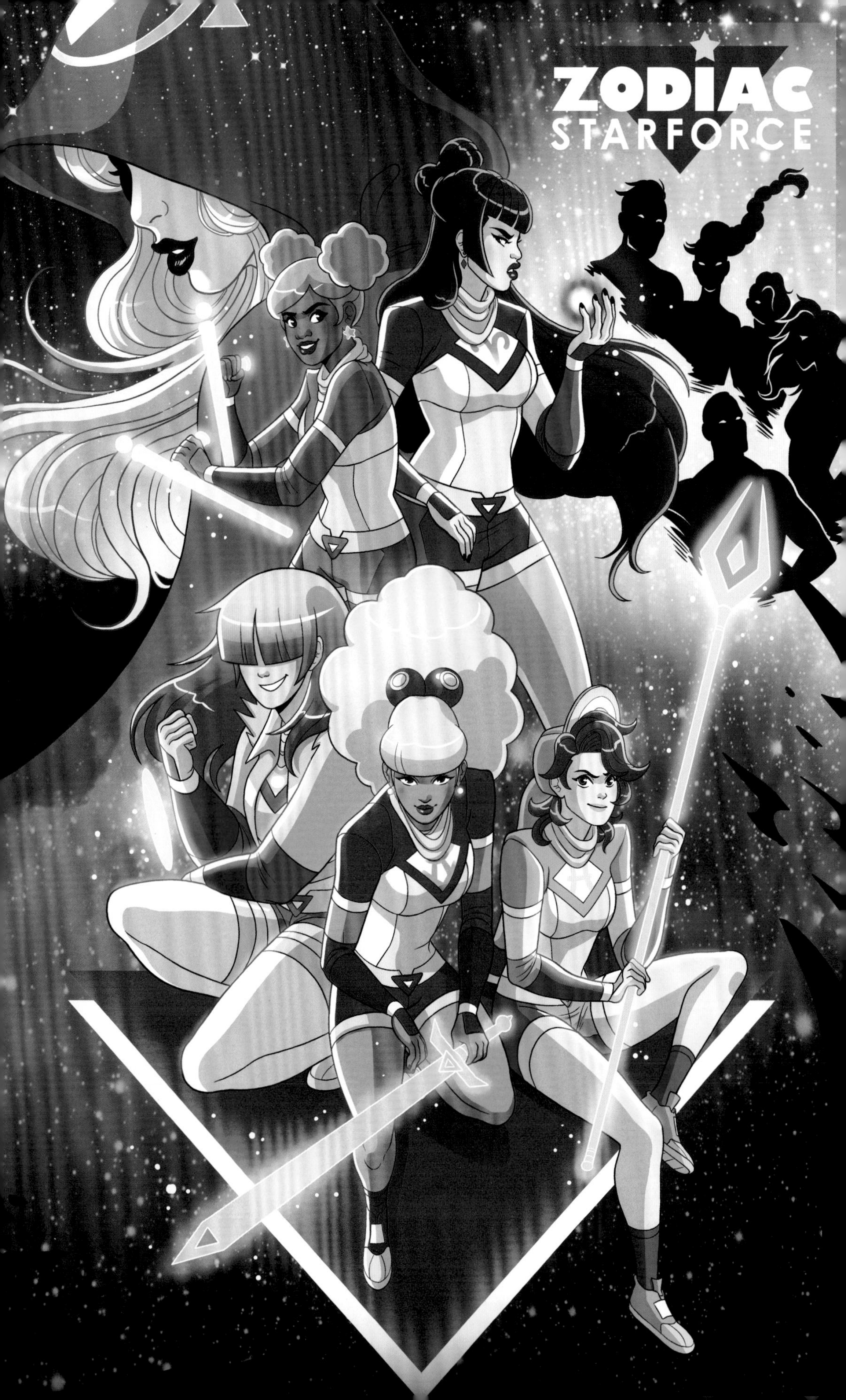
ZODIAC
STARFORCE

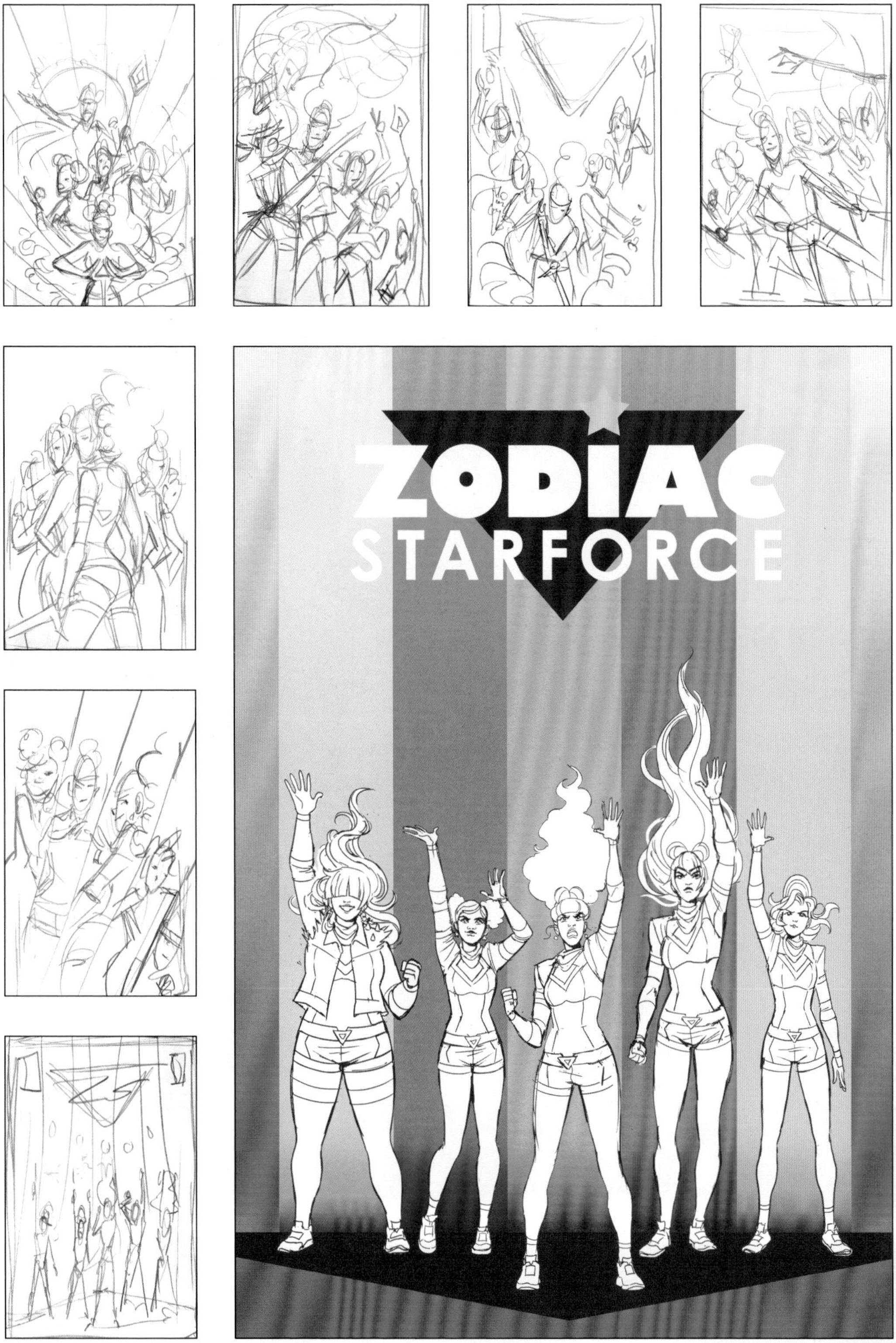
ZODIAC
STARFORCE

ZODIAC STARFORCE #1 COVER

P: I didn't get to do covers for the first series so I was really pumped to do them for this one. Also, look at that Jen Bartel variant cover (*facing*). I mean have you ever seen anything so beautiful?

K: We had a bunch of cool covers in *By the Power of Astra*, but I was super happy to have Paulina covers on *Cries of the Fire Prince*! We went through a lot of options for the first issue, but I'm really happy with the final cover.

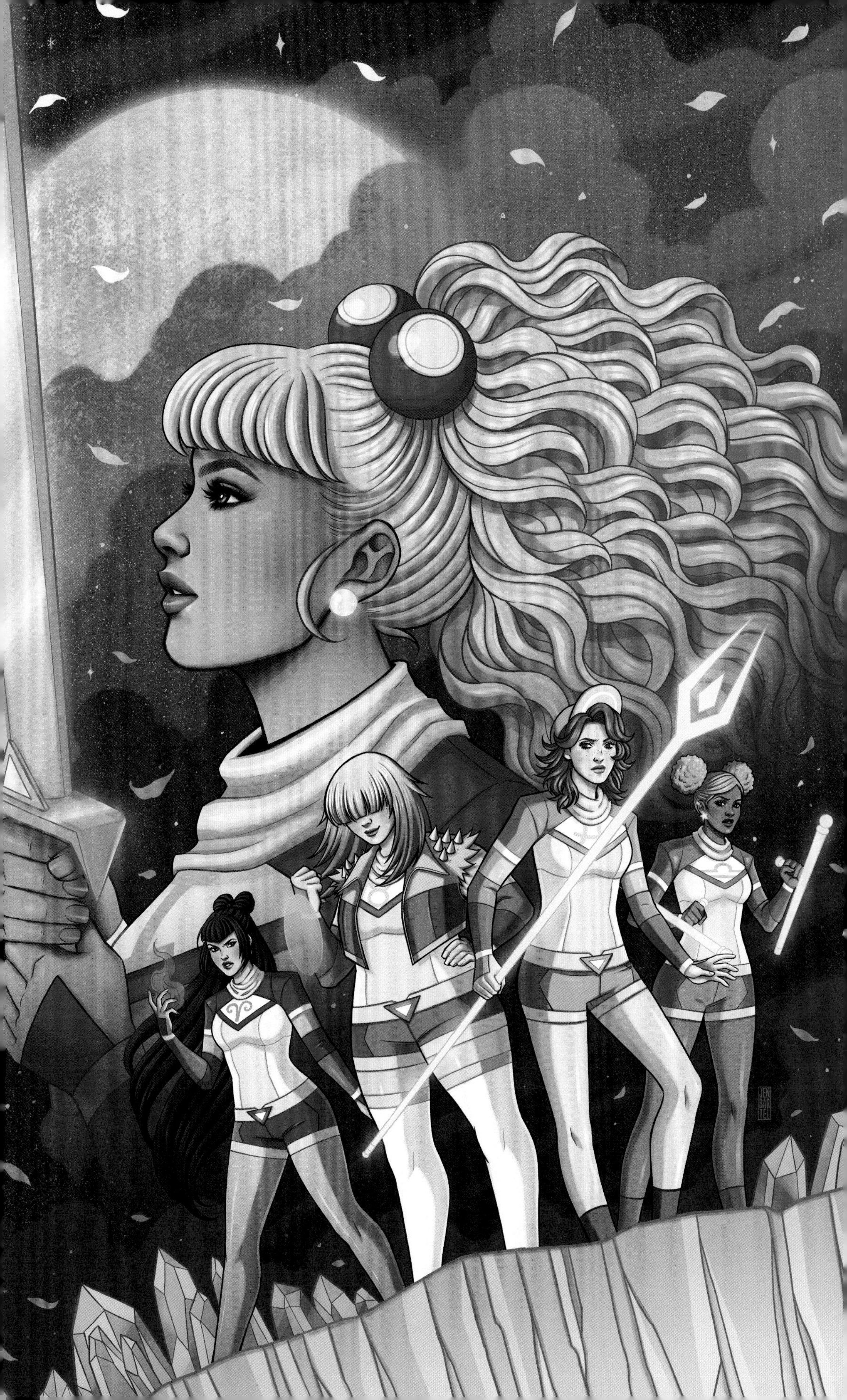
JEN BAR TEL

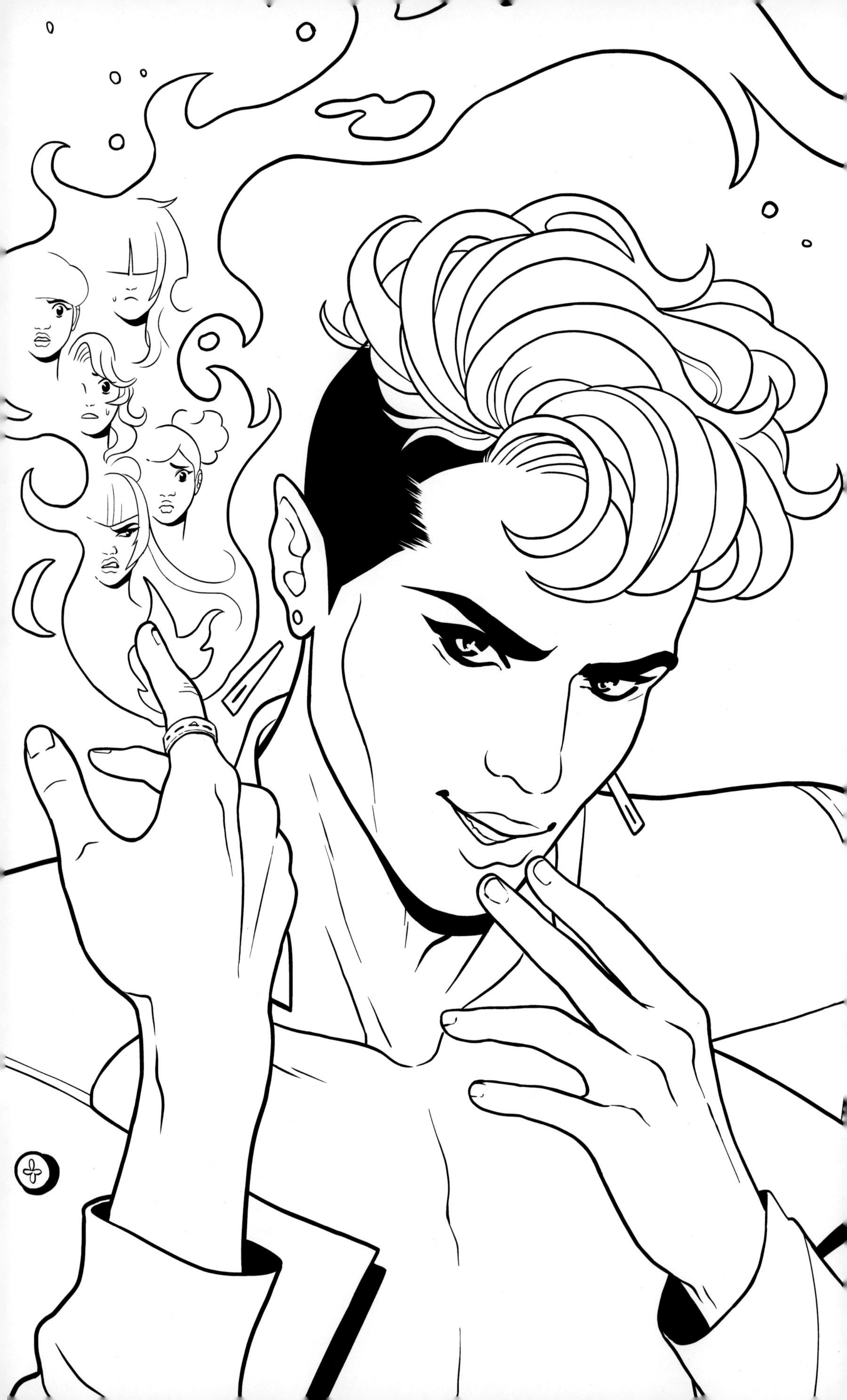

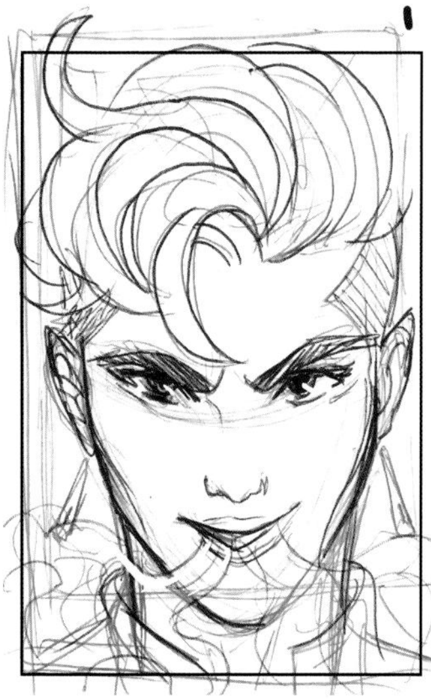
1

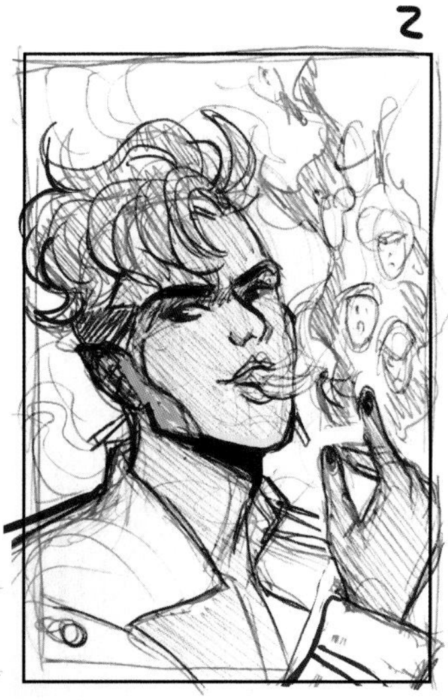
2

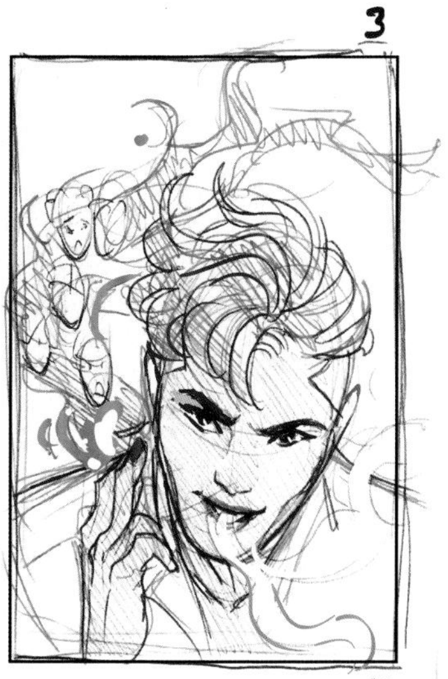
3

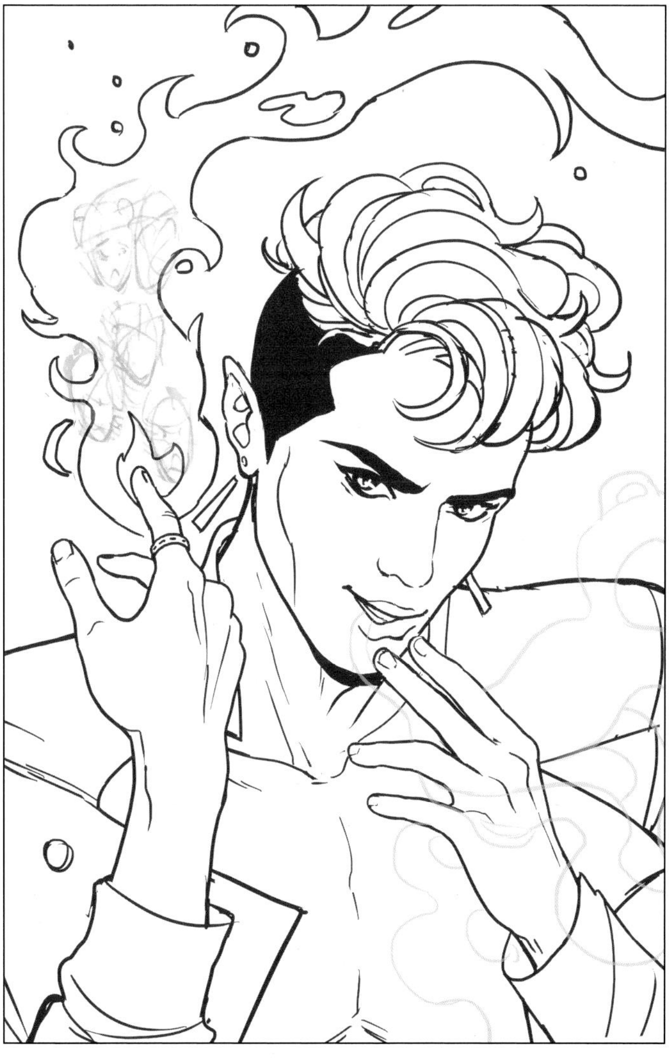

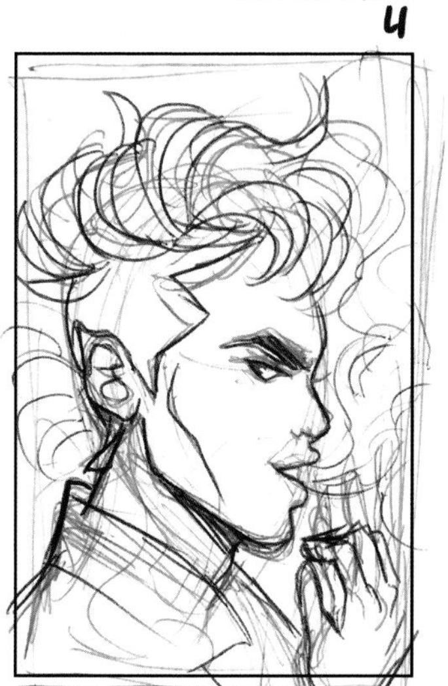
4

ZODIAC STARFORCE #2 COVER

P: I came up with the idea for the smoke exhalation "cool down power mode" thing Pavos does while I was thumbnailing this cover. I think it's a really fun visual. (Issue #2 showcases it a lot if you missed it!)

K: I'm so mad at this cover. Why is Pavos so hot?! It's annoying!

P: Pavos is hot. Deal with it, Kevin.

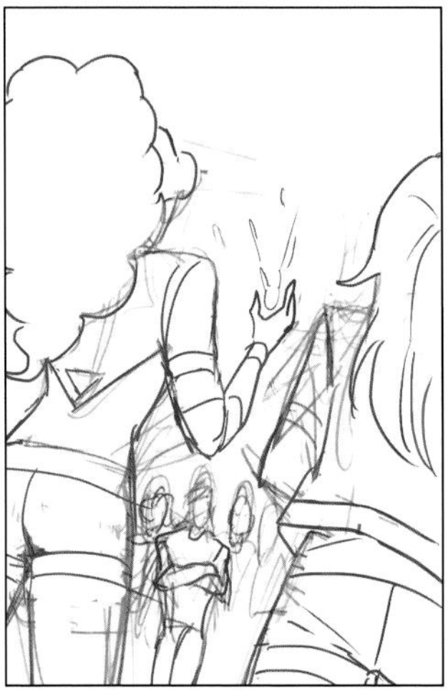

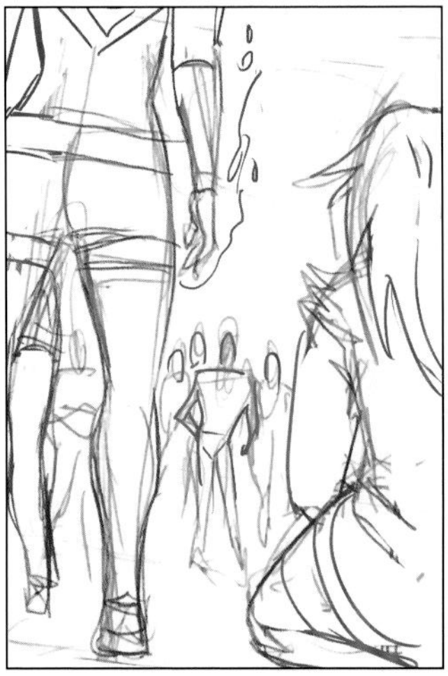

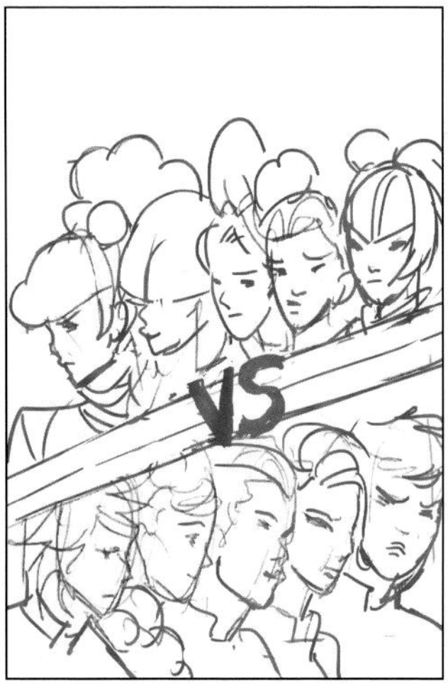
VS

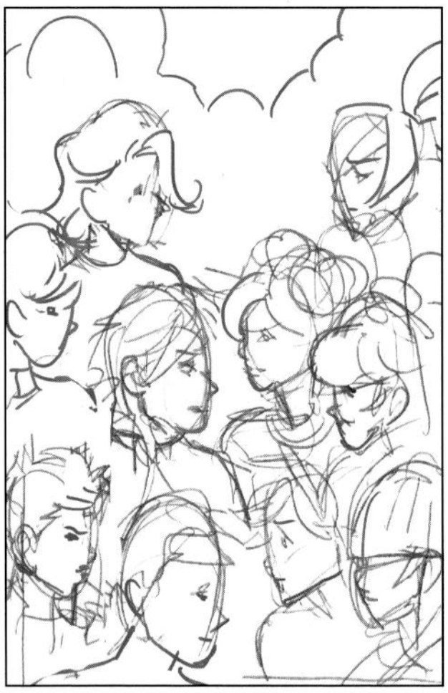

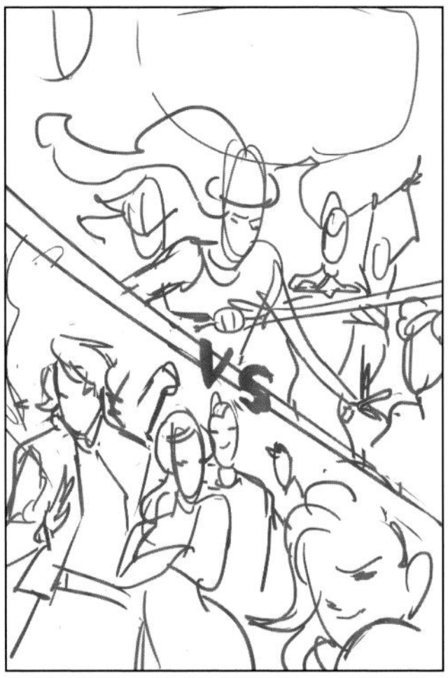
VS

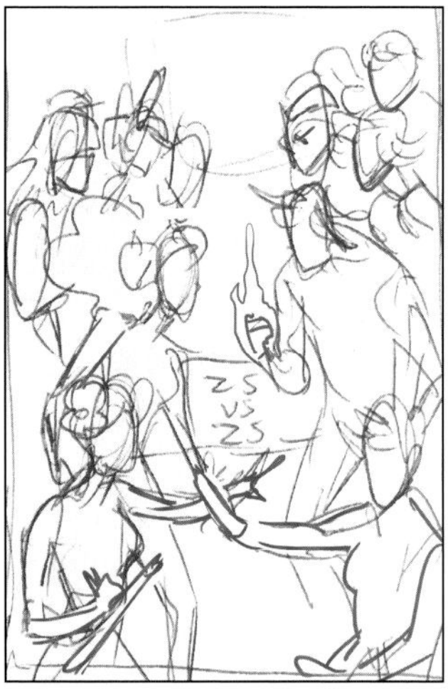

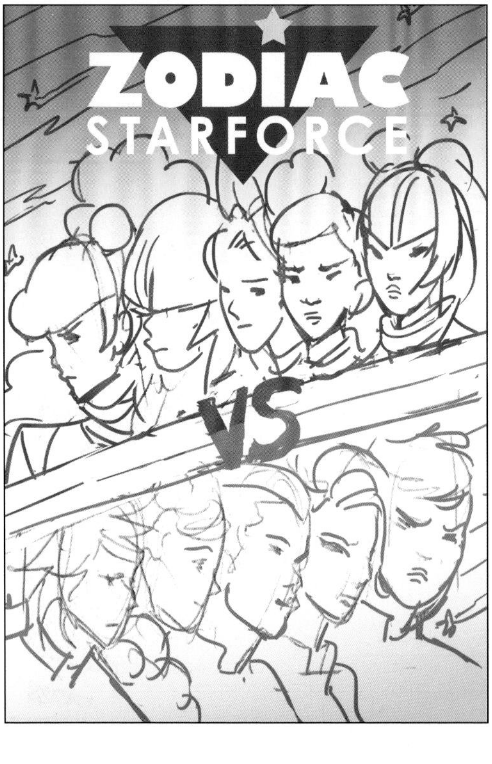
ZODIAC
STARFORCE
VS

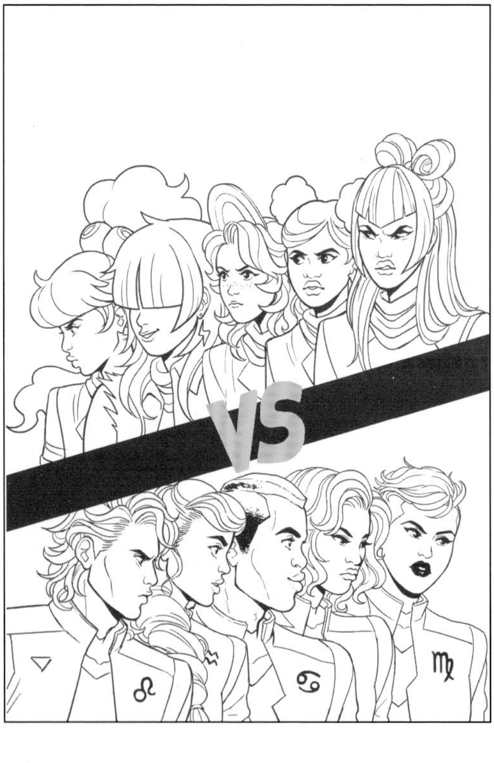
VS

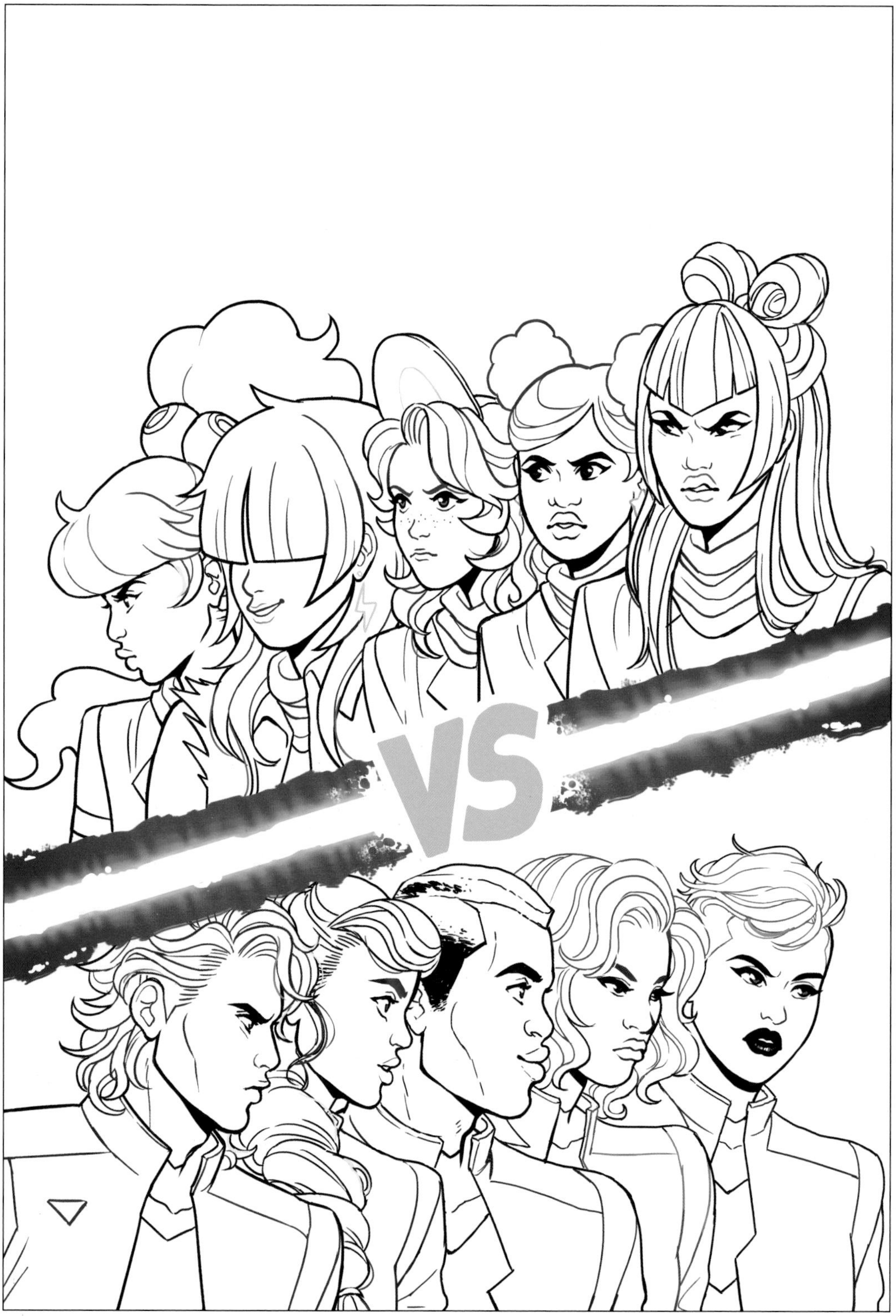
VS

ZODIAC STARFORCE #3 COVER

P: I did this cover in a hotel room while attending C2E2 in 2017 on a laptop with a tiny Wacom tablet, and I can't believe it's still one of my favorite covers I've ever done! It's been my Twitter banner since last year. I just love the colors, simplicity, and the fighting game style VS theme of it.

K: We were still trying to keep the UK ZS a secret when we first revealed this cover so they were all silhouettes. It's fun to be mysterious!

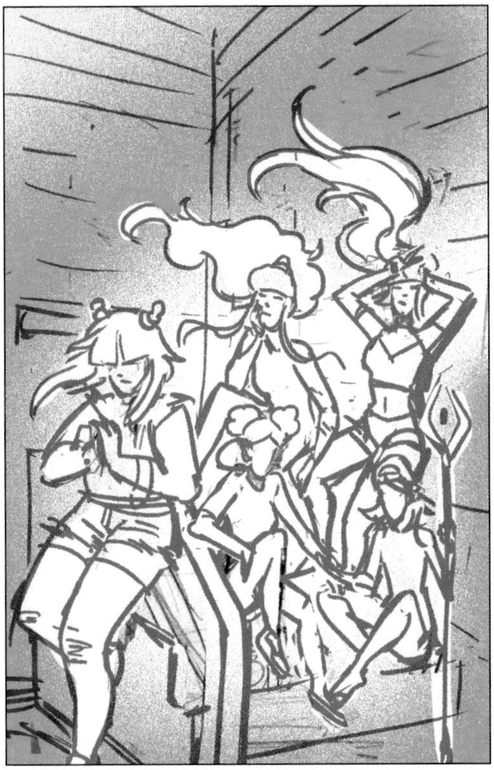

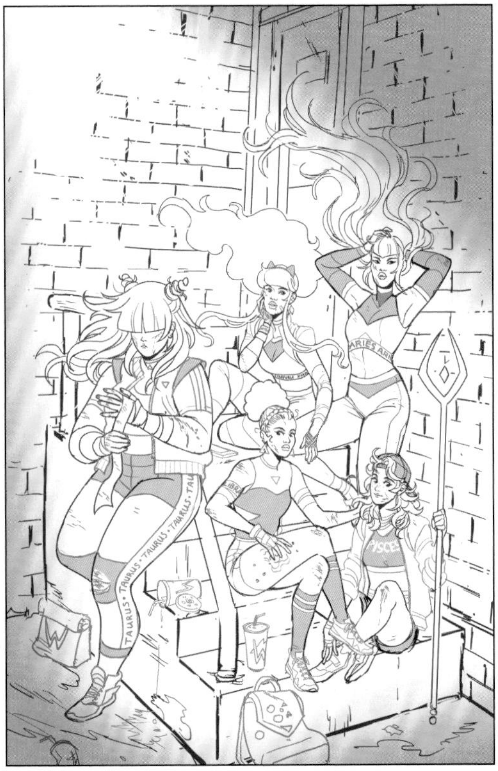

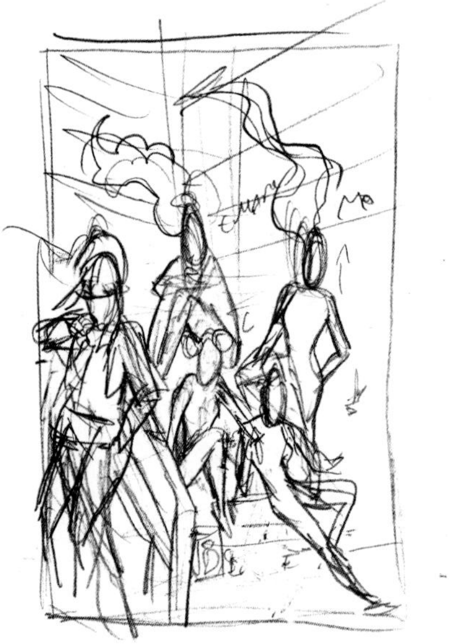

ZODIAC STARFORCE #4 COVER

P: This though is probably my favorite Zodiac Starforce drawing. When can I release a line of *ZS* inspired athletic wear?

K: Was this athleisure cover my idea?

P: I can't remember.

K: Okay, I'm gonna take credit then. LOOK AT MY GREAT IDEA!

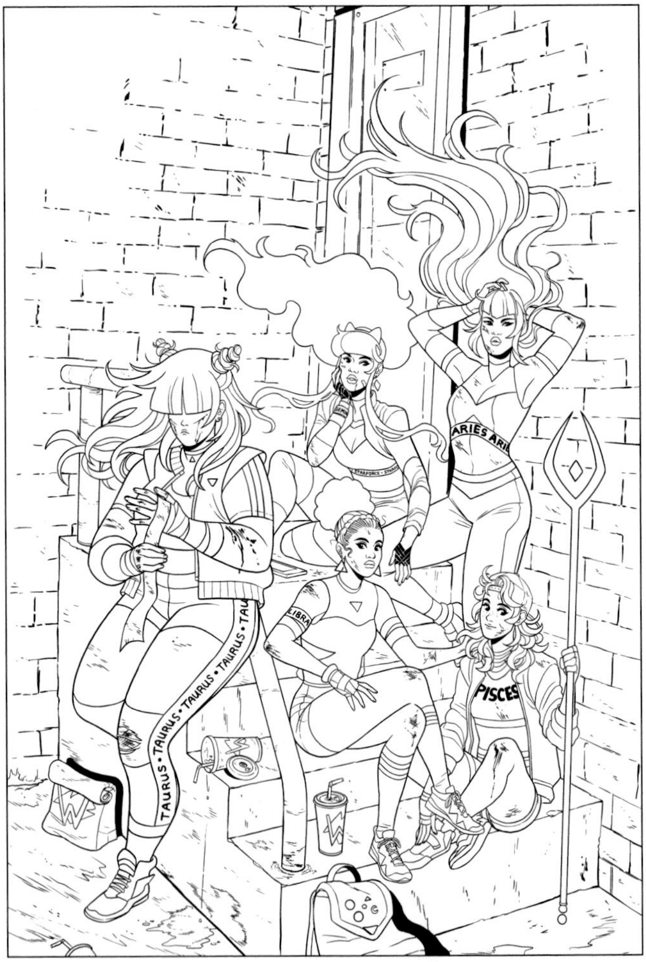
ARIES ARI
LIBRA
PISCES

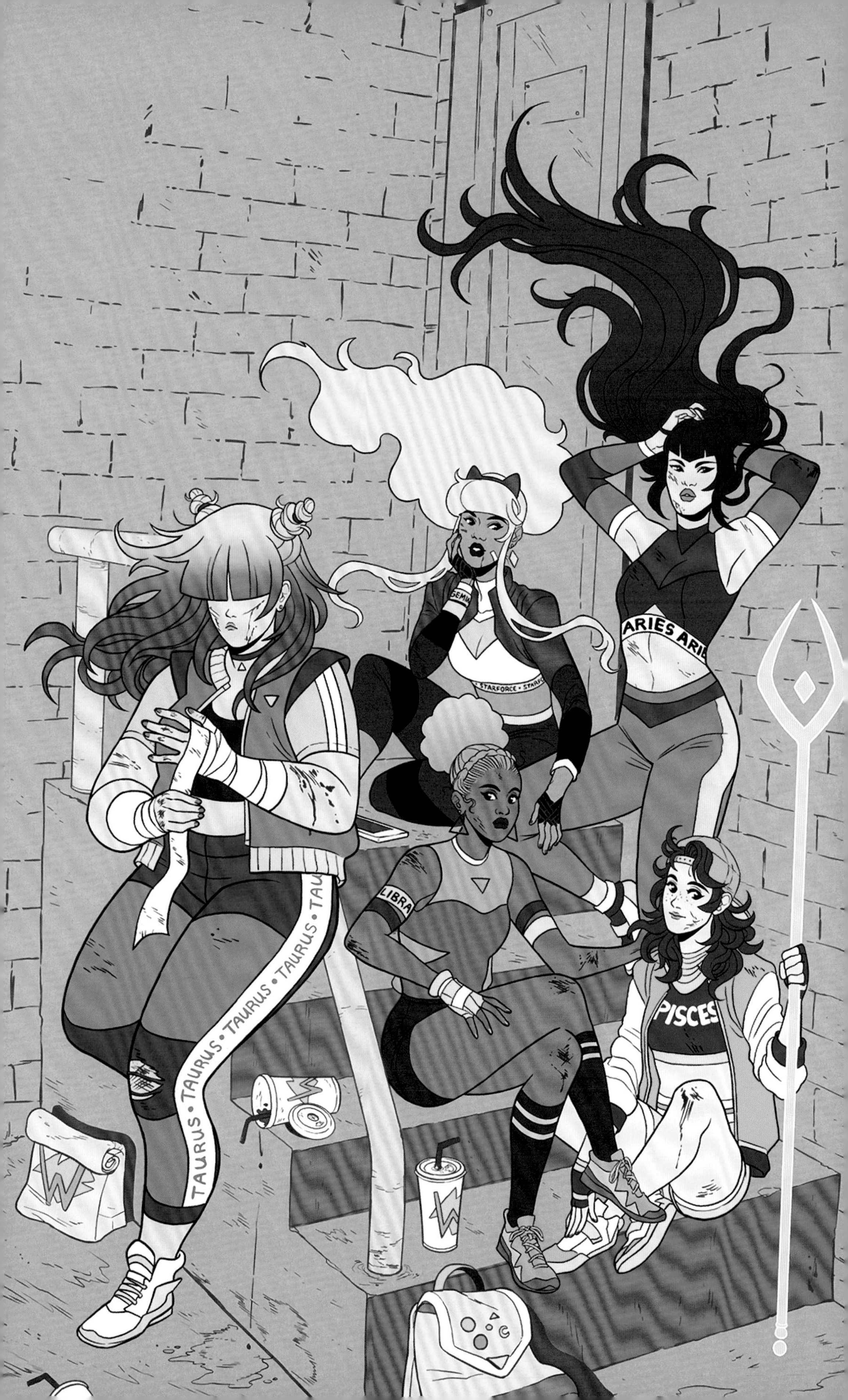
ARIES
STARFORCE
TAURUS • TAURUS • TAURUS • TAURUS
LIBRA
PISCES

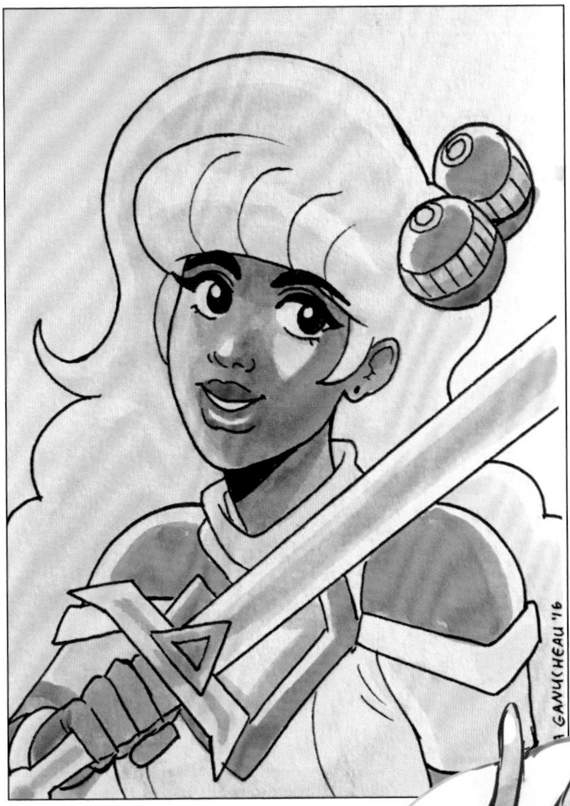
GANUCHEAU '16

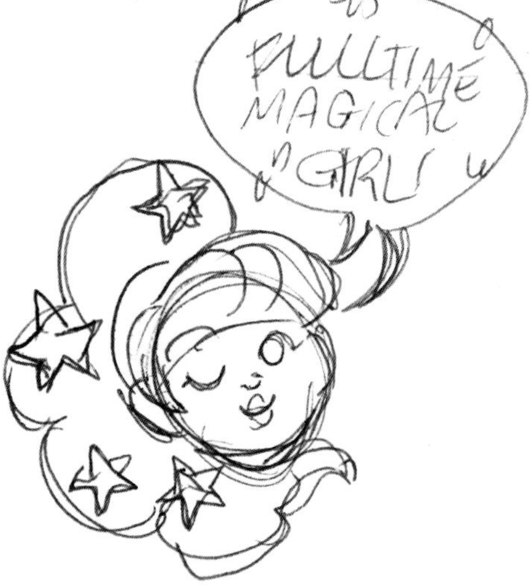
FULLTIME
MAGICAL
GIRL

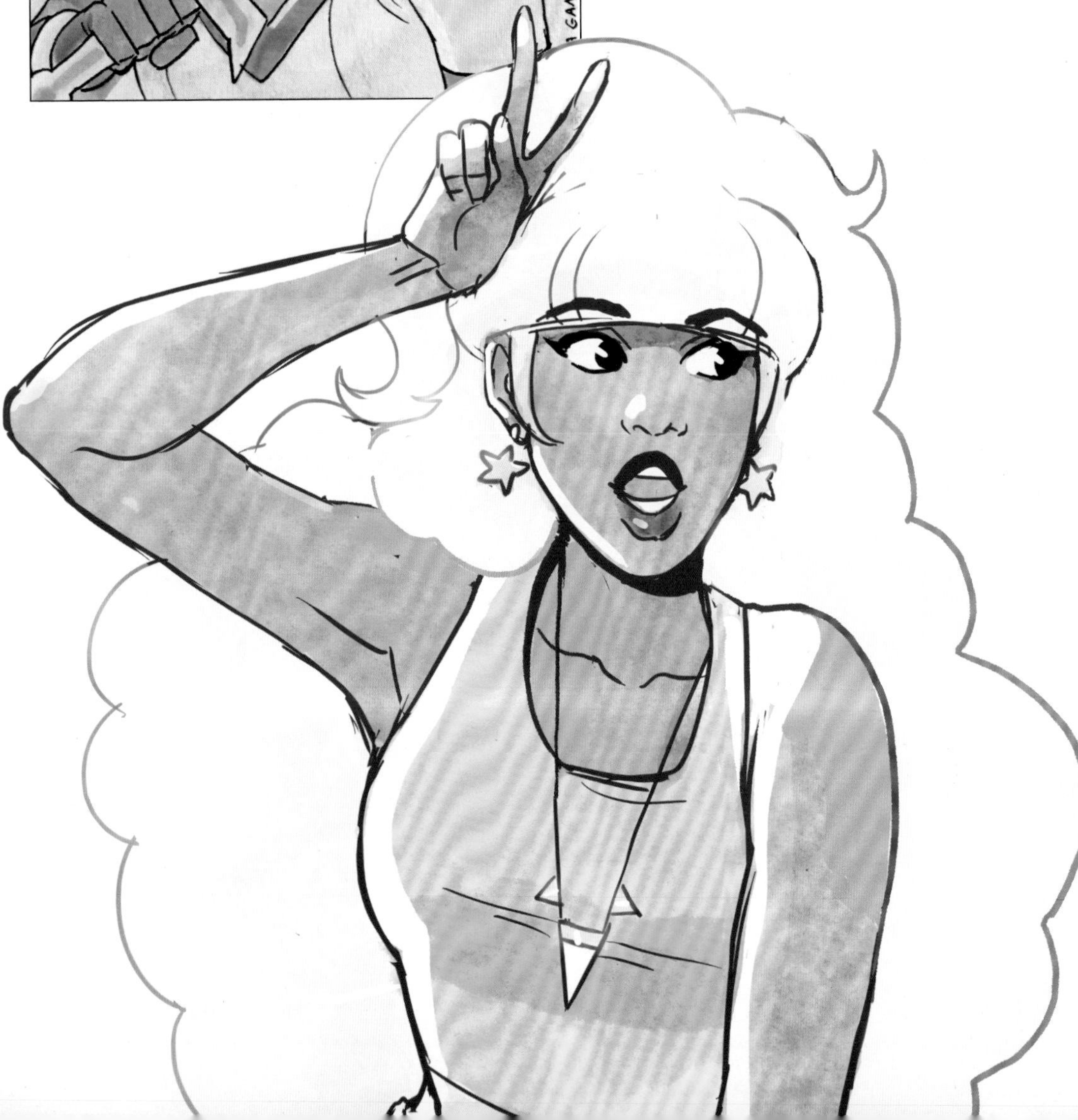

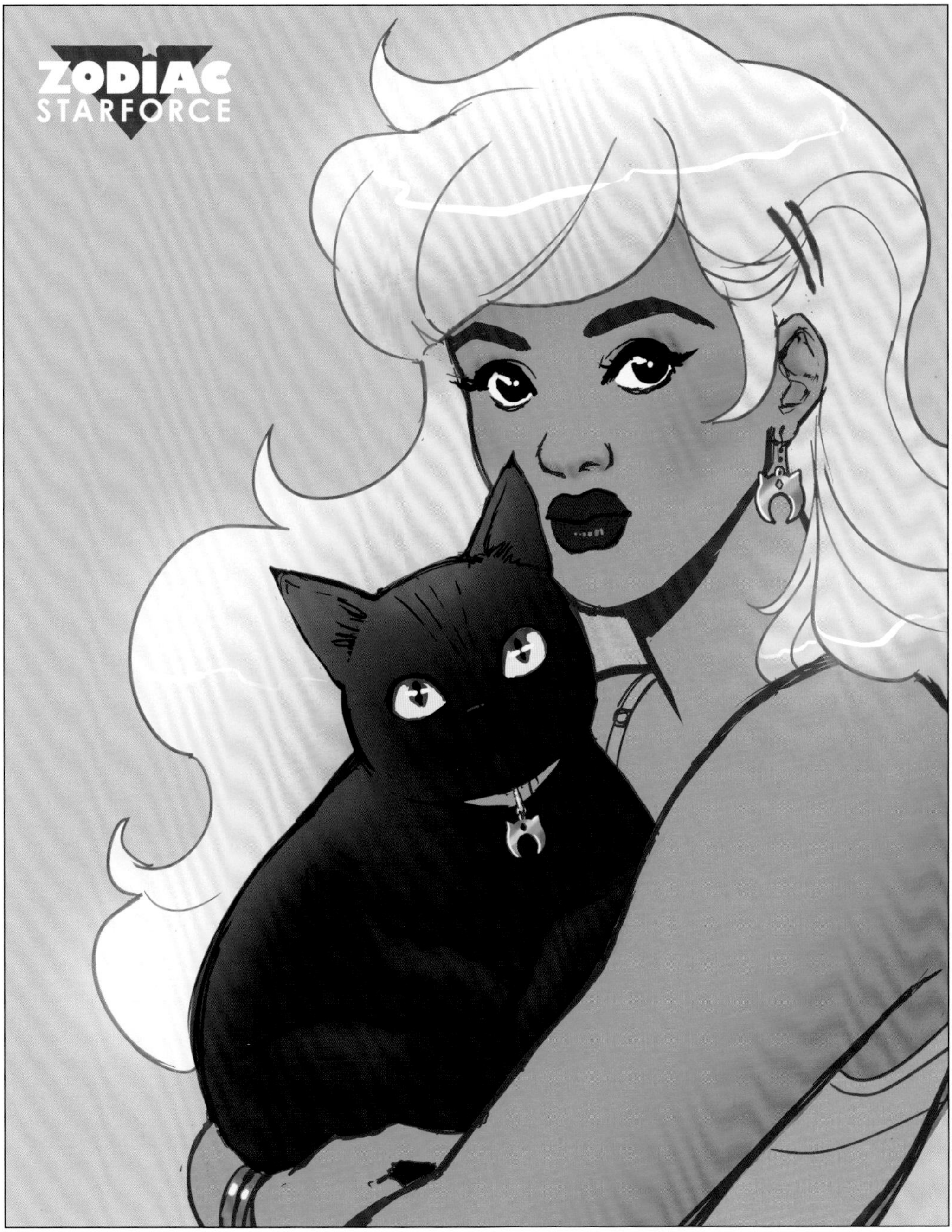
ZODIAC
STARFORCE

EMMA

K: Emma is on a little bit of a relationship rollercoaster in this series. She's been dating Luke but he's more of a fan than a boyfriend. Then she meets Jack and he's hot, but that seems like a potential mess. Maybe Emma needs to be on her own for a little while.

P: Ugh, I had boyfriends like that. Emma, you do YOU.

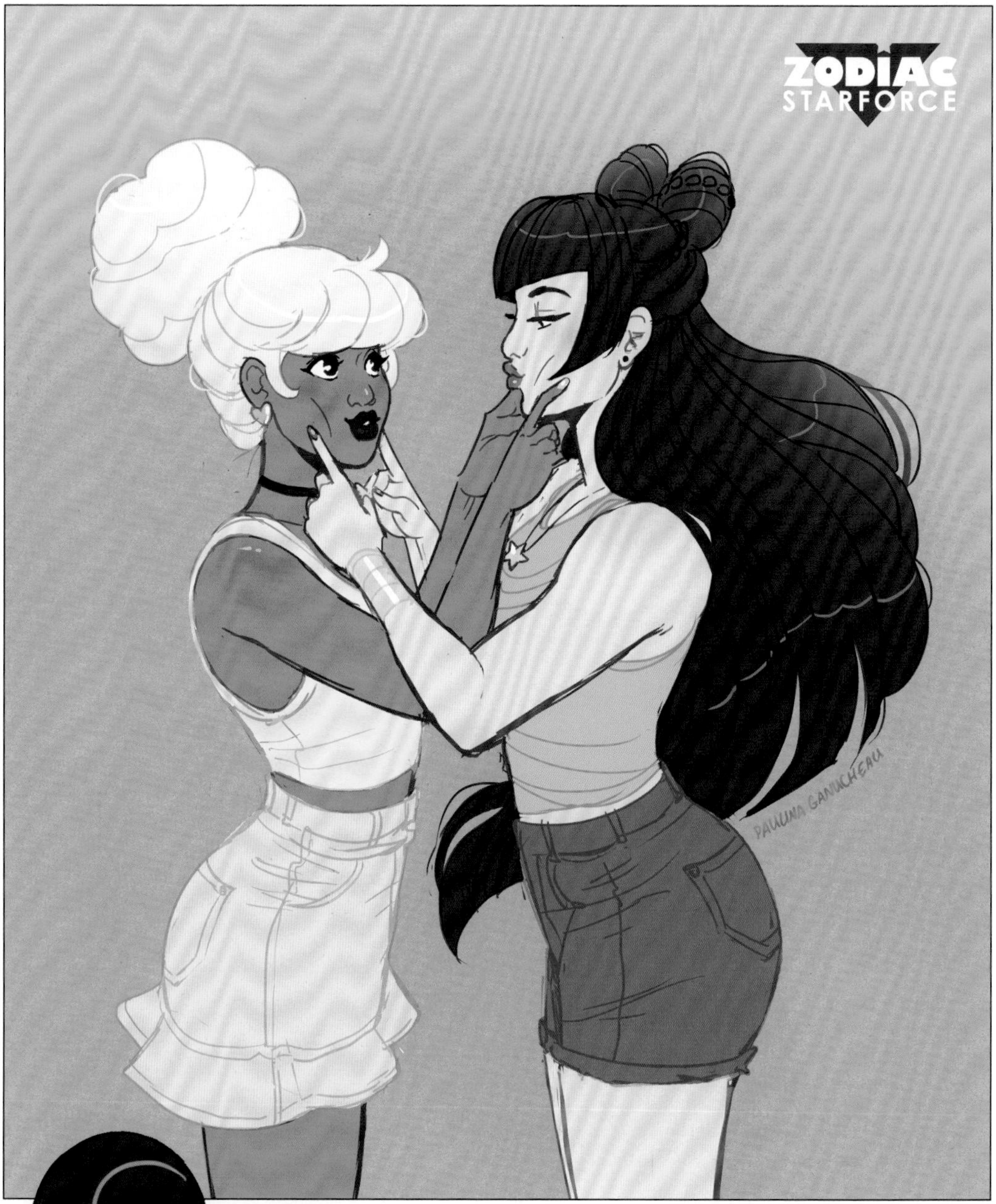
ZODIAC
STARFORCE
PAULINA GANUCHEAU

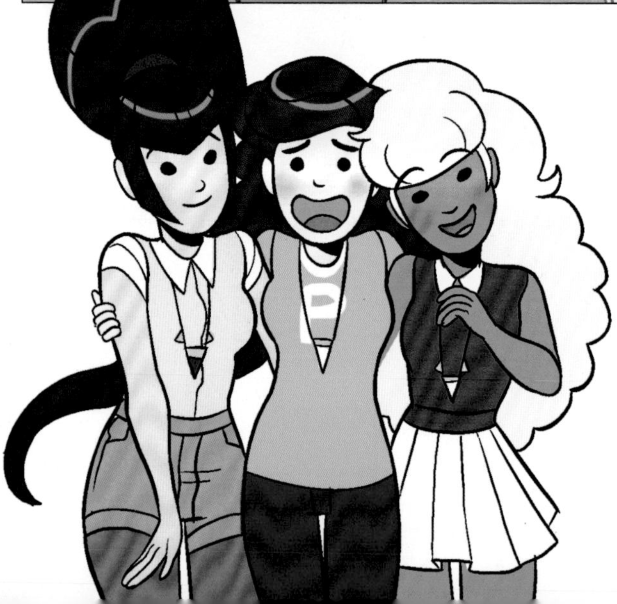

EMMA AND MOLLY

P: See that drawing of me with Emma and Molly? Yeah, that's real life 'cause they're my most favorite for all time.

K: I think they're everybody's favorites. Shipping "MOMMA" is very popular amongst *ZS* fans.

P: MOMMA 4 LIFE

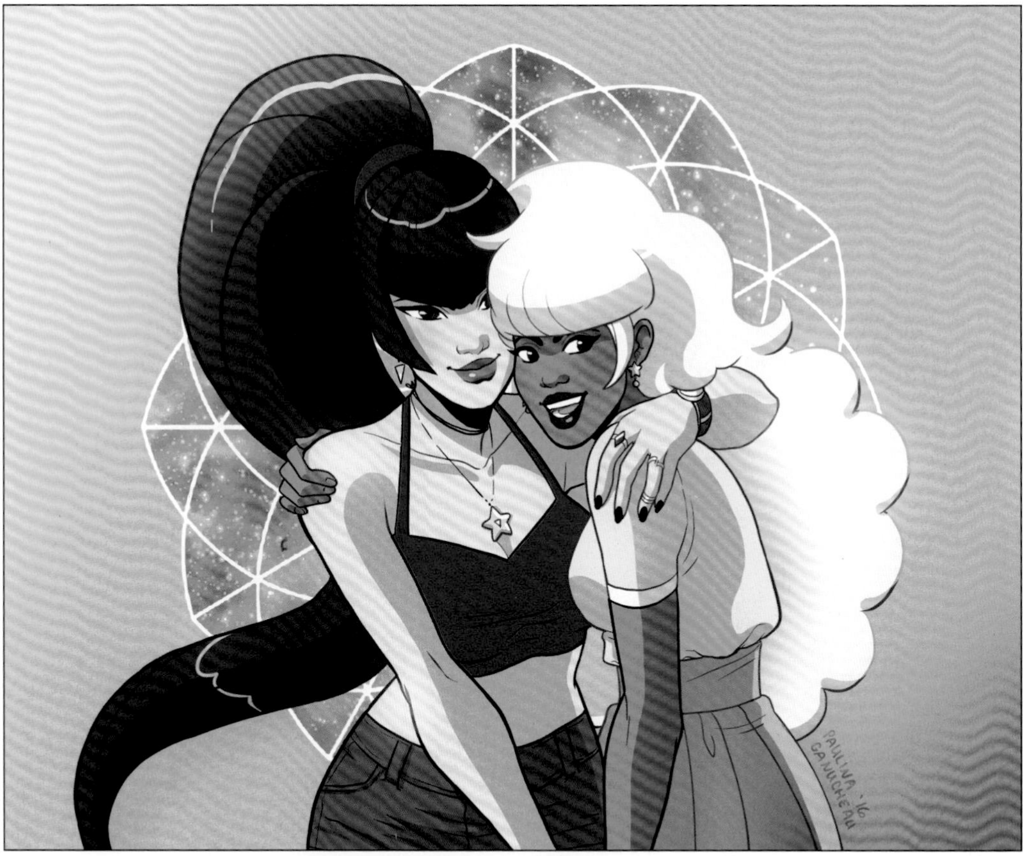
PAULINA GANUCHEAU '16

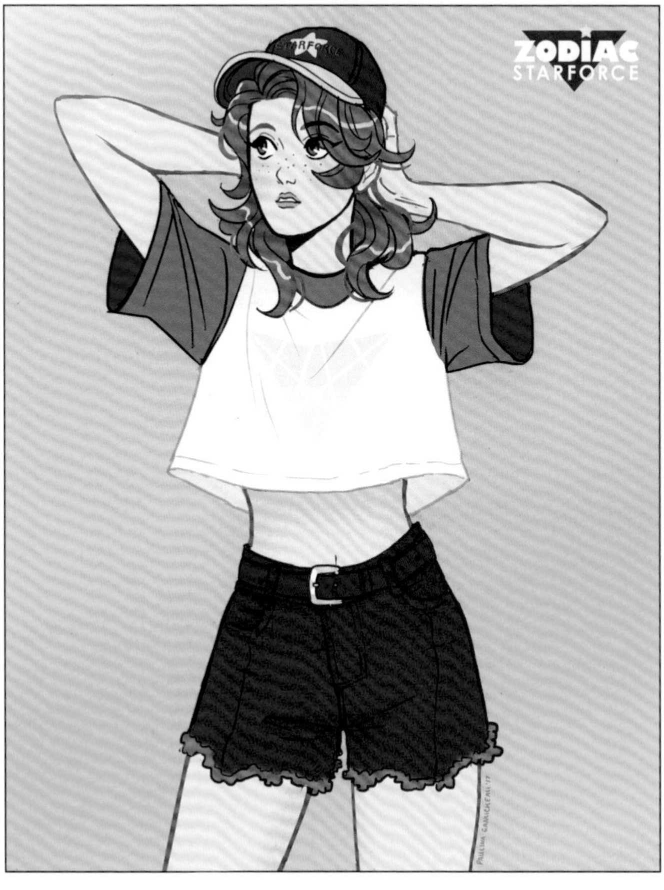
ZODIAC
STARFORCE

SAVI

K: We're gonna talk more about Savi's storyline in two pages but right now I just want to say this is a good look for Savi. Baseball hat, crop top, cool shorts. Very snazzy.

P: This is fashion Savi. She's very put together. Also, should we make those hats one day?

K: I would buy one.

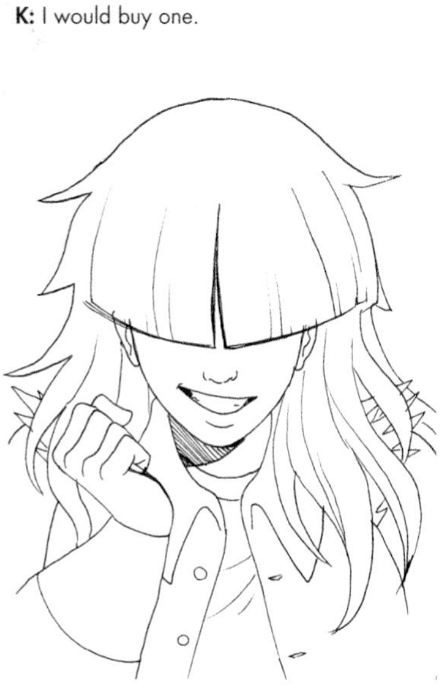

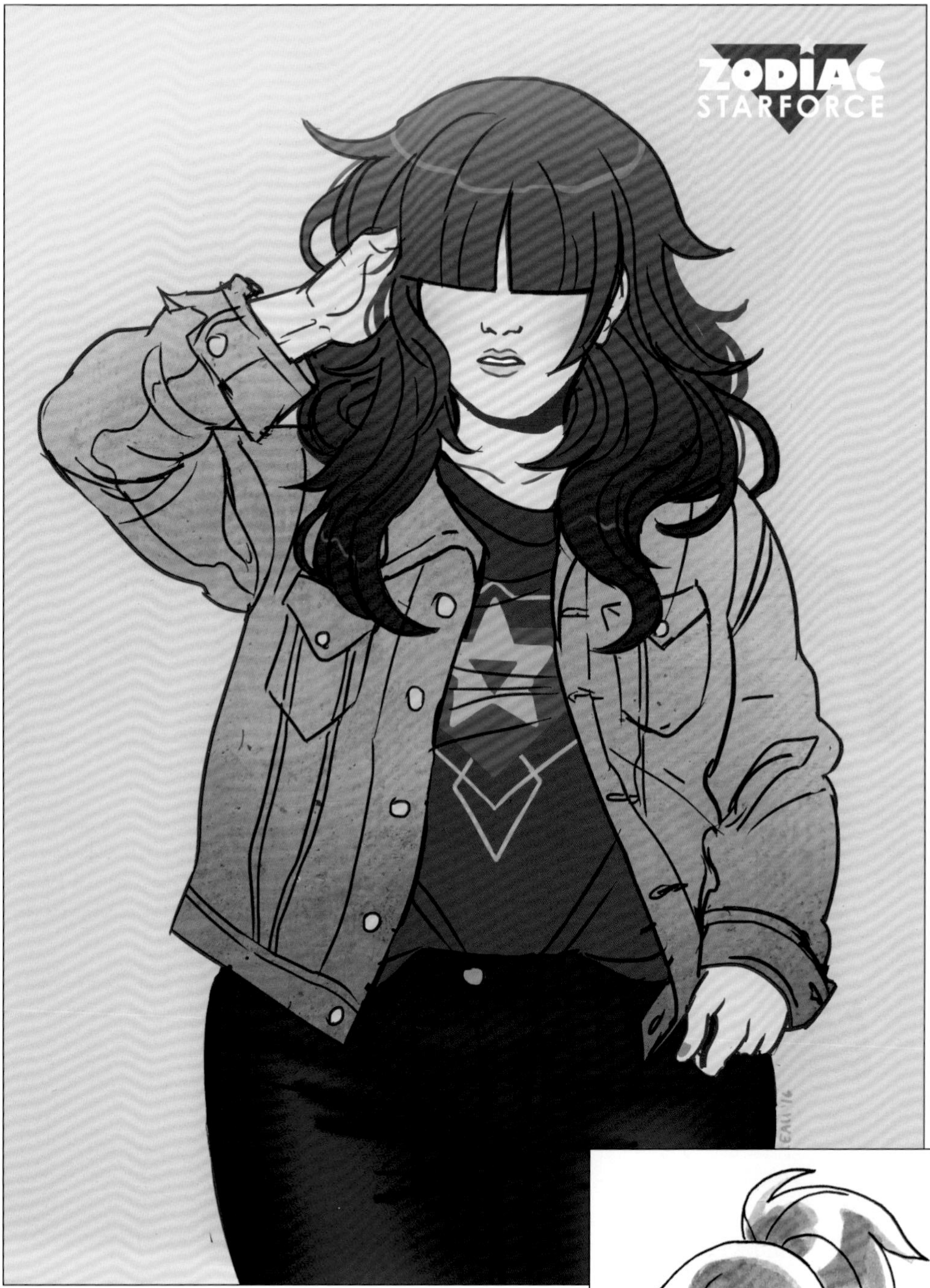
ZODIAC
STARFORCE

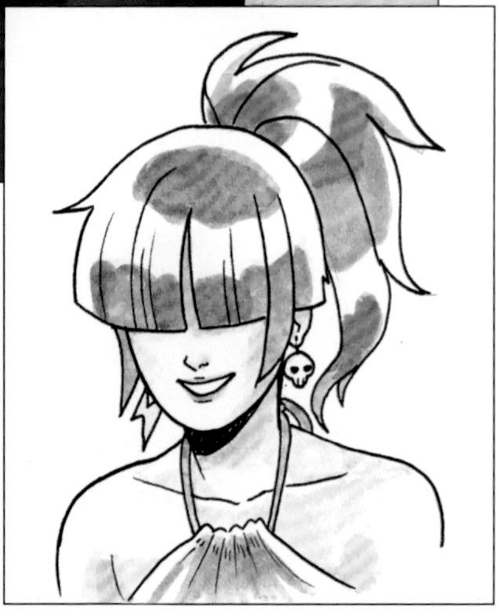

KIM

K: I always wanted Kim to become a wrestler, and it was exciting to explore that in this volume. She has a really small but cute character arc where she's just learning to use wrestling moves in the first issue and the last issue she's drop kicking monsters off of airships. I love it.

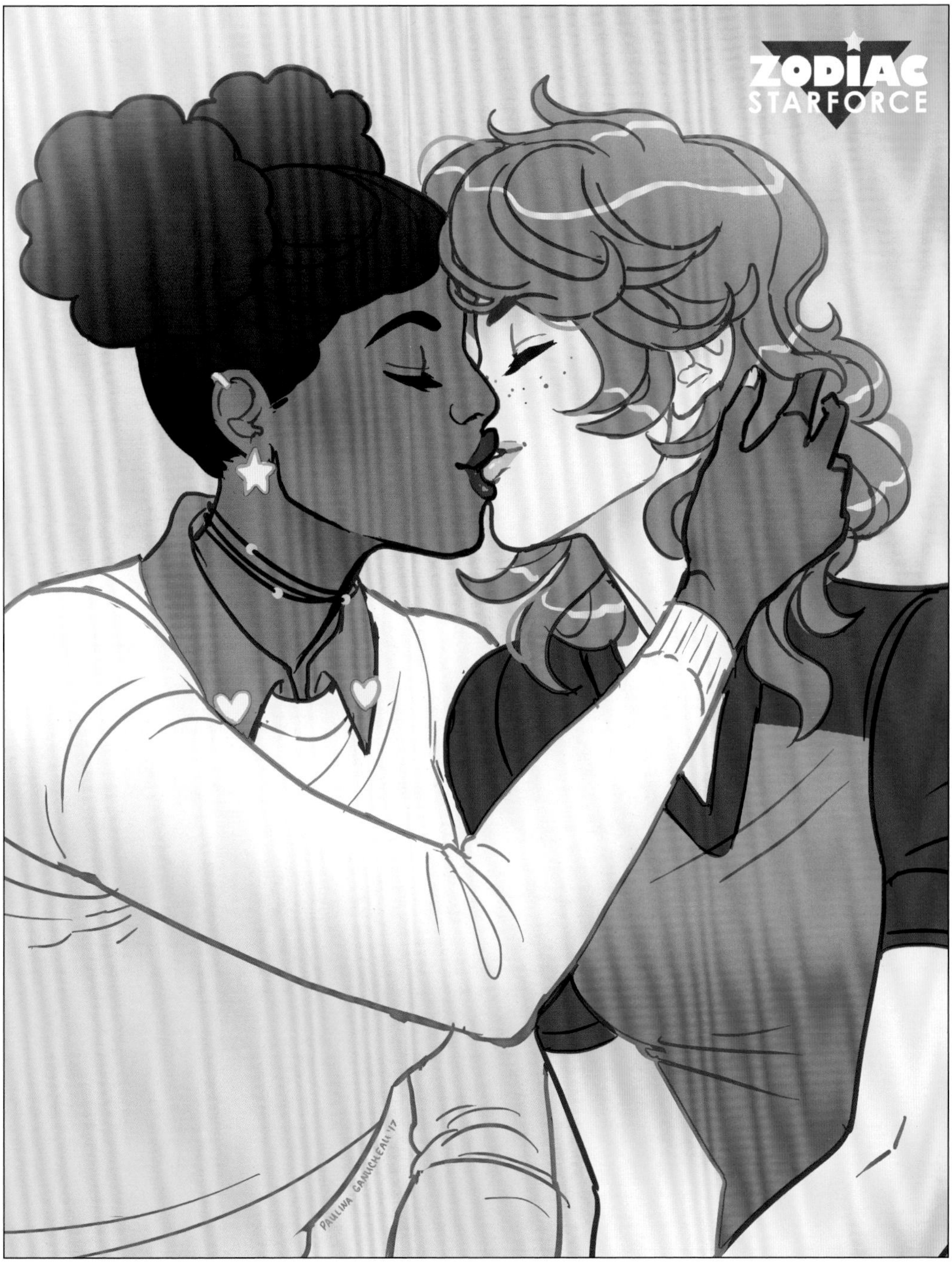
ZODIAC
STARFORCE
PAULINA GANUCHEAU '17

LILY AND SAVI

P: My two favorite love birds. Note to self: please draw more cute pictures of them being in love. Especially now that they've both said "I love you!" *sniff* So beautiful.

K: Savi & Lily's story in this series is my fave. They are struggling in their relationship, but they just need to COMMUNICATE MORE! A good lesson for everybody, IMHO.

P: It's so thrilling seeing Lily find her own power literally and figuratively!

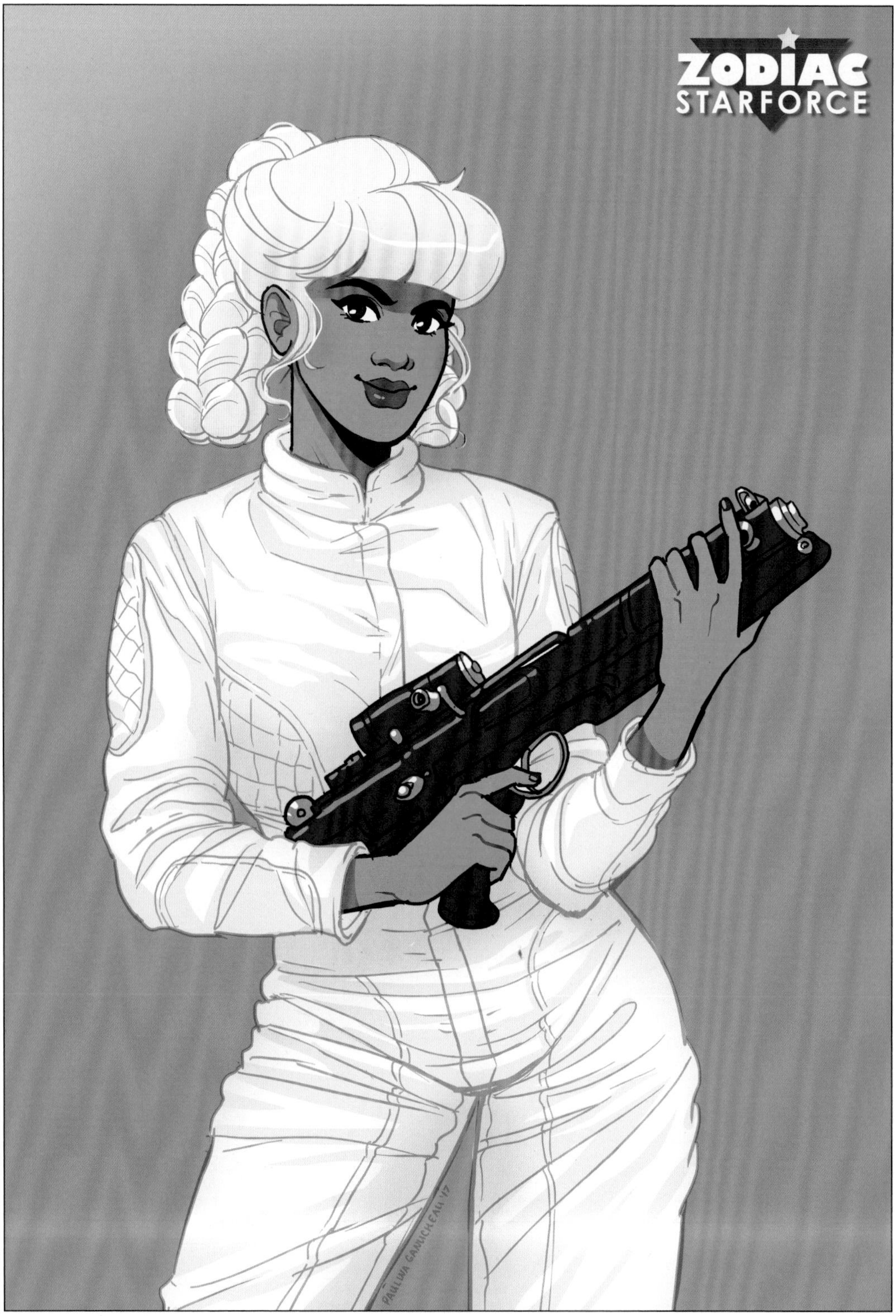
ZODIAC
STARFORCE
PAULINA GANUCHEAU '17

ZODIAC STAR WARS

P: Okay so this illustration series was born out of both of our unhealthy obsessions with *Star Wars*.

K: It was one of those "Which *Star Wars* character would Molly be?" kind of things and then Paulina drew Molly Han Solo and it was like, YES DO MORE!

P: I'm honestly sad I never finished the Kim Poe Dameron! I should do that . . .

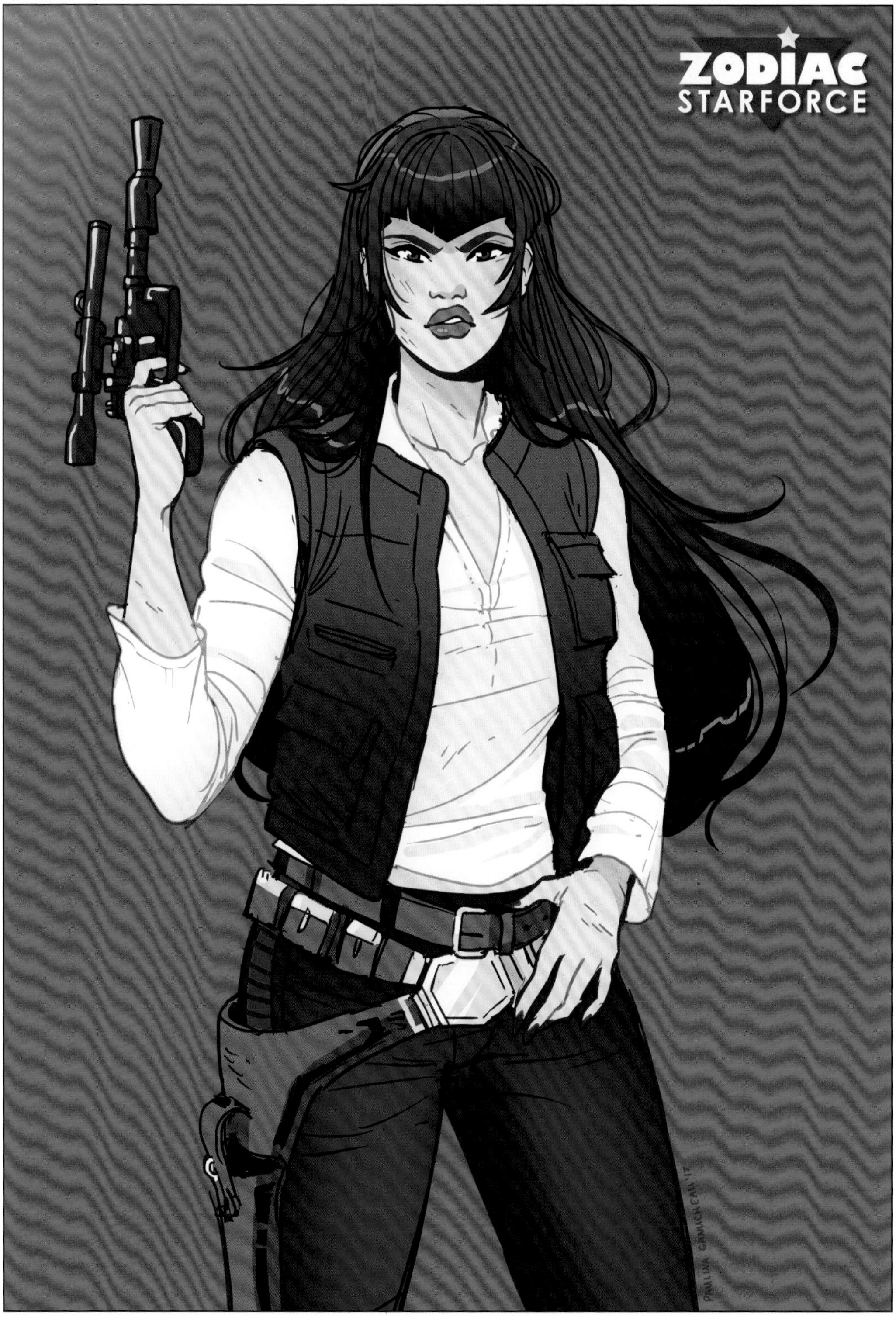
ZODIAC
STARFORCE

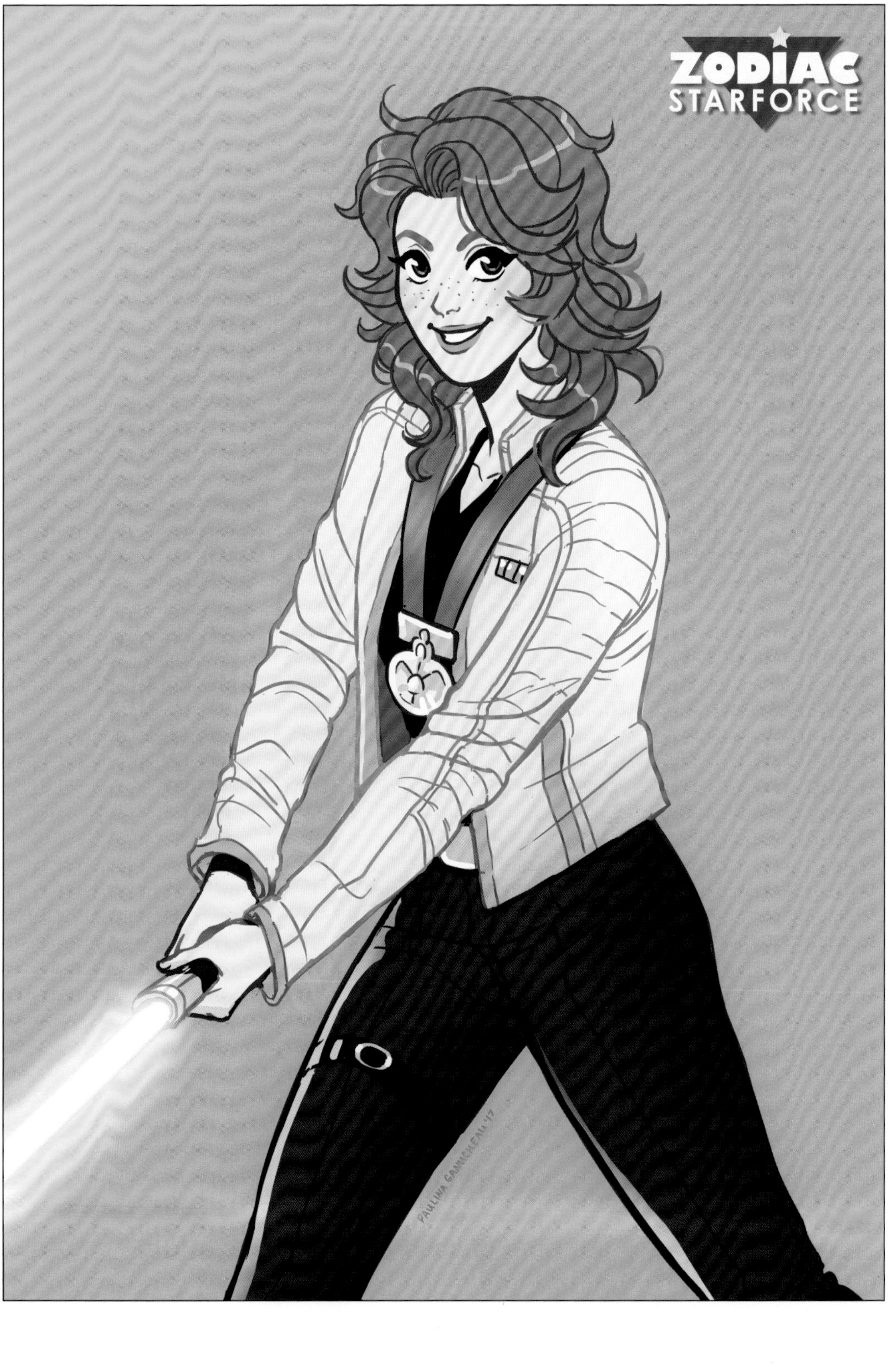
ZODIAC
STARFORCE

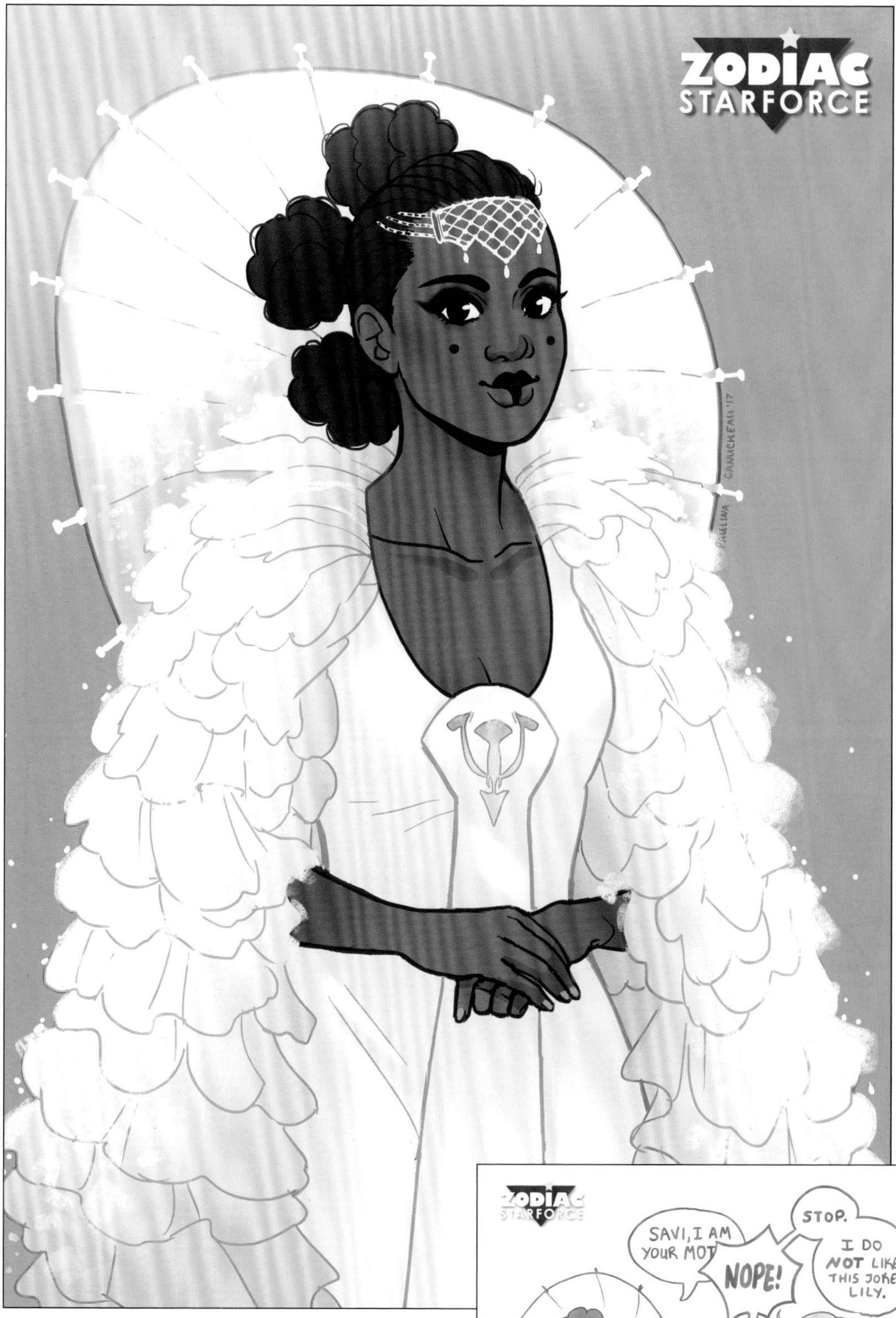
ZODIAC
STARFORCE
PAULINA GANUCHEAU '17

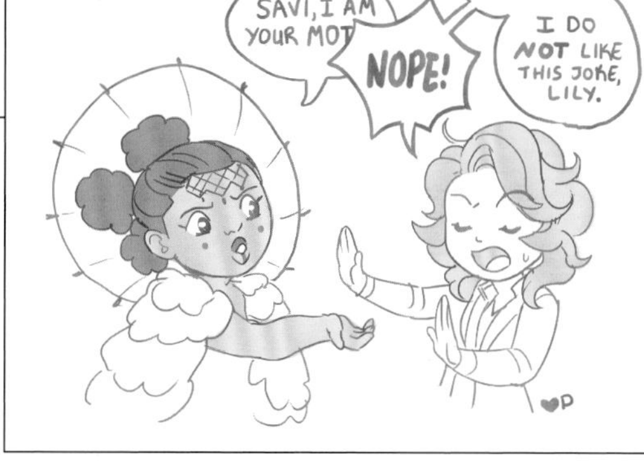
ZODIAC
STARFORCE
SAVI, I AM YOUR MOT
NOPE!
STOP.
I DO NOT LIKE THIS JOKE, LILY.

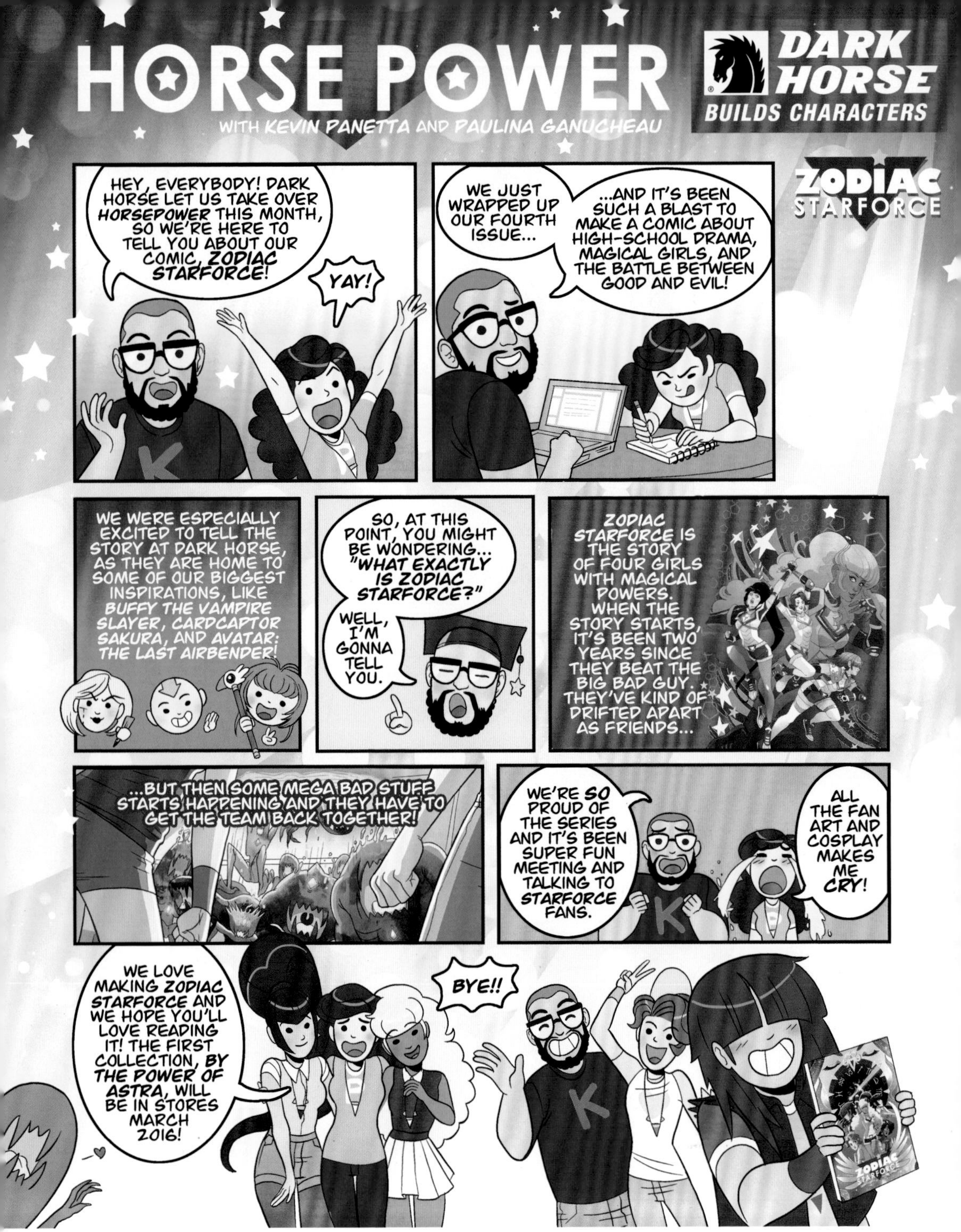
HORSE POWER
WITH KEVIN PANETTA AND PAULINA GANUCHEAU
DARK HORSE
BUILDS CHARACTERS
ZODIAC STARFORCE
HEY, EVERYBODY! DARK HORSE LET US TAKE OVER HORSEPOWER THIS MONTH, SO WE'RE HERE TO TELL YOU ABOUT OUR COMIC, ZODIAC STARFORCE!
YAY!
WE JUST WRAPPED UP OUR FOURTH ISSUE...
...AND IT'S BEEN SUCH A BLAST TO MAKE A COMIC ABOUT HIGH-SCHOOL DRAMA, MAGICAL GIRLS, AND THE BATTLE BETWEEN GOOD AND EVIL!
WE WERE ESPECIALLY EXCITED TO TELL THE STORY AT DARK HORSE, AS THEY ARE HOME TO SOME OF OUR BIGGEST INSPIRATIONS, LIKE BUFFY THE VAMPIRE SLAYER, CARDCAPTOR SAKURA, AND AVATAR: THE LAST AIRBENDER!
SO, AT THIS POINT, YOU MIGHT BE WONDERING... "WHAT EXACTLY IS ZODIAC STARFORCE?"
WELL, I'M GONNA TELL YOU.
ZODIAC STARFORCE IS THE STORY OF FOUR GIRLS WITH MAGICAL POWERS. WHEN THE STORY STARTS, IT'S BEEN TWO YEARS SINCE THEY BEAT THE BIG BAD GUY. THEY'VE KIND OF DRIFTED APART AS FRIENDS...
...BUT THEN SOME MEGA BAD STUFF STARTS HAPPENING AND THEY HAVE TO GET THE TEAM BACK TOGETHER!
WE'RE SO PROUD OF THE SERIES AND IT'S BEEN SUPER FUN MEETING AND TALKING TO STARFORCE FANS.
ALL THE FAN ART AND COSPLAY MAKES ME CRY!
WE LOVE MAKING ZODIAC STARFORCE AND WE HOPE YOU'LL LOVE READING IT! THE FIRST COLLECTION, BY THE POWER OF ASTRA, WILL BE IN STORES MARCH 2016!
BYE!!

HORSEPOWER AD

K: This was a fun comic strip that Dark Horse asked us to make to explain what *Zodiac Starforce* is. It showed up in the back of a bunch of Dark Horse books. It's still crazy to think we are being published by the company that puts out *Buffy*, *Cardcaptor Sakura*, and *Avatar: the Last Airbender*!

P: It's amazing and I'm so grateful to be amongst so many great creators and books!

K: Okay. What do we say to end this sketchbook commentary? "Stay cool"? "Never change"? "Have an awesome summer"?

P: 2 COOL 2 BE 4 GOTTEN!

K: Nice.

MORE TITLES YOU MIGHT ENJOY

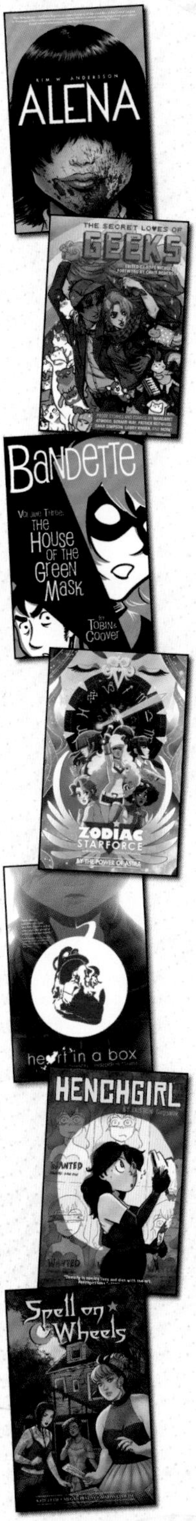
ALENA
THE SECRET LOVES OF GEEKS
BANDETTE
THE HOUSE OF THE GREEN MASK
TOBIN & COOVER
ZODIAC STARFORCE
BY THE POWER OF ASTRA
heart in a box
HENCHGIRL
Spell on Wheels

ALENA

Kim W. Andersson

Since arriving at a snobbish boarding school, Alena's been harassed every day by the lacrosse team. But Alena's best friend Josephine is not going to accept that anymore. If Alena does not fight back, then she will take matters into her own hands. There's just one problem . . . Josephine has been dead for a year.

$17.99 | ISBN 978-1-50670-215-5

ASTRID: CULT OF THE VOLCANIC MOON

Kim W. Andersson

Formerly the Galactic Coalition's top recruit, the now-disgraced Astrid is offered a special mission from her old commander. She'll prove herself worthy of another chance at becoming a Galactic Peacekeeper . . . if she can survive.

$19.99 | ISBN 978-1-61655-690-7

BANDETTE

Paul Tobin, Colleen Coover

A costumed teen burglar by the *nome d'arte* of Bandette and her group of street urchins find equal fun in both skirting and aiding the law, in this enchanting, Eisner-nominated series!

$14.99 each

Volume 1: Presto!
ISBN 978-1-61655-279-4

Volume 2: Stealers, Keepers!
ISBN 978-1-61655-668-6

Volume 3: The House of the Green Mask
ISBN 978-1-50670-219-3

BOUNTY

Kurtis Wiebe, Mindy Lee

The Gadflies were the most wanted criminals in the galaxy. Now, with a bounty to match their reputation, the Gadflies are forced to abandon banditry for a career as bounty hunters . . . 'cause if you can't beat 'em, join 'em—then rob 'em blind!

$14.99 | ISBN 978-1-50670-044-1

HEART IN A BOX

Kelly Thompson, Meredith McClaren

In a moment of post-heartbreak weakness, Emma wishes her heart away and a mysterious stranger obliges. But emptiness is even worse than grief, and Emma sets out to collect the pieces of her heart and face the cost of recapturing it.

$14.99 | ISBN 978-1-61655-694-5

HENCHGIRL

Kristen Gudsnuk

Mary Posa hates her job. She works long hours for little pay, no insurance, and worst of all, no respect. Her coworkers are jerks, and her boss doesn't appreciate her. He's also a supervillain. Cursed with a conscience, Mary would give anything to be something other than a henchgirl.

$17.99 | ISBN 978-1-50670-144-8

THE ONCE AND FUTURE QUEEN

Adam P. Knave, D.J. Kirkbride, Nick Brokenshire, Frank Cvetkovic

It's out with the old myths and in with the new as a nineteen-year-old chess prodigy pulls Excalibur from the stone and becomes queen. Now, magic, romance, Fae, Merlin, and more await her!

$14.99 | ISBN 978-1-50670-250-6

MISFITS OF AVALON

Kel McDonald

Four misfit teens are reluctant recruits to save the mystical isle of Avalon. Magically empowered and directed by a talking dog, they must stop the rise of King Arthur. As they struggle to become a team, they're faced with the discovery that they may not be the good guys.

$14.99 each

Volume 1: The Queen of Air and Delinquency
ISBN 978-1-61655-538-2

Volume 2: The Ill-Made Guardian
ISBN 978-1-61655-748-5

Volume 3: The Future in the Wind
ISBN 978-1-61655-749-2

THE SECRET LOVES OF GEEK GIRLS

Hope Nicholson, Margaret Atwood, Mariko Tamaki, and more

The Secret Loves of Geek Girls is a nonfiction anthology mixing prose, comics, and illustrated stories on the lives and loves of an amazing cast of female creators..

$14.99 | ISBN 978-1-50670-099-1

THE SECRET LOVES OF GEEKS

Gerard Way, Dana Simpson, Hope Larson, and more

The follow-up to the smash hit *The Secret Loves of Geek Girls*, this brand new anthology features comic and prose stories from cartoonists and professional geeks about their most intimate, heartbreaking, and inspiring tales of love, sex, and dating. This volume includes creators of diverse genders, orientations, and cultural backgrounds.

$14.99 each | ISBN 978-1-50670-473-9

ZODIAC STARFORCE: BY THE POWER OF ASTRA

Kevin Panetta, Paulina Ganucheau

A group of teenage girls with magical powers have sworn to protect our planet against dark creatures. Known as the Zodiac Starforce, these high-school girls aren't just combating math tests—they're also battling monsters!

$12.99 | ISBN 978-1-61655-913-7

SPELL ON WHEELS

Kate Leth, Megan Levens, Marissa Louise

A road trip story. A magical revenge fantasy. A sisters-over-misters tale of three witches out to get back what was taken from them.

$14.99 | ISBN 978-1-50670-183-7

THE ADVENTURES OF SUPERHERO GIRL

Faith Erin Hicks

What if you can leap tall buildings and defeat alien monsters with your bare hands, but you buy your capes at secondhand stores and have a weakness for kittens? Faith Erin Hicks brings humor to the trials and tribulations of a young, female superhero, battling monsters both supernatural and mundane in an all-too-ordinary world.

$16.99 each | ISBN 978-1-61655-084-4

Expanded Edition | ISBN 978-1-50670-336-7

DARKHORSE.COM

AVAILABLE AT YOUR LOCAL COMICS SHOP OR BOOKSTORE | TO FIND A COMICS SHOP IN YOUR AREA, VISIT COMICSHOPLOCATOR.COM

For more information or to order direct: • On the web: DarkHorse.com • Email: mailorder@darkhorse.com • Phone: 1-800-862-0052 Mon.–Fri. 9 AM to 5 PM Pacific Time.

AXE COP
Malachai Nicolle, Ethan Nicolle
Bad guys, beware! Evil aliens, run for your lives! Axe Cop is here, and he's going to chop your head off! We live in a strange world, and our strange problems call for strange heroes. That's why Axe Cop is holding tryouts to build the greatest team of heroes ever assembled.

Volume 1	ISBN 978-1-59582-681-7	$14.99
Volume 2	ISBN 978-1-59582-825-5	$14.99
Volume 3	ISBN 978-1-59582-911-5	$14.99
Volume 4	ISBN 978-1-61655-057-8	$12.99
Volume 5	ISBN 978-1-61655-245-9	$14.99
Volume 6	ISBN 978-1-61655-424-8	$12.99

THE ADVENTURES OF DR. MCNINJA OMNIBUS
Christopher Hastings
He's a doctor! He's a ninja! And now, his earliest exploits are collected in one mighty omnibus volume! Featuring stories from the very beginnings of the Dr. McNinja web comic, this book offers a hefty dose of science, action, and outrageous comedy.

$24.99 | ISBN 978-1-61655-112-4

BREATH OF BONES: A TALE OF THE GOLEM
Steve Niles, Matt Santoro, Dave Wachter
A British plane crashes in a Jewish village, sparking a Nazi invasion. Using clay and mud from the river, the villagers bring to life a giant monster to battle for their freedom and future.

$14.99 | ISBN 978-1-61655-344-9

HARROW COUNTY
Cullen Bunn, Tyler Crook
Emmy always knew that the woods surrounding her home crawled with ghosts and monsters. But on the eve of her eighteenth birthday, she learns that she is connected to these creatures—and to the land itself—in a way she never imagined.

$14.99 each
Volume 1: Countless Haints	ISBN 978-1-61655-780-5
Volume 2: Twice Told	ISBN 978-1-61655-900-7
Volume 3: Snake Doctor	ISBN 978-1-50670-071-7
Volume 4: Family Tree	ISBN 978-1-50670-141-7
Volume 5: Abandoned	ISBN 978-1-50670-190-5

SPACE-MULLET!
Daniel Warren Johnson
Ex–Space Marine Jonah and his copilot Alphius rove the galaxy, trying to get by. Drawn into one crazy adventure after another, they forge a crew of misfits into a family and face the darkest parts of the universe together.

$17.99 | ISBN 978-1-61655-912-0

EI8HT
Mike Johnson, Rafael Albuquerque
Welcome to the Meld, an inhospitable dimension in time where a chrononaut finds himself trapped. With no memory or feedback from the team of scientists that sent him, he can't count on anything but his heart and a stranger's voice to guide him to his destiny.

$17.99 | ISBN 978-1-61655-637-2

REBELS
Brian Wood, Andrea Mutti, Matthew Woodson, Ariela Kristantina, Tristan Jones
This is 1775. With the War for Independence playing out across the colonies, Seth and Mercy Abbott find their new marriage tested at every turn as the demands of the frontlines and the home front collide.

Volume 1: A Well-Regulated Militia
$24.99 | ISBN 978-1-61655-908-3

HOW TO TALK TO GIRLS AT PARTIES
Neil Gaiman, Gabriel Bá, Fábio Moon
Two teenage boys are in for a tremendous shock when they crash a party where the girls are far more than they appear!

$17.99 | ISBN 978-1-61655-955-7

NANJING: THE BURNING CITY
Ethan Young
After the bombs fell, the Imperial Japanese Army seized the Chinese capital of Nanjing. Two abandoned Chinese soldiers try to escape the city and what they'll encounter will haunt them. But in the face of horror, they'll learn that resistance and bravery cannot be destroyed.

$24.99 | ISBN 978-1-61655-752-2

THE BATTLES OF BRIDGET LEE: INVASION OF FARFALL
Ethan Young
There is no longer a generation that remembers a time before the Marauders invaded Earth. Bridget Lee, an ex–combat medic now residing at the outpost Farfall, may be the world's last hope. But Bridget will need to overcome her own fears before she can save her people.

$10.99 | ISBN 978-1-50670-012-0

MUHAMMAD ALI
Sybille Titeux, Amazing Ameziane
Celebrating the life of the glorious athlete who metamorphosed from Cassius Clay to become a three-time heavyweight boxing legend, activist, and provocateur, Muhammad Ali is not only a titan in the world of sports but in the world itself, he dared to be different and to challenge and defy. Witness what made Ali different, what made him cool, what made him the Greatest.

$19.99 | ISBN 978-1-50670-318-3

THE FIFTH BEATLE: THE BRIAN EPSTEIN STORY
Vivek J. Tiwary, Andrew C. Robinson, Kyle Baker
The untold true story of Brian Epstein, the visionary manager who discovered and guided the Beatles to unprecedented international stardom. The Fifth Beatle is an uplifting, tragic, and ultimately inspirational human story about the struggle to overcome the odds..

$19.99 | ISBN 978-1-61655-256-5
Expanded Edition $14.99 | ISBN 978-1-61655-835-2

THE USAGI YOJIMBO SAGA
Stan Sakai
When a peace came upon Japan and samurai warriors found themselves suddenly unemployed and many of these ronin turned to banditry, found work, or traveled the musha shugyo to hone their spiritual and martial skills. Whether they took the honest road or the crooked path, the ronin were less than welcome. Such is the tale of Usagi Yojimbo.

$24.99 each
Volume 1	ISBN 978-1-61655-609-9
Volume 2	ISBN 978-1-61655-610-5
Volume 3	ISBN 978-1-61655-611-2
Volume 4	ISBN 978-1-61655-612-9
Volume 5	ISBN 978-1-61655-613-6
Volume 6	ISBN 978-1-61655-614-3
Volume 7	ISBN 978-1-61655-615-0
Legends	ISBN 978-1-50670-323-7

DARKHORSE.COM AVAILABLE AT YOUR LOCAL COMICS SHOP OR BOOKSTORE | TO FIND A COMICS SHOP IN YOUR AREA, CALL 1-888-266-4226
For more information or to order direct: •On the web: DarkHorse.com •Email: mailorder@darkhorse.com •Phone: 1-800-862-0052 Mon.–Fri. 9 AM to 5 PM Pacific Time.
Axe Cop™ © Ethan Nicolle and Malachai Nicolle. The Adventures of Dr. McNinja™ © Chris Hastings. Breath of Bones™ © Steve Niles, Matt Santoro, and Dave Wachter. EI8HT™ © Rafael Albuquerque and Mike Johnson. Harrow County™ © Cullen Bunn and Tyler Crook. How to Talk to Girls at Parties™ © Neil Gaiman. Nanjing™, The Battles of Bridget Lee™ © Ethan Young, Rebels™ © Brian Wood and Andrea Mutti. Space-Mullet!™ © Daniel Warren Johnson. Muhammad Ali™ © EDITIONS DU LOMBARD (DARGAUD-LOMBARD S.A.), by Amazing Améziane, Sybille Titeux de la Croix. The Fifth Beatle™ © Tiwary Entertainment Group Ltd. Produced under license by M Press. Usagi Yojimbo © Stan Sakai. Dark Horse Books® and the Dark Horse logo are registered trademarks of Dark Horse Comics, Inc. All rights reserved. (BL 6051)